EXTERN SISTERS IN MONASTERIES OF NUNS

This dissertation was approved by the Reverend Romaeus W. O'Brien, O.Carm., M.A., J.C.D., Associate Professor of Canon Law, as director, and by the Right Reverend Clement V. Bastnagel, S.T.L., J.U.D., Dean of the School of Canon Law, and the Reverend Meletius M. Wojnar, O.S.B.M., S.T.L., J.C.D., as readers.

THE CATHOLIC UNIVERSITY OF AMERICA
CANON LAW STUDIES
NO. 430

Extern Sisters in Monasteries of Nuns

A DISSERTATION

SUBMITTED TO THE FACULTY OF THE SCHOOL OF CANON LAW OF THE CATHOLIC UNIVERSITY OF AMERICA IN PARTIAL FULFILLMENT OF THE REQUIREMENTS FOR THE DEGREE OF DOCTOR OF CANON LAW

BY

REV. DISMAS W. BONNER, O.F.M., A.B., J.C.L.

PRIEST OF THE PROVINCE OF THE SACRED HEART

THE CATHOLIC UNIVERSITY OF AMERICA
WASHINGTON, D.C.
1963

NIHIL OBSTAT:
REVEREND MARCIAN J. MATHIS, O.F.M.
Censor Provinciae

IMPRIMI POTEST:
VERY REV. DOMINIC LIMACHER, O.F.M.
Minister Provincial

September 11, 1963

NIHIL OBSTAT:
REVEREND ROMAEUS O'BRIEN, O.CARM.
Censor Deputatus

IMPRIMATUR:
✠ PATRICK A. O'BOYLE
Archbishop of Washington

June 20, 1963

The *nihil obstat* and *imprimatur* are official declarations that a book or pamphlet is free of doctrinal or moral error. No implication is contained therein that those who have granted the *nihil obstat* and the *imprimatur* agree with the content, opinions or statements expressed.

Printed by The Abbey Press, St. Meinrad, Indiana, U.S.A.

To

My Mother and Father

FOREWORD

The special condition of cloistered nuns demands the service of certain persons outside the cloister, who are destined to care for the business and affairs of the monastery. In fact, from its beginning, the very nature of the cloistered life has created such a necessity. On the one hand, there exists a group of nuns, bound to the observance of an enclosure which, while varying in strictness throughout history, has at all times provided severe limitations to their ability to leave the enclosed area. On the other hand, it is evident that, in connection with the operation of a monastery, a number of matters will of necessity demand attention outside the cloistered area to which the nuns are restricted. The Sacred Congregation of Religious, issuing the Instruction and Statutes for Extern Sisters in 1961 observed that there have always been pious women to meet these needs of monasteries of nuns. These women, who cared for the external service of the monasteries, generally remained outside the cloister and were not bound by any vows, or at most by vows which were not those of the religious life.

It is the purpose of the historical part of this dissertation to examine the various forms which this external service of monasteries of nuns has taken in the past, together with the ecclesiastical legislation pertinent to the subject. At various periods of history, external service was provided for monasteries by priests, monks and lay servants attached to the convent, as well as by the nuns themselves. The history of this development culminated in the comparatively recent evolution of the present day concept of extern sisters, which was crystallized by the Holy See in the Statutes for Extern Sisters, promulgated in 1931. Detailed attention is given to these Statutes since an understanding of them is most important in order to appreciate in its proper perspective the current legislation concerning extern sisters.

The second part of this dissertation contains a canonical commentary on the present Statutes for Extern Sisters, which were promulgated in 1961. Special attention is given to the relation of these Statutes to the particular law of the various Orders of nuns. Some emphasis is placed upon the particular law of the Order of St. Clare and that of the Poor Clare Colettines; examples are drawn from the Constitutions of both these Orders to illustrate the practical application of the norms of the Statutes. It is hoped that this method of presentation will be of assistance in the sometimes difficult task of harmonizing the particular laws of various institutes with the norms of the Statutes.

The writer wishes to express his gratitude to the Very Reverend Dominic Limacher, O.F.M., Minister Provincial of the Franciscan Province of the Sacred Heart, for the opportunity of engaging in advanced studies in Canon Law. He is most grateful to the Dean and Faculty of the School of Canon Law of the Catholic University of America for their helpful guidance and advice, especially to the Reverend Romaeus W. O'Brien, O.Carm., J.C.D., who directed the dissertation. Special thanks are due to the Reverend Marcian Mathis, O.F.M., J.C.D., Professor of Canon Law at St. Joseph Seminary, Teutopolis, Illinois, for his gracious assistance, and to the nuns and extern sisters of the Order of St. Clare and the Poor Clare Colettines, who, by their kind cooperation and prayers, assisted greatly in the completion of this dissertation.

TABLE OF CONTENTS

PART TWO
CANONICAL COMMENTARY

CHAPTER VIII

CHAPTER IX

PART ONE
HISTORICAL SYNOPSIS

CHAPTER I

THE COMMISSARIES (*APOCRISIARII*) IN ROMAN LAW

The *Codex Iustinianus* laid down the precept that those who lived in monasteries were not permitted to go out of them; much less were they to be permitted to frequent the cities.[1] The law, however, permitted an exception to this rule in favor of the commissaries or representatives (*apocrisiarii*[2] or *responsarii*[3]). The Justinian Code provided that, in addition to one priest and one deacon who were to care for the spiritual needs of the monastery, the bishop of the city should appoint one old man to carry on the necessary occupations and transactions of women living by themselves.[4] Later in the *Novellae* it was prescribed that there be two or three men for the service of each monastery; if possible, they were to be eunuchs, in any case, men of proven chastity. The duties of these representatives were to carry on the affairs of the monastery, and also to administer the Holy Eucharist to the nuns at the proper times.[5] Thus, it

1 "Iis, qui in monasteriis degunt, non liceat monasteriis egredi vel etiam in Antiochena aliisve civitatibus versari: ..."—*Corpus Iuris Civilis*, Vol. II, *Codex Iustinianus*, quem recognovit et retractavit P. Krueger, ed. 10 (Berolini: apud Weidmannos, 1928), (1.3) 29 (hereafter cited as *C.*).

2 "... exceptis solis apocrisiariis qui vocantur, quibus licentiam damus, si velint, propter necessarias tamen apocrises intrandi."—*Loc. cit.*

3 *Corpus Iuris Civilis*, Vol. III, *Novellae Constitutiones*, quos recognovit R. Schoell; opus Schoellii morte interceptum absolvit G. Kroll, ed. 5 (Berolini; apud Weidmannos, 1928), (135.5) (hereafter cited as *N.*).

4 "Ad necessaria autem negotia mulierum per se viventium unus senex a beatissimo civitatis episcopo designetur, ..."—*C.* (1.3) 43, 5.

5 "Et non solum si virorum monasterium, sed si etiam mulierum contingat, esse duos aliquos aut tres viros aut eunuchos, si possibile est, aut senes et castitatis testimonium habentes qui causas agant et ineffabilem eis praebeant communionem, cum huius tempus fuerit."—*N.* (135.5).

seems that, according to the *Novellae,* these commissaries took over the functions not only of the old man mentioned in the *Codex Iustinianus,* but even of the priest and deacon assigned to the monastery. It is not surprising that they should have been entrusted with the sacred ministry, since the *Novellae* refer to the representatives *(responsarii)* of monasteries of men as "old men who have already proven themselves in the monastic life and are not readily subject to bodily passions, and who are engaged in the affairs and service of the monks."[6] This text, together with the fact that the *Codex* refers to the commissaries *(apocrisiarii)* as men "who dwell in monasteries,"[7] indicates that those who filled this office in the monasteries of men were actually taken from among the monks themselves. While it did not indicate that the eunuchs and men of proven chastity who were commissaries in monasteries of women were actually monks, the law did invest them with a sort of quasi-monastic character.

Although the commissaries in monasteries of men were monks actually living in the monastery itself, the law took precautions to provide a strict separation between the nuns and their representatives. They were to perform only those services and duties specifically allotted to them; under no circumstances were they to dwell in the monastery itself.[8] In discussing the business affairs of the monastery, or even of any one particular nun, the commissaries were permitted to speak only with the abbess, and not with any of the other nuns; contact with the abbess was to be made in some way by the intervention of the portresses of the monastery.[9]

[6] "... viros senes et iam monachicum certamen superantes et non facile corporales violentias passuros, qui eorum rebus et eorum occupentur utilitatibus."—*Loc. cit.*

[7] *C.* (1.3) 29.

[8] *C.* (1.3) 43, 5.

[9] "Si vero de aliqua monasterii utilitate aut ad unam reverentissimarum ascetriarum pertinente dicere aliquid necessariorum voluerint, loquentur abbatissae et alteri penitus nulli feminarum quae in monasterio sunt, haec per reverentissimas ostiarias agentes."—*N.* (135.5).

With regard to the actual carrying out of their duties, the law sought to impress upon the commissaries the importance of their role as representatives of the monasteries. Justinian warned those who might be assigned to this office to take care not to engage in disputes and arguments about dogma and religious matters. Especially were they to avoid stirring up the simple people to seditions and riots. Those who transgressed this command were threatened with the severe punishment of the law.[10]

[10] "Atque hi ipsi qui ingrediuntur caveant, ne de religioso cultu vel dogmate disputent vel consiliis quae ad seditionem vel tumultum tendant simpliciores populi animos pervertant, cum sciant, si nostrae pietatis iussa praetermiserint, legum severitati se subici."—*C.* (1.3) 29.

CHAPTER II

DEVELOPMENTS AMONG BENEDICTINE AND CENOBITIC NUNS

SECTION I

THE BENEDICTINE NUNS

Among the Benedictine nuns, the law and practice relating to the observance of the enclosure was, from the beginning, not at all uniform.[1] Thus, in the year 528, there were nuns entering one cloister "never to go out of it, unless a reasonable cause, or a matter of some great utility should so demand."[2] Again, in the middle of the seventh century, some nuns observed an inviolable enclosure, although dispensations even from this were allowed in some instances for the abbess; other nuns, however, were not so rigidly bound to the observance of the cloister that they could not leave it for necessary and proper reasons.[3] From this it is evident that, in those monasteries where the enclosure was less strictly observed, the outside necessities were simply taken care of, at least in some measure, by the nuns themselves. Certainly such tasks must have fallen within the necessary and reasonable causes permitted by the rules in force in these monasteries.

[1] "Atqui omnes tum monachae non eadem severitate reclusionis leges servabant, sicut illae, quae Caesarii regulam profitebantur."—J. Mabillon, *Annales Ordinis S. Benedicti*, ed. prima Italica a quamplurimis mendis, quae in Parisienses irrepserant, ad auctoris mentem expurgata (6 vols., Lucae: Typis Leonardi Venturini, 1739), I, 54, ad annum 528.

[2] ". . . numquam egressurae, nisi causa rationabilis, vel magnae cuiusdam utilitatis id exigeret."—*Loc. cit.*

[3] "Aliae inviolabilem reclusionem servabant . . . tametsi aliquando cum abbatissis earum dispensatum; aliae non ita claustris suis addictae erant, ut non aliquando pro causis honestis ac necessariis egrederentur."—*Ibid.*, p. 406, ad annum 656; II, 9, ad annum 704; II, 134, ad annum 748.

The most common means of meeting the problem of the outside work in these monasteries of nuns was to place several monks at the disposal of each. It was their duty to provide for the spiritual as well as the temporal needs of the nuns, although they were not to be reduced to the status of servants *(familiares)*. The monks were to tend the farms and estates, construct buildings, and, in general, provide for the temporal well-being of the monastery entrusted to their care.[4] In certain monasteries, the men placed in charge of this work were not monks, but clerics appointed by the Bishop of the place. But, whether monks or clerics, these procurators were designated as overseers *(praepositi)* of the monastery.[5] A mid-eighth century council makes express mention of the overseers or agents *("praepositi vel missi")* in monasteries of nuns,[6] and the Sixth Council of Paris held in 839 mentions the special permission to approach monasteries of nuns which is granted only to those monks who are duly employed there.[7] The exact relation of these monks to the monasteries of nuns seems to have varied considerably from one place to another. There are records of monasteries which were completely dependent on neighboring monasteries of monks, and which had absolutely no male or fe-

[4] "Leguntur in quinto concilio Aurelianensi pro xenodochio Lugdunensi a Childeberto rege constructo: . . . Absit enim, ut monachos (quod etiam dictu nefas est) Christi virginibus familiares esse velimus, sed . . . longe discretos atque sejunctos, eorum tantum easdem gubernaculis deputamus; constituentes, ut unus monachorum probatissimus eligatur, cujus curae sit, praedia earum rustica vel urbana intendere, fabricas exstruere, vel si quid ad necessitatem monasterii providere: ut Christi famulae, pro animae suae tantum utilitate sollicitae, solis divinis cultibus vivant, operibusque suis inserviant."—*Ibid.*, I, 287, ad annum 618.

[5] "Ejusmodi procuratores clericos aut monachos in coenobiis puellarum posteri praepositos appellarunt."—*Ibid.*, p. 211, ad annum 594.

[6] "Concilii Vernensis decreta pro monachis"—*Ibid.*, II, 164, ad annum 755; Hardouin, *Acta Conciliorum et Epistolae Decretales ac Constitutiones Summorum Pontificum* (12 vols., Parisiis, 1714-1715), III, 1996; Mansi, *Sacrorum Conciliorum nova et amplissima Collectio* (53 vols., Florentiae, Venetiis, Parisiis, Arnhem, Lipsiae, 1759-1927), XII, 581.

[7] Mabillon, *op. cit.*, II, 485, ad annum 829; Hardouin, *op. cit.*, IV, 1325; Mansi *op. cit.*, XIV, 566.

male servants of their own.[8] Again there were monasteries where the overseers were under no abbot at all, but were directly attached to the monastery of the nuns and subject to the abbess.[9] Still another means of caring for the work outside the cloister was the fact that a number of male and female servants were attached to many of the monasteries. It seems that both male and female servants were used inside as well as outside the monastery.[10] The early twelfth century Rule of Abelard mentions lay women *(conversae)* who left the world to serve the nuns "clad in a religious garb, but not the monastic habit."[11] These sisters were employed in the outside work of the monastery in which the cloistered nuns were not able to engage.[12] At the same period, the *Vita des hl. Gilbert* indicates that, in some monasteries, the outside service was performed by "certain poor girls who served the convent while clad in secular garb."[13] Eventually, it seems that these particular maids were obliged to wear some type of habit and, after a novitiate of one year, make profession, the reason being "that it was not safe to have young lay women serving the religious."[14]

[8] Mabillon, *op. cit.*, V, 549, ad annum 1113.

[9] "... paucos habens in disparatis aedibus sine abbate monachos, quot scilicet ad sacra eis ministranda sufficiebant ... ; qui ad nutum abbatissae et sanctimonialium admittebantur, eisque ministrabant; ... abbatissae et sanctimonialibus quodam modo subjecti."—*Ibid.*, p. 396, ad annum 1100.

[10] "... certas villas ad victum usumque sanctimonialium, eisque servientium assignaverunt, hoc pacto, ut essent in illa congregatione sanctimoniales feminae ducentae-sexdecim, famulae in monasterii clausura consistentes, eisque in diversis officiis et officinis ministrantes quadraginta; in gynoecio extra laborantes triginta; viri quoque ad diversa officia destinati, intra vel extra monasterium servientes, centum-triginta."—*Ibid.*, III, 66, ad annum 858.

[11] Migne, *Patrologiae Cursus Completus*, Series Latina (Paris, 1844-1864), CLXXVIII, col. 267s.

[12] P. Hofmeister, "Von den Nonnenklöstern," *Archiv für katholisches Kirchenrecht*, CXIV (1934), 426.

[13] *Loc. cit.*

[14] *Loc. cit.*

SECTION II
THE CISTERCIAN REFORM

The Cistercian nuns, like the Benedictines, were obliged to the observance of a very strict enclosure, although, at least in the early days of the Order, the nun in charge of supplies, the *celleraria,* was permitted to go out of the cloister to perform her duties.[15] Just as was the practice among the Benedictines, monks and lay brothers *(conversi)* of the male branch of the Order were employed to care for a large share of the burdens. At first, there seems to have been a reluctance on the part of the monks to perform this service. Thus the General Chapter warned them not to dare eat, or much less spend the night, at a certain nunnery near Paris;[16] only a few years later, the Chapter petitioned the Pope himself no longer to compel the monks and lay brothers to dwell with the nuns and provide for their temporal welfare.[17] This request did not do away with the service of the nuns as far as the lay brothers *(conversi)* were concerned, but it did bring about a change in the status of these men. No longer were they members of the male branch of the Order, but were actually incorporated into the monastery of the nuns. These lay brothers of the nuns *(conversi monialium)* ordinarily wore a habit like that of the regular Cistercians,[18] and had their own form of life, as did certain clerics who also were attached in this manner to the monasteries of the nuns.[19] There even existed a "Form of profession of the brothers, chaplains, clerics and lay brothers of the nuns in our Order." It provided for a novitiate to be made in the nuns' monastery, followed by

[15] Canivez, *Statuta Capitulorum Generalium Ordinis Cisterciensis,* ab anno 1116 ad annum 1786 (8 vols., Louvain: Bureaux de la Revue, 1933), I, 517, ad annum 1220.

[16] *Ibid.,* I, 405, ad annum 1213-1214.

[17] "Supplicandum Domino Papae ne compellat nos ad mittendos monachos nostros et conversos ad cohabitandum cum monialibus, et in temporalibus eisdem providendis."—*Ibid.,* II, 19, ad annum 1222.

[18] *Ibid.,* p. 76, ad annum 1229.

[19] *Ibid.,* p. 253, ad annum 1242.

profession made into the hands of the abbess.[20] Although the Chapter of 1267 changed the designation of these providers *(provisores)* from overseers *(praepositi)* to procurators *(procuratores)*, and demanded that permission be obtained in order to have them in the monastery, the institution continued to flourish.[21] By the end of the thirteenth century, they were promising the abbess to observe not only obedience, but poverty and chastity as well.[22] In the next century, the institution was even made mandatory by the Chapter of 1321;[23] subsequent chapters continued to prescribe these procurators "to provide for the nuns in regard to food and other necessities."[24] These same Chapters continued to enforce the rule of obtaining permission to establish procurators in a given monastery. Apparently, in some places at least, it was the custom for them to live within the cloister; for the Chapter of 1458 found it necessary to prohibit this practice, and to demand that they live outside the cloister in separate and remote buildings.[25] This institution continued until the early seventeenth century, when it was finally suppressed.[26]

Section III
The Cenobites

Among the Camaldulese was found an institution very much like the Cistercian procurators. Evidence shows that

[20] "Forma professionis fratrum capellanorum, clericorum et conversorum monialium nostri Ordinis: promitto vobis obedientiam de bono usque ad mortem."—*Ibid.*, pp. 399-400.

[21] *Ibid.*, III, 49, ad annum 1267.

[22] *Ibid.*, p. 285, ad annum 1296.

[23] *Ibid.*, p. 355, ad annum 1321.

[24] "...ad providendum eis in victu et aliis necessariis."—*Ibid.*, p. 589, ad annum 1390; IV, 608, ad annum 1448.

[25] "...ne ammodo permittant suos procuratores saeculares intra claustra ipsorum monasteriorum habitare, sed in locis ab ipsis claustris separatis et remotis habitationes eorum disponantur."—*Ibid.*, V, 20, ad annum 1458.

[26] "In monasteriis monialium de cetero nulli conversi habitant, nec ab abbatissa recipiantur."—*Ibid.*, VII, 278, ad annum 1609.

there were priests and laymen called *conversi* who lived in the monasteries of nuns, cared for the business of the monastery, and served its needs. There they received the habit, and promised obedience to the abbess.[27] The Camaldulese also made use of a group of women called *devotae* or oblates *(oblatae)* who formed a class which was distinct from the nuns and lay sisters *(conversae)*; these women dwelt in the monasteries and performed the menial tasks.[28]

The Carthusian nuns had in their monastery lay persons called *conversae* and *donatae* who were the female counterparts of the laymen known as *conversi* and *donati* in the monasteries of the monks.[29] In the organization of Carthusian life, the members of these classes were completely separated from the other religious, being assigned their own cloister and choir, their separate refectory and dormitory.[30] From what the annals of the Carthusian Order tell of the condition and work of the lay brothers among the monks, it appears that their female counterparts were engaged mostly in the physical labor necessary to maintain the monastery, caring also for all the external works.[31]

27 "Conversos insuper tum presbyteros, tum laicos legimus monasteriorum sanctimonialium, apud quas habitum recipiebant, regulam profitebantur, abbatissis obedientiam praestabant . . . et ad partem negotiorum rerumque agendarum vocabantur."—Mittarelli-Costadoni, *Annales Camaldulenses Ordinis S. Benedicti* (9 vols., Venetiis, 1755), I, 411, ad annum 1267.

28 "Devotas etiam reperimus in sacrarum virginum monasteriis commorantes, atque a monialibus et a conversabus distinctas, sed facile nomen hoc tribuebatur Oblatis et familiaribus mulieribus."—*Ibid.*, p. 425, ad annum 1220.

29 "Praeter Moniales sunt apud eas Conversae et Donatae, sicut apud nos sunt Conversi et Donati."—C. le Couteulx Monstrolii, *Annales Ordinis Cartusiensis* ab anno 1084 ad annum 1429 (7 vols., Typis Cartusiae S. Maraie de Pratis, 1888), II, 37, ad annum 1145.

30 *Ibid.*, I, 39, ad annum 1085.

31 "Illi mentem, hi corpus maxime exercent; illi cancellatis manibus divinis rebus vacant, hi manibus expansis terrenis incumbunt; illi demum cellae solitudini dant operam, hi vero externis operibus occupantur."—*Ibid.*, p. 41, ad annum 1085.

CHAPTER III

THE MENDICANT NUNS

Section I
The Serving Sisters

The rise of the mendicant nuns in the thirteenth century is, for the most part, the history of the Order of St. Clare at that time. A study of the various Rules approved for use in the monasteries of the Poor Clares indicates that an important factor in solving the problem of outside work and questing for alms was the serving sisters (*sorores servientes*).

These sisters appeared in the Rule of Cardinal Hugolino, which was approved by Pope Honorius III in 1224.[1] The Rule gave detailed directions concerning the manner in which they were to carry out their work. The sisters were ordered not to delay for a long time outside the monastery, unless some evident necessity should so require. Their conduct was to be edifying to those with whom they came into contact; at the same time they were to avoid becoming too closely involved in the difficulties of outside affairs. This latter was emphasized by an admonition to avoid suspicious intimacy and even to refrain from acting as godmothers to men or women. Especially was it prohibited to bring worldly news into the monastery, or to spread abroad tales of happenings in the monastery which might prove a scandal. Those who failed in this regard were subject to punishment at the hands of the abbess.[2] In the light of these prescriptions, it seems

[1] Wadding, *Annales Minorum*, ed. 3 accuratissima auctior et emendatior ad exemplar editionis P. Josephi Mariae Fonseca ad Ebora (30 vols., Ad Claras Aquas, Florentia, 1931-1951; 1 vol., Romae, 1956), II, 88.

[2] "Sorores servientes extra Monasterium longam moram non faciant, nisi causa manifestae necessitatis requirat. Et honeste debeant ambulare, et parum loqui ut aedificari valeant semper intuentes. Et firmiter caveant ne habeant suspecta consortia vel consilia aliquorum, nec fiant

that the serving sisters were in much the same status as the others, with the single exception that they were allowed to go out to provide for the needs of the monastery. They must have had contact with the other religious, if the prohibition against spreading worldly news in the convent was to have any meaning at all. The Rule made no mention of any separate place within the monastery for them. It seems best to say that they were nuns just as the others, for whom an exception was made in this one regard. These same regulations for the serving sisters were repeated in the Rule approved by Pope Innocent IV in 1253.[3]

In 1247, Innocent IV approved a Rule for certain monasteries of the Order of St. Clare which gave an even clearer picture of the status of the serving sisters.[4] This Rule made a much sharper distinction between the strictly cloistered nuns and the sisters who were permitted to go out. In death, for instance, it ascribed the right to burial within the cloister to "deceased religious, both nuns and serving sisters."[5] For some evident necessity or manifest utility, the visitor might transfer these sisters from one monastery to another.[6] At the same time, the Rule showed clearly that they were considered true nuns just as the others. After listing the qualities of those to be received, the demand for a novitiate of one year and the form of profession of the nuns, the Rule stated: "This is also to be firmly observed in a similar man-

commatres virorum aut mulierum, ne hac occasione murmuratio vel turbatio oriatur. Nec praesumant rumores de saeculo referre in Monasterio; et firmiter teneantur de his, quae intus dicuntur vel aguntur, extra Monasterium aliquid non referre, quod possit aliquod scandalum generare; et si aliqua simpliciter in his duobus offenderit, sit in providentia Abbatissae misericorditer sibi poenitentiam injungere."—*Ibid.*, p. 94.

3 Bulla "Solet annuere," 9 aug. 1253, cap. IX—*Bullarum Diplomatum et Privilegiorum Sanctorum Romanorum Pontificum,* Taurinensis ed. (24 vols., Augustae Taurinorum, 1857-1872), III, 575 (hereafter cited as *Bull. Rom.*).

4 Bulla "Cum omnis vera religio," 6 Aug. 1247—*Ibid.*, p. 527.

5 "...morientes vero tam Sorores quam servientes."—*Ibid.*, p. 528.

6 *Ibid.*, p. 534.

ner for the serving sisters."[7] The serving sisters lived in the cloister like the others, and it was necessary for them to secure permission in order to leave to perform their outside duties.[8] The Rule continued describing the good character and proper age of the sisters engaged in serving the monastery, granting them, as well as all the nuns of the monastery, permission to wear sandals.

A definite time of returning to the monastery was to be assigned to the sisters when they went out, and none of them was ever to eat, drink or sleep outside the monastery without special permission. When outside the monastery, they were never to become separated from each other, much less to secretly enter the buildings set aside for the *conversi* or brothers who served the monastery. Like the Rule of Honorius III, this Rule too directed the sisters to avoid suspicious situations and familiarity with secular persons, not to repeat worldly gossip in the cloister, and to go about their business in such a manner that those who observed them would be edified. Lastly they were to hand over whatever they managed to collect to the abbess or her representative.[9]

[7] "Quod etiam de servientibus firmiter modo simili observetur."—*Ibid.*, pp. 528-529.

[8] "De servientibus Sororibus, quae semper manere clausae sicut aliae non tenentur, districtius volumus observari, ut sine licentia nulla claustrum egrediatur..."—*Ibid.*, p. 533.

[9] "...quae emittuntur honestae sint, et convenientis aetatis, et calceamentis honestis, tam ipsae, quam Sorores illae quas aliquando emitti contigerit, pro casibus suprascriptis calceatae incedant. Ceteris autem intus manentibus, si voluerint liceat istud idem. Egredientibus vero assigentur certus terminus redeundi. Nec alicui ipsarum conceditur extra Monasterium sine speciali licentia comedere, bibere, vel dormire, nec ab invicem separari, vel alicui in secreto, seu Capellani Monasterii, aut Conversorum, vel Fratrum ibidem morantium domicilium introire. Quod si aliqua contrarium fecerit, graviter puniatur. Et sollicite caveant, ne ad loca suspecta divertant vel cum personis malae famae familiaritatem habeant, nec in suo reditu saecularia, vel inutilia Sororibus referant, per quae dissolvi valeant, vel turbari; et quamdiu extra fuerint, taliter studeant se habere, quod de conversatione honesta ipsarum aedificari valeant intuentes, et quidquid eis datum fuerit, vel promissum, resignent et renuncient Abbatissae, vel alii, cui haec commiserit vices suas."—*Ibid.*, pp. 533-534.

Chapter XIX of the Rule approved in 1264 by Urban IV repeats the prescriptions of the Rule of 1247, making only a few minor changes in wording, and omitting the phrase "*vel Fratrum ibidem morantium.*"[10]

Still another Rule which made provisions for serving sisters was that of the Lesser Sisters of the Monastery of the Humility of Blessed Mary (*Sorores Minores Monasterii Humilitatis beatae Mariae*) in the diocese of Paris. This particular Rule repeated most of the foregoing specifications regarding the character of these sisters and their work, but added the necessity of obtaining permission from the Minister General of the Friars Minor in order to leave the cloister.[11] A similar arrangement was prescribed for the Dominican lay sisters in the second half of the thirteenth century.[12]

This development of a class of professed nuns who could also care for the external necessities of the monasteries and go out on the quest for alms was dealt a severe blow by the strict cloister prescribed in the *Liber Sextus.* Affecting all nuns whatsoever, both present and future and in each and every Order, the observance of a perpetual cloister in the monasteries was demanded. No one who had professed the vows of religion even tacitly was to have permission to leave the enclosure, outside the case of serious illness which might prove a danger to the others.[13]

Apparently, this regulation was not well observed, at least among the Poor Clares, since it was necessary for Benedict

[10] Bulla "Beata Clara," 18 oct. 1264—*Ibid.*, p. 717.

[11] Bulla "Religionis augmentum," 27 iul. 1263—Wadding, *op. cit.*, IV, 575.

[12] Hofmeister, *op. cit.*, p. 428.

[13] "... sancimus, universas et singulas Moniales praesentes atque futuras, cuiuscumque religionis sint vel ordinis, in quibuslibet mundi partibus existentes, sub perpetua in suis monasteriis debere decaetero permanere clausura: ita quod nulli earum religionem tacite vel expresse professae, sit vel esse valeat quacunque ratione vel causa (nisi forte tanto et tali morbo evidenter earum aliquam laborare constaret, quod non posset cum aliis absque gravi periculo seu scandalo commorari) monasteria ipsa deinceps egrediendi facultas ..."—C. un., *de statu regularium,* III, 16, in VI°.

XII in 1336 to point out to them the fact that, although the Rule allowed them to have serving sisters who were not bound to observe the enclosure, it would be necessary for these to observe a perpetual cloister just like the other nuns. It was permitted that their duties be assumed by a few secular women of good repute and mature age; they were to be clad in secular garb and were never to enter the enclosure, devoting themselves to carrying on the business of the monastery and caring for the needs of the nuns.[14]

SECTION II

THE FRIARS ALMSGATHERERS

(*Fratres Eleemosynarii*)

"If the two facts of the enclosure and absolute poverty of the early Claresses are taken in conjunction with each other it is at once clear that in the long run they must have proved incompatible. If the nuns were to hold no property they must be dependent on chance alms, yet their Rule of enclosure forbade them leaving the convent in order to collect such alms. A way out of this difficulty was found in the assistance given by the Friars Minor."[15] In addition to the

[14] "Quamvis autem in regula dictarum monialium Sanctae Clarae sequens clausula inter alia sit inserta, videlicet: Possint autem in singulis monasteriis recipi aliquae, licet paucae, sub Servitialium nomine vel sororum, ad huiusmodi professionis observantiam astringendae: praeterquam in articulum de clausura etc. Nos tamen honestati et famae tam ipsarum Monialium Sanctae Clarae, quam Minorissarum et Sancti Damiani praedictarum in hac parte providere volentes, ordinatione praesenti perpetuo valitura districte praecipimus, quod huiusmodi servitiales seu sorores, ad observantiam professionis astrictae, et quae de caetero astringentur, quemadmodum et caeterae moniales debeant sub perpetua clausura manere; possint tamen singula monasteria dictarum monialium habere aliquas paucas tamen mulieres, moribus et aetate maturas, providas et honestas in saeculari honesto tamen habitu incedentes, quae dictam clausuram nullatenus ingredi permittantur; sed negocia monasterii ac necessitates monialium, prout eis commissum fuerit, fideliter exterius peragant et procurent."—*Bull. Rom.*, IV, 414.

[15] Bourdillon, *The Order of Minoresses in England*, British Society of Franciscan Studies, Vol. XII (Manchester: University Press, 1926), p. 5.

serving sisters then, the services of certain friars were also employed in order to meet the difficulties caused by living the cloistered life. From the inception of the Poor Clares, members of the Order of Friars Minor cared not only for the spiritual but also the temporal needs of the nuns. Such was the case at the monastery of *San Damiano* in Assisi, as is evident from a letter written by St. Clare to Pope Gregory IX, who was threatening to prevent the spiritual care of the nuns by the friars. She went so far as to send away the friars who collected alms in protest.[16]

At the beginning, when the numbers of the Clares were so few that a small number of friars were able to provide for their material necessities, it was no great burden upon the friars to render this service to the nuns. But as the Poor Ladies spread and became more numerous, the situation threatened to reduce a large number of the friars to mere attendants on their material necessities.[17] Most of the documents concerning the ensuing controversy between the Clares and the friars deal directly with the government and spiritual care of the nuns. But these documents contain references which make it quite clear that the government of the nuns included also the responsibility of providing for their temporal welfare, at least in a number of the monasteries. In 1246, Pope Innocent IV introduced the Bull *Licet olim,* which placed the spiritual care of the Clares on the friars, by recalling former letters in which he had burdened them with temporal service in order to leave the nuns free for their life

[16] "Cum semel dominus Papa Gregorius prohibuisset, ne aliquis Frater ad monasteria Dominarum sine sua licentia pergeret, dolens pia Mater cibum sacrae doctrinae rarius habituras sorores, cum gemitu dixit: Omnes nobis auferat de caetero Fratres, postquam vitalis nutrimenti nobis abstulit praebitores. Et statim omnes Fratres ad Ministrum remisit, nolens habere eleemosynarios, qui panem corporalem acquirerent, postquam panis spiritalis eleemosynarios non haberet." —Bollandistae (Sollerio-Pinio-Cupero-Boschio), *Acta Sanctorum,* ed. novissima (68 vols., Parisiis et Romae, 1863-), Aug. II, Cap. V, p. 762C.

[17] Cf. Bourdillon, *op. cit.,* p. 7.

of contemplation.[18] These former letters were written only shortly before that Bull, and provided papal sanction for what had already become customary in regard to the care of the Clares by the friars.[19] Heretofore the care of the Poor Ladies had been enjoined on the friars by special mandate or local custom; now it was in virtue of the Bull of Innocent IV.[20]

This care as imposed by papal sanction was short-lived, for in 1250 Pope Innocent IV declared that the friars were no longer bound to undertake the care of the nuns, even by future Apostolic letters, unless those letters made specific mention of this particular exemption.[21] Again in 1253 the Pope declared expressly "that the friars may not be forced to take upon themselves or assume the care of these ladies."[22]

Even this failed to resolve the question, however, for the friars in many instances continued to care for the Clares,

[18] "Licet olim quibusdam vestrum per nostras litteras formas dissimiles continentes quaedam Monasteria Ordinis Sancti Damiani duxerimus committenda, cupientes tamen eorum utilitatibus sic vestro ministerio provideri, ne sanctae contemplationis otium occursu occupationum multiplicium valeat impediri, praesentium . . ."—Bulla "Licet olim," 12 iulii 1246—*Bullarium Franciscanum*, ed. a. J. Sbaralea (4 vols., Romae, 1759-1780), I, 420 (hereafter cited as *Bull. Fran.*).

[19] "Nostras Litteras: anno 1245, die 8 Novembris incip. Paci, et saluti etc. Generali, et Marchiae Anconitanae Provinciali Ministris datas, et hoc anno 1246, die 2 Junii Cum sicut ex parte etc. iisdem pro Monialibus Asculanis, nonnullisque aliis Monasteriis."—*Loc. cit.*

[20] "Hinc et ex superioribus constat unde cura Monialium primum Ordini demandata est, nempe ex mandato Innocentii ad instantiam ipsarum Monialium, quantumlibet alias quorumdam Monasteriorum regimen ad Fratres spectabat ex speciali mandato, vel Protectoris, vel Praelatorum, vel Sedis Apostolicae, vel particulari quorumdam locorum consuetudine."—Wadding, *op. cit.*, III, 190.

[21] ". . . recipere curam Monialium, seu Religiosarum quarumlibet nulli Fratrum vestrorum de cetero per litteras Apostolicas teneantur; nisi expresse de hac indulgentia fecerint mentionem."—Bulla "Inspirationis divinae," 6 martii 1250—*Bull. Fran.*, I, 538.

[22] Innocentius IV, Bulla "Petitio vestra," 24 iun. 1253—Alessandri-Pennacchi, *Bullarium Pontificium quod exstat in Archivo Sacri Conventus S. Francisci Assisiensis* (Ad Claras Aquas prope Florentiam, 1920), p. 16, n. 84.

and it was even enjoined upon them again by Pope Alexander IV, "notwithstanding the constitution of your Order, or any favor of the Apostolic See granted to your Order."[23] So strongly did the controversy burn after the death of Alexander IV that separate Cardinal Protectors were assigned for the friars and the Poor Clares. Hoping to establish some measure of peace, Urban IV in the Bull *Inter personas,* of August 19, 1262, made concessions to both parties in the quarrel and ordered the friars to care for the Clares until the Chapter of 1263 when, if they so wished, they might be absolutely free of this burden.[24] Although Urban IV in the Bull *Spiritus Domini,* of May 15, 1263, exhorted the Chapter to continue to assist the nuns as in the past, it is not easy to decide just what the Chapter actually determined, since the *acta* are not available today. Subsequent facts and documents seem to bear out the conclusion that no definite determination was reached.[25] It is known, for instance, that, after the Chapter, Cardinal Cajetan was made Protector of both the friars and the Clares; in this position he urged the friars to continue to care for the Clares as in the past. St. Bonaventure, who was Minister General, acceded to this request, but only on condition that, for each particular monastery served, there be given a public document of freedom, declaring that this service was not of obligation and that no right could arise therefrom.[26] Again in 1274 the Cardinal Protector of the Order pleaded with the friars to continue the service they were so anxious to abandon, and again the Gen-

[23] "...non obstantibus constitutione vestri Ordinis, aut aliqua Sedis Apostolicae indulgentia Ordini vestro concessa."—Cf. Wadding, *op cit.*, I, 537, ad annum 1258 Regesti Pontificii; pp. 548-549, ad annum 1259 Regesti Pontificii; p. 567, ad annum 1260 Regesti Pontificii.

[24] "...'ex tunc Ordo Fratrum Minorum, et ipsi Fratres, si voluerint, ac ipsum Capitulum Generale eo ipso quod hoc voluerit' a quacumque obligatione erga Moniales 'sint liberi penitus et immunes.' "—Lazzeri, "Documenta controversiam inter FF. Minores et Clarissas spectantia (1262-1297)," *Archivum Franciscanum Historicum,* III (1910), 669.

[25] *Ibid.,* p. 676.

[26] *Loc. cit.*

eral Chapter acquiesced, provided the document of freedom was given.[27] At length, in 1296, Pope Boniface VIII returned the situation to its status during the early times of the controversy by renewing all the provisions of the Bull *Licet olim*, which placed the care of the Poor Ladies on the friars.[28]

It is known that the burden of this temporal service of the Clares, along with their government and spiritual care, continued until the Chapter of 1532. In the time which intervened, still further responsibilities were placed upon the friars. Thus, the Constitutions of St. Colette, which were approved by the Minister General in 1434 and confirmed by Pius II in 1458, prescribed that four friars, two priests and two lay brothers, were to be placed at the service of each Colettine monastery.[29] In 1517 the government of most of the Clares, including the Colettines, was imposed upon the Observant Friars.[30] All of this led the Chapter of 1532 to complain of the great trouble and labor caused by this care of the nuns, which also resulted in spiritual harm to the friars. Hence it proceeded to decree that no new monasteries of nuns be accepted without the consent of the General Chapter; moreover, the monasteries of nuns were forbidden to place the care of their temporalities on the brethren, since

[27] *Ibid.*, IV (1911), 91.

[28] Bulla "Quasdam litteras," die 4 iunii 1296—*Bull. Fran.*, IV, 396; Wadding, *op. cit.*, V, 570-571.

[29] "Praeterea, cum dicta forma vitae contineat, quod *Sorores Capellanum cum uno Clerico bonae famae, discretionis providae, et duos Fratres laicos sanctae conversationis et honestatis amatores, in subsidium paupertatis misericorditer ab Ordine Fratrum Minorum semper habeant.* Quae quidem verba declaramus ita debere intelligi, et fieri in modum, qui sequitur, videlicet: Quod in quocumque Conventu dictarum Monialium Sorores habeant, vel habere valeant quatuor Fratres de Ordine Fratrum Minorum, . . . Et alii duo Fratres sint laici, qui, sicut dicit forma vitae, debent esse sanctae conversationis et honestatis amatores."—Wadding, *op. cit.*, X, 289, ad annum 1435; cf. Holzapfel, *Manuale Historiae Ordinis Fratrum Minorum*, Latine redditum a G. Haselbeck (Friburgi Brisgoviae, 1909), p. 589.

[30] Holzapfel, *op. cit.*, p. 590.

secular people, according to the Chapter, might just as easily perform this work in the future.[31]

SECTION III
LAY SERVANTS AND BROTHERS (*Conversi*)

Still a third means of meeting the difficulties caused by the conflict between enclosure and outside necessities was the use of male and female lay servants, as well as brothers (*conversi*). According to the 1247 Rule of Innocent IV, and the 1264 Rule of Urban IV, which followed the same dispositions in this matter, the friars to whom the monasteries of the Poor Clares were committed were not bound to reside in the convents; in their stead were to be appointed a chaplain and some laymen or brothers (*conversi*) who would promise obedience directly to the abbess, vowing stability, poverty and chastity.[32] Like the serving sisters, these brothers (*conversi*) could be transferred by the visitor to another monastery for necessary or useful purposes. They were expected to observe the fasts prescribed, just as were the sisters, although the abbess was empowered to grant a dispensation in this regard. They were bound to recite a daily Office consisting of seventy-two *Paters*, and were to be clad in a habit which was described by the Rule in minute detail. Moreover, they were subject to the visitor in all things.[33]

In 1336, as has been shown, Benedict XII forbade the serving sisters to leave the cloister. In order to fill the need created by this rule, each monastery was permitted to have a few good and prudent women of mature age and manner. These women were to be clad in secular garb, and were not permitted to enter the cloister. Their function was to faith-

[31] "Igitur decretum est, ne qua domus nova acciperetur absque consensu capituli generalis, simulque monasteria monialium prohibita sunt curam rerum temporalium fratribus imponere, quia huic muneri saeculares satisfacere possent."—*Ibid.*, p. 591.

[32] "... Capellanus et conversi secundum dispositionem visitatoris promittant obedientiam abbatissae, voventes loci stabilitatem, et perpetuo vivere sine proprio et in castitate: ..."—*Bull. Rom.*, III, 534.

[33] *Ibid.*, pp. 534-535.

fully carry on the outside business of the monastery and to provide for the necessities of the nuns, insofar as these tasks might be committed to them.[34] In all likelihood, such women were in attendance on the needs of the nuns even before the permission granted by Benedict XII. "It is fairly certain that from the early years of the Order onwards it was quite usual to have lay people staying within the precincts of each house."[35] In England, for example, it was quite common to have in religious houses men and women called *corrodians*. In return for their services, these persons received food and lodging within the monastic precincts.[36]

[34] *Ibid.*, IV, 414; cf. *supra*, p. 17.
[35] Bourdillon, *op. cit.*, p. 65.
[36] *Ibid.*, p. 66.

CHAPTER IV

PAPAL CONSTITUTIONS OF THE SIXTEENTH CENTURY

SECTION I
PRECEDING DEVELOPMENTS

The strict cloister demanded by Boniface VIII apparently ruled out any further employment of professed nuns in the exterior duties of the monastery.[1] Perhaps the most practical solution to this very strict cloister, and one which approximated quite closely the notion of the extern sister today, was to be found in the fourteenth century Rule of the Nuns of St. Jerome, so named because the Rule was falsely attributed to that saint.[2] This Rule provided that strict enclosure, in accordance with the papal mandate, be observed by all the nuns, but not by those women who, wearing a type of religious habit and bound by a vow, frequented the cities and towns in order to provide food and other necessities for the monasteries.[3] These women were to dwell outside the cloister, there to minister to the needs of the enclosed nuns, at the same time leading such a life as to give evidence of the interior sanctity of the monastery. To this end the Rule warned them to be guarded in speech, not to take nourishment outside the monastery in private homes, and to give a good example to all. To avoid distraction and harm to the nuns, it was forbidden for these women to hold any secret conversations with them. They were bound to the fasts and

[1] Cf. *supra*, p. 15.

[2] "Indigna prorsus, quae Hieronymo affigeretur, doctis probisque hominibus visa est. Sane neque est, in quo consarcinatoris diligentiam laudes."—Migne, *op. cit.*, XXX, col. 391-392.

[3] "... numquam, si fieri potest, exire permittatur. Non etiam mulieres illae quae religionis habitum gestant, et voto obligatae noscuntur coenobio, per civitatem et vicos, victus et necessaria quaerant."—*Ibid.*, col. 413.

observances of the institute. Over the observance of all these matters the abbess kept watch, with power to punish those who violated these rules.[4]

It does not seem that these women were extern sisters in the strict sense of the word, since they were not professed in the Order. It is true that, according to the Rule, they were bound by a kind of vow (*"voto obligatae"*) ; however this vow is interpreted as a private vow or promise, and not as any sort of public profession. In fact, the Rule mentioned absolutely nothing about a novitiate or profession for these women.[5]

This particular solution to the problems created by the strict enclosure was not very widespread. The use of lay servants, both male and female, continued to grow, however, and the service of the nuns by monks, brothers (*conversi*) and friars was still in existence. In fact these were now the sole means of providing for the needs of the monasteries of nuns. The serving sisters had been definitely ruled out by Boniface VIII in 1298 and by Benedict XII in 1336.[6] New statutes, like those of the Benedictine nuns at *Marienberg bei Boppard* in 1437, demanded that the lay sisters (*conversae*) observe the enclosure just as the other nuns, demanding much more serious reasons for egress than the mere day to day necessities of the monastery.[7] A set of statutes dating from around 1480 simply stated that the lay sisters were bound to the same enclosure as the nuns.[8]

[4] *Loc. cit.*

[5] "Ob diese '*servitrices*' wirklich '*Schwestern im Sinne des Rechts*' d. h. Frauen mit den Ordensgelübden waren, ist freilich keineswegs sicher. Von einem Noviziat und einer Profess berichtet diese Regel nichts; . . ."—Hofmeister, *op. cit.*, pp. 428-429.

[6] Cf. *supra*, pp. 15-16.

[7] " 'Insuper et de conversis sororibus idem per omnia volumus observari, quas Magistra sicut nec alias sorores extra claustrum monasterii emittere potest, nisi ex magna et nobili necessitate aut evidente utilitate monasterii, quod tunc de consilio et consensu conventus seu maioris partis conventus facere poterit; quod si secus fecerit, per visitatores sui reatus penam [sic] luat.' "—Hs. 1258/1819 der Stadtbibliothek Trier f. 2r—cited by Hofmeister, *op. cit.*, p. 65.

[8] *Ibid.*, pp. 65-66.

In many instances it was not easy to find lay servants to provide for the needs of a monastery of nuns; the situation was rendered even more acute in 1532, when the Friars Minor refused to provide for the temporal care of the Poor Clares on the grounds that secular people should be used for such tasks.[9] Despite these difficulties, the attitude of the Church toward the strict observance of the enclosure remained unflinching. The Council of Trent renewed the dispositions of Boniface VIII in this regard, ordering the bishops to restore the enclosure where it had been violated and to maintain the *status quo* where it had been faithfully observed. No nun after making profession was allowed to leave the enclosure without the special permission of the bishop; all contrary indults and privileges were revoked.[10] Realizing the detriment which was being caused to the nuns by this strict enclosure coupled with increasing difficulties in obtaining adequate outside help, the Holy See attempted to remedy the situation in two closely connected papal constitutions. The first of these was the Constitution of Pius V, *Circa pastoralis,* dated May 29, 1566.[11] Closely following was the Constitution of Gregory XIII, given on December 30, 1572, and entitled *Deo sacris.*[12]

SECTION II
THE PAPAL CONSTITUTIONS

The Constitution *Circa pastoralis* made provision for an

[9] Cf. *supra,* pp. 20-21.

[10] "Bonifacii octavi constitutionem, quae incipit: Periculoso, renovans sancta synodus universis episcopis sub obtestatione divini iudicii et interminatione maledictionis aeternae praecipit, ut in omnibus monasteriis sibi subiectis ordinaria, in aliis vero sedis apostolicae auctoritate, clausuram sanctimonialium ubi violata muerit, diligenter restitui, et ubi inviolata est, conservari maxime procurent... Nemini autem sanctimonialium liceat post professionem exire a monasterio, etiam ad breve tempus, quocunque praetextu, nisi ex aliqua legitima causa ab episcopo approbanda, indultis quibuscunque et privilegiis non obstantibus."—Conc. Trident., sess. XXV, *de regularibus et monialibus,* Cap. V, *Clausurae monialium.*

[11] *Fontes,* I, n. 112.

[12] *Ibid.,* n. 143.

exception to the inviolable rule of enclosure for all professed nuns. According to Pius V (1566-1572), this was done lest the strict cloister prove a source of detriment and harm to the nuns, especially in the matter of procuring their daily sustenance.[13] Pius placed upon the ordinaries and superiors of the nuns the responsibility of seeing to it that the alms of the faithful were collected for their needs. This was to be done by lay sisters (*conversae*) who were not professed; if, however, these sisters had been professed, it was demanded that they be forty years of age, and that they dwell outside the monastery in houses which were nearby. These sisters (*conversae*), even though they might be professed, were not to enter the enclosure of the other nuns, except in cases permitted by their particular constitutions. Moreover, they were not to leave their own houses to collect alms without the permission of the ordinary or their superiors.[14]

In the case of those professed lay sisters (*conversae*) who were employed in collecting alms, the law of the Constitution *Circa pastoralis* amounted to a temporary exclaustration for these women, who were true nuns just as were those who remained in the cloister. This is evident even from the Constitution itself, which forbade them, while performing this outside service, to enter the enclosure of the *other nuns* (*"aliarum Monialium"*).[15] Commentators on the Constitution support this interpretation. Pellizzari refers to them as lay nuns, *"moniales conversae"*;[16] the same terminology is

[13] "Porro ne Moniales, vel Tertiariae praedictae propter hanc clausuram, detrimentum aut incommodum aliquod in earum necessitatibus, maxime in pertinentibus ad illarum victum patiantur, sed ut eis opportune consulatur . . ."—*Ibid.*, n. 112.

[14] ". . . praecipimus, atque mandamus Ordinariis, et Superioribus earum, ut curent colligi fidelium eleemosynas per conversas, quae non sint professae, vel si professae fuerint, sint tamen aetatis annorum quadraginta, et in domibus contiguis, extra tamen Monasterium, degant, et non ingrediantur clausuram aliarum Monialium, nisi in casibus ex earum Constitutionibus permissis, et de earum domibus exire non possint pro huiusmodi eleemosynis colligendis, nisi de licentia Ordinarii, vel earum Superiorum."—*Loc. cit.*

[15] *Loc. cit.*

[16] Pellizzari, *Tractatio de monialibus* (Venetiis, 1651), p. 137.

used by Bonacina.[17] But, although he permitted these professed lay sisters to leave the cloister if necessary, Pius showed in this Constitution that the mind of the Church was still that all professed nuns remain perpetually in the enclosure; this he indicated by forbidding the reception of any more professed lay sisters (*conversae*) even with the permission of the superiors, even going so far as to annul and invalidate any such future reception.[18]

Should this collection of alms by means of lay sisters prove inadequate to sufficiently meet the needs of the monasteries, Pius commanded the ordinaries and superiors of the nuns to provide other pious persons in order to collect the necessary alms, or, should it seem better and more fitting in the judgment of the authorities, to determine that the nuns help support themselves through their own labors.[19]

Even these concessions, however, were inadequate to meet the problems which existed. Thus, only a little more than six years later, Gregory XIII (1572-1585) was led to make still further provisions in the Constitution *Deo sacris*. This Constitution was occasioned by the fact that many monasteries of nuns were still in need, and no sufficient means had been provided to care for their necessities, despite the command of Pius V.[20] In order to ensure a regular and ade-

[17] Bonacina, *Tractatus de clausura, et poenis eam violantibus impositis* (Venetiis, 1626), p. 23.

[18] "Et de cetero nullae aliae conversae professae recipi amplius etiam de consensu suorum Superiorum, vel Praelatorum possint; quod si adversus hanc nostram prohibitionem receptae fuerint, illarum receptio nulla, irrita, et inanis sit, prout ex nunc nullam irritam facimus, et annullamus."—*Fontes*, n. 112.

[19] "Quo si praedicto modo mecessitatibus Monialium, et mulierum Tertiariarum praedictarum succurri sufficienter non poterit, mandamus ipsis Ordinariis, et Superioribus earum, ut ipsi provideant de aliis personis piis, et Deo devotis, quae fidelium eleemosynas colligant, vel alias eo meliori, et commodiori modo, quo fieri poterit, etiam ex opere manuum ipsarum Monialium, et mulierum praedictarum, arbitrio Ordinariorum, et Superiorum earumdem, et prout eis congruentius expedire videbitur, provideatur, et succurratur."—*Loc. cit.*

[20] "Cum autem, sicut accepimus, multae Moniales, etiam quae Tertiariae vocantur, sub solemni Religionis voto, perpetuaque clausura

quate income for needy monasteries of nuns, Gregory levied a tax for their support on certain types of benefices; moreover, he prescribed that half of all the alms collected for the poor throughout the world be conferred on needy monasteries of nuns located in the places where the alms were supposed to be distributed. The only exceptions to this rule were the alms designated for certain particular poor persons, and the alms destined for uses other than the alleviation of the needs of the poor.[21]

With such provisions for the support of the monasteries, it was naturally no longer so necessary for the lay sisters to quest for alms.[22] Hence, where the necessity ceased to exist, there was no longer need to maintain the exclaustration of professed sisters (*conversae*) as permitted by Pius V. Consequently, Gregory provided that, in monasteries where the daily sustenance was adequately provided by any means whatsoever without this collection of alms by the lay sisters, the ordinaries were to place them under the same enclosure as the other nuns. Likewise they were not to be permitted to go out again in the future.[23]

Those lay sisters who were not professed and who were no longer needed in the monastery, if they did not wish to make profession and observe the enclosure, were directed to

degentes, aliaeque talibus literis comprehensae, et in ipsa clausura permanentes, multis praeterea ad se sustentandas necessariis egeant, neque usque ad hoc tempus ullo sufficienti remedio earum necessitatibus subventum sit."—*Ibid.*, n. 143.

[21] *Loc. cit.;* cf. Bonacina, *op. cit.*, p. 24.

[22] "Verum tamen est, hoc tempore raro fieri posse, ut moniales conversae iustam habeant causam exeundi ad colligendas eleemosinas, . . ." —Bonacina, *op. cit.*, p. 24.

[23] "Ceterum quod attinet ad Conversas professas, quas praedictus Pius Praedecessor per praedictas literas sub certis conditionibus ibi contentis permisit posse manere extra Monasteria pro colligendis eleemosynis, eisdem locorum Ordinariis iniungimus, ut quibus Monasteriis praedictarum Monialium quotidianis laboribus computatis, supradicta, vel alia qualibet ratione de sufficienti subventione, et sustentatione provisum esse cognoverit, easdem Conversas sub eadem clausura cum aliis Monialibus reducant, neque a suis Monasteriis amplius exire permittant."—*Fontes*, I, n. 143; cf. Pellizzari, *op. cit.*, p. 137.

remove their habits and return to their homes in the world, and they could not be received in the future unless they were willing to make profession and abide under a perpetual enclosure.[24] Such an order seemed to conflict with the prohibition of Pius V against the admission of any more lay sisters (*conversae*) to profession; Gregory obviated this objection by declaring that the prohibition of the Constitution *Circa pastoralis* should be interpreted as not including those who dwelt outside the monastery in nearby houses.[25]

SECTION III
EFFECTS OF THE PAPAL CONSTITUTIONS ON THE LAY SISTERS

In the Constitutions *Circa pastoralis* and *Deo sacris,* it had been the mind of the Holy See to meet the needs of the monasteries by permitting the use of professed lay sisters outside the enclosure. At the same time it had wished to limit as strictly as possible the number of situations in which the exclaustration of a professed lay nun might be permitted. After these Constitutions, it was attitude of the Holy See that, where the needs of a monastery could not conveniently be met through the assistance of other persons, the lay sisters might continue to quest, observing the conditions laid down by these Constitutions, but qualified by a declaration of the Sacred Congregation of Bishops and Regulars which was issued in 1573. According to this declaration, the number of such sisters who might be sent out to collect alms was limited to a maximum of eight nuns, who were of good character and in at least their fortieth year of age. They were always to go out two by two, and never to be separated from

24 "Conversas vero non professas, et profiteri nolentes, dimisso habitu domum remittant, neque alias in futurum, nisi professionem suo tempore emissuras, atque sub perpetua clausura mansuras in Monasteria huiusmodi recipi permittatur."—*Fontes,* I, n. 143.

25 "Quod autem id. Pius Praedecessor statuit, de cetero nullas alias Conversas professas recipi amplius, etiam de consensu suorum Superiorum posse, ita esse intelligendum declaramus, praeter illas Conversas, quae extra Monasterium in domibus contiguis degerent."—*Loc. cit.*

each other. It was forbidden to spend the night outside of towns where there were monasteries, unless special permission of the bishop was obtained; in such a case, they were to sleep together.[26]

The interpretation placed upon these conditions by the Holy See was rather strict. A certain monastery of tertiary nuns in Assisi had received permission from the episcopal visitor to go out on the quest, despite the fact that the nuns were not lay sisters (*conversae*). The Sacred Congregation of Bishops and Regulars declared that such a faculty granted to monasteries of Tertiaries was against the provisions of the Council of Trent and against the papal constitutions. Without an express grant by the Holy See, such a permission simply could not be given.[27]

In the light of the severe limitations placed on the reception of lay sisters by the papal constitutions, it might be expected that the institution would almost have died. Such, however, was not the case, for professed lay sisters continued to exist in almost all the institutes of nuns. One argument used in justification of this continued practice was that the law did not mean to completely forbid the reception of all lay sisters, but sought to bar the reception of those who did not wish to become true religious, i.e., of those who desired

[26] "Octavo licitum esse monialibus conversis e Monasterio exire ad petendas eleemosinas conventui necessarias, dum eas per alios commode petere non possunt, servatis tamen conditionibus praescriptis in motu Pii Quinti, qui incipit, *Circa pastoralis,* et in alio motu Gregorii Decimitertii, qui incipit, *sacris virginibus,* ac denique in quadam Sacrae Congregationis declaratione apud Zechium capitulo tertio, numero decimoquinto versiculo nono, titulo de regulis edita anno MDLXXIII ubi decernitur, et declaratur, ad colligendas eleemosinas non plures conversas mittendas esse, quam octo, quae binae incedant, nec disiungantur, et sint probatae vitae, excedentesque annos triginta novem, nec pernoctent extra oppida, ubi habent Monasteria, nisi de Episcopi licentia, et tunc simul dormiant."—Bonacina, *op. cit.,* p. 23.

[27] "La facoltà concessa alli monasterii delle tertiarie di poter uscire a questuare in certo numero, è contro il Concilio[3] [[3]Sess. XXV, de regularibus, c. 5] et bolle et pero senza espresso ordine di S. S. non si può dar loro tal licentia."—S.C. Ep. et Reg., Assisinaten., 7 oct. 1573, al Vescovo d'Ascoli Visitatore in Assisi, *Fontes,* IV, n. 1310.

to enter only for the purpose of collecting alms.[28] Moreover, the reception of lay sisters was justified on the basis of a custom which as the authors held, could safely be followed, as long as these sisters made profession like the other nuns.[29] This custom was upheld as reasonable and safe in practice, since otherwise those women who were not apt for choir duty, or who could not raise the demanded dowry, would be excluded from the religious life entirely. Moreover, just as, in institutes of men, some were admitted for the care of temporalities, so, by analogy, this should be permitted in institutes of women.[30]

Among the various monasteries of Poor Clares, the faculty to receive lay sisters was dependent upon which particular Rule a given monastery followed. Those who followed the primitive Rule were not permitted to retain their lay sisters. However, Urban IV in his mitigated Rule had permitted a few of these serving sisters (*servitiales*) or lay sisters (*conversae*) in each monastery, with the same obligations and vows as the other nuns. The Holy See declared that the prohibition of receiving lay sisters (*conversae*) applied only to the Clares who observed the first Rule. The others might continue to have such sisters if such had been the custom of the monastery. It was not permitted, however, to begin the practice where no such custom had existed in the past.[31]

[28] "Ratio est. Tum quia in praecitatis iuribus non interdicitur simpliciter conversarum receptio, sed illarum, quae fieri nolunt verae religiosae, seu quae eleemosinis colligendis deputatae sunt."—Bonacina, *op. cit.*, p. 23.

[29] ". . . potest talis consuetudo tuto servari; dummodo dictae conversae legitimam faciant professionem: . . ."—Pellizzari, *op. cit.*, p. 279; "Respondeo moniales conversas posse adhuc ob receptam consuetudinem recipi, et ad professionem admitti."—Bonacina, *op. cit.*, p. 23.

[30] Bonacina, *op. cit.*, p. 23.

[31] "Differentia notabilis est inter ipsas Moniales, ac reliquas, quae sub Regula mitigata vivunt, nedum quoad majorem rigorem habitus, et penitentiarum, ut Cherubin. notat in margine utriusque Bullae; sed praesertim, quia illae observantes hanc primaevam Regulam non possunt retinere Conversas, seu Ancillas, quas permittit Urbanus in mitigatione Regulae cap. 19 ubi Servitiales huiusmodi Conversas appellat,

Although the lay sisters (*conversae*) still continued to exist in the monasteries of nuns, they became more and more exclusively cloistered as a result of the prescriptions of the Holy See, and performed the menial tasks within the enclosure. The outside work and questing were, for the most part, taken over by lay servants and extern sisters which began to develop during this period.[32] Thus the Cistercian nuns were ordered by their General Chapter to cease cultivating their own farms and to turn them over to seculars, in order to put a stop to the scandals resulting from the frequent trips of the lay sisters to the fields. If such places could not conveniently or quickly enough be turned over to the care of seculars who were willing to move on to the land and cultivate it, the work was to be done by secular women who dwelt ouside the enclosure, and no longer by the lay sisters, whose performance of this work would entail a violation of the cloister.[33]

The actual egress of nuns from their monasteries in order to quest became more and more of a rarity as other means became common. In 1809 permission was granted to a monastery in Nepi, Italy, for some of the nuns to go out to pro-

et cap. 2 permittit etiam eas, sed paucas cum obligatione votorum earundem Monialium. Hinc Sacra Congregatio Episcoporum 6. Martii 1596. rescripsit Archiepiscopo Ulyssiponen. quod prohibitio Monialibus Franciscanis facta de non recipiendis Conversis, intelligatur de Monialibus primam Regulam observantibus . . . imo nec ipsis Monialibus Regulam mitigatam servantibus permittuntur, si eas retinere non consueverint."—Petra, *Commentaria ad Constitutiones Apostolicas seu Bullas Singulas Summorum Pontificum in Bullario Romano contentas secundum collectionem Cherubini* (Romae, 1708), III, 99-100.

[32] Cf. *infra*, Chapters V and VI.

[33] "Praeterea statuitur et ordinatur ut deinceps abbatissae et praefectae monasteriorum abstineant a laboribus et cultura propriorum praediorum, illaque dent ad firmam locationem saecularibus . . . ad obviandum scandalis quae plerumque ex egressu sororum conversarum ad agros evenire solent. Quod si commode vel tam cito id fieri non potest ad huiusmodi administrationem et oeconomiam domesticam extra claustra utantur, in quantum fieri poterit, opera et ministerio mulierum saecularium et non amplius sororum conversarum, ne occasione frequentis illarum egressus clausura violetur."—Canivez, *op. cit.*, VII, 338, ad annum 1618.

cure the necessary sustenance of the convent; but this permission was granted for only three years and subject to the vigilance of the bishop. Moreover, the nuns destined for the quest were to be mature and over forty years of age; they were never to go out alone, but always in pairs, and with their faces duly veiled. They were to remain out no longer than necessary to procure the needed alms. Insofar as possible they were to live in a place apart from the others, but were never to sleep outside the enclosure. On those days when they were not engaged in the quest, they were to make their spiritual exercises in the church, just as the other nuns were required to do. Moreover, during the three years of the indult, the monastery was not allowed to accept, invest, or much less profess other nuns, until the monastery was possessed of sufficient income to support the religious.[34] The mind of the Holy See, then, was to permit the exit from the cloister of professed nuns only when it was absolutely necessary, under subjection to stringent regulations, and only for as long a time as was needed until some other arrangement could be made.

[34] *Collectanea in usum Secretariae Sacrae Congregationis Episcoporum et Regularium*, cura A. Bizzarri Archiepiscopi Philippensis Secretarii edita (Romae, 1885), p. 409.

CHAPTER V

LAY SERVANTS

As the practice of permitting professed lay sisters (*conversae*) to leave the cloister became less common, one of the principal means of caring for the necessities of the monasteries was the employment of secular servants, both male and female. These servants were employed both within the cloister, and outside of it. Those who worked inside the enclosure are not of concern here, since it was strictly required that, for the duration of their service, they observe the enclosure just as the nuns observed it.[1] Hence, insofar as outside work and questing for alms might be entrusted to lay servants, such tasks had to be performed by those who lived permanently outside the enclosure.

These outside servants were attached to many monasteries of various institutes of nuns. Thus the Cistercian nuns made use of secular women;[2] and, among the Poor Clares, the abbess was empowered to appoint laymen for the service of the monastery.[3] So closely united were these servants to the monasteries that they were, according to the instructions of the Holy See, to be counted among the number of individual persons to be supported by the monastery. This was an important factor, inasmuch as the total number of nuns, lay sisters (*conversae*), and extern persons (*personae exterae*) was not permitted to exceed the number who could be cared for by the income of the convent.[4]

[1] Bouix, *Tractatus de Jure Regularium* (2 vols., Parisiis, 1857), Tom. I, pp. 669 et 673; Pellizzari, *op. cit.*, p. 190; Ferraris, *Bibliotheca canonica iuridica moralis theologica*, ed. novissima (9 vols., Romae, 1885-1899), V, 584; Const. Benedicti XIV, "Per binas," 24 ian. 1747—*Fontes*, II, n. 375.

[2] Canivez, *op. cit.*, VII, 338, ad annum 1618.

[3] Petra, *op. cit.*, III, 345.

[4] "In praefixione numeri distingui debent separatim, quot debeant esse moniales velatae, quot conversae, et quot aliae personae exterae

The houses where these servants lived were in no wise considered a part of the monastic enclosure, but were usually located near the monastery. Access to these places was, therefore, absolutely forbidden to the nuns.[5] If no other arrangement could be made, a servant was permitted to live in a room located in the parlor of the monastery, but always with the provision that the room be located outside the cloister.[6] These servants were permitted to enter the cloister only when it was necessary to perform tasks that could not conveniently be done by the nuns or by the lay sisters (*conversae*) and female servants within the enclosure.[7] Thus, the Sacred Congregation of Bishops and Regulars allowed the admission of servants in order to handle large wine casks and to perform other such necessary services.[8]

It was generally conceded that these servants, while re-

monasterii redditibus sustinendae. Sacra Congreg. Episc. et Regul. in Placent. 6 Novemb. 1695; in Comen. 23 Julii 1602; in una Civit. Castelli 13 Maii 1603; in una nullius Castri Durantis, 29 Augusti 1614."—Ferraris, *op. cit.*, V, 600.

5 "Hinc sequitur primo Moniales non posse ad domos Monasterio contiguas accedere, etiamsi domos illas inhabitent tantummodo feminae eleemosinis colligendis, vel servitiis Monasterio praestandis deputatae; cum enim ad huiusmodi domos saecularibus pateat accessus, intra Monasterii septa non connumerantur, nec clausurae terminis clauduntur."—Bonacina, *op. cit.*, p. 3.

6 "Factor, si non patiatur exceptiones, habitare poterit in cubiculo intra collocutorium, sed extra clausuram, Navarien. 5. Decembris 1600, Ianven. 15. Martii 1606."—Lucidi, *De Visitatione Sacrorum Liminum*, Instructio S. C. Concilii, ed. 3, purgata et aucta per P. Iosephum Schneider (3 vols., Romae, 1883), II, 156.

7 "Non posse, nec debere ingredi, nisi in iis casibus, in quibus Moniales se ipsis non possunt commode praestare illud servitium (quod est dicere in casibus necessitatis moraliter urgentis) et, si citra tales casus ingrediatur, delinquit contra clausuram et incurrit excommunicationem quod bene debent advertere etiam Moniales; quae interdum sunt nimis faciles in admittendis propriis famulis, etiam ad ea obsequia, quae iudicio prudentis possunt commode praestari a Monialibus Conversis."—Pellizzari, *op. cit.*, p. 192.

8 "Poterit etiam ingredi, prout moris est, ad apte locanda dolia, recondendum vinum, et alia necessaria ministeria exercenda. Perusin. 9. Oct. 1618. apud Nicol. loc. cit."—Lucidi, *op. cit.*, II, 156.

maining lay persons, were invested with a quasi-religious dignity in favorable matters, and this by reason of their intimate connection wth the nuns and their special dedication to the service of God. Often they even wore a type of religious habit. On this basis, it was regarded as a probable opinion that such servants enjoyed the privilege of the forum (*privilegium fori*).[9] This same doctrine was extended to the privilege of the canon (*privilegium canonis.*)[10] This privilege likewise included the female lay servants who dwelt inside the enclosure.[11]

Although the servants living in the vicinity of the monasteries of nuns were considered to have a quasi-religious status, they were nevertheless under the spiritual care of the pastor of that parish in which the monastery was located. According to several declarations of the Sacred Congregation of the Council, they were to receive the sacraments from this pastor, who also had the right and duty to care for their burial at death.[12] In regard to this matter of their spiritual

[9] "Immo, *Bonac. D. I. de censur. in partic. c. 16. sect. I. p. 3. n. 18.* et cum eo *Diana p. 4. tr. I. resol. 31.* aliique; et non improbabiliter sustinent homines laicos, qui, assumpto habitu religioso, adhibentur ad obsequia Monialium, et ad petendam pro ipsis eleemosynam, gaudere hoc eodem privilegio fori: quippe in materia favorabili censentur quasi religiosi, utpote intimius pertinentes ad personas religiosas, et speciali quadam ratione Deo devoti: quod iuxta superius dicta videtur sufficere, ad hoc ut quis dicatur gaudere privilegio fori, quamvis alias sit laicus."—Pellizzari, *op. cit.*, p. 320.

[10] "Quin etiam docet *Bonac. D. 2. de censur. in com. q. 4. p. I. n. 9.* homines illos, qui, assumpto habitu religioso, adhibentur ad servitia, ac obsequia Monialium, et ad petendas pro ipsis eleemosynas, frui privilegio canonis, et hoc maxime ob rationem paulo ante allatam ex Suarez."—*Ibid.*, p. 323.

[11] "Addo privilegium canonis competere foeminis, quae, mutato habitu sub clausura cum velo albo, ac obligatione recitandi quotidie certas preces admittuntur ad famulatum monasterii absque emissione votorum substantialium religionis. . . ."—*Ibid*, p. 321.

[12] "Monialium famuli et famulae habitantes in mansionibus intra atria monasteriorum, tenentur recipere sacramenta ab illis parochis, in quorum parochia sita sunt monasteria. Sacra Congr. Conc. in Ulixbonen. Occidentalis 19 sept. 1722; et iam decreverat in Leodien. 14 apr. 1685, et in Spoletana 19 apr. 1691. Ubi etiam, quod ad

care, these male and female servants were also in a privileged position because of their connection with the monastery, for, during the time of interdict, they were permitted to attend religious services at the monastery. This included all who in any way could be called servants of the convent.[13]

Gradually the employment of such servants began to decline. The lay sisters (*conversae*) within the cloister were able to perform the tasks that the cloistered servants (*ancillae*) had done, and the growing number of extern sisters displaced many of the outside servants. Although some vestige of these servants remains today in the caretakers often found associated with monasteries of nuns, by far the principal answer to the problems created by the cloistered life has become the extern sister.

dictos parochos spectat eos associare ad sepulturam."—Ferraris, *op. cit.*, V. 665.

[13] Pellizzari, *op. cit.*, p. 340.

CHAPTER VI

EXTERN SISTERS

Extern sisters, in the present day concept, are women religious of simple vows, who, attached to a monastery of nuns as members of the religious family, care for the external necessities of the convent.[1] It is generally agreed that this institution originated in its present form with the Constitutions of the Visitation Nuns, which were sanctioned by St. Francis de Sales in 1618 and approved by Urban VIII in 1626.[2] A study of these *Soeurs Tourières* is of importance, since they served as the pattern on which the extern sisters of other institutes were based.

SECTION I

EXTERN SISTERS OF THE VISITATION

The first Constitution of the Sisters of the Visitation divided the religious into three classes, viz. choir nuns, associated sisters and domestic sisters; the extern or outsisters were not even mentioned at this point.[3] However, the entire forty-second Constitution dealt with these sisters, and made it quite evident that they were considered *bona fide* members of the monastery and true sharers in the religious life of the institute.[4]

The monasteries were directed to be rather reserved in admitting these sisters, two or three being regarded as both

[1] "Sorores externae sunt Religiosae votorum simplicium, quae Monasteriis Monialium, tamquam membra familiae adscriptae, quibusvis externis singuli Monasterii necessitatibus inserviunt."—V. la Puma, "De Sororibus Externis," *Commentarium pro Religiosis*, XII (1931), 426.

[2] *Loc. cit.;* Hofmeister, *op. cit.*, p. 429; A. Vermeersch, "De externis monasteriorum Sororibus," *Periodica*, XXI (1932), 44.

[3] *Règles de St. Augustin et Constitutions de la Visitation*, (Annecy, 1889), Const. I, *Des trois rangs des Soeurs*, pp. 119-120. (Hereafter cited as *Const.*).

[4] *Ibid.*, XLII, *Des Soeurs Tourières*, pp. 293-300.

necessary and sufficient for the service of a convent.[5] Above all, the superior was directed to receive only those who desired to serve the Lord in laboring for the community; moreover, because of the practical needs they were destined to serve, it was demanded that they be of a strong body and healthy physical constitution.[6] In addition, a certain degree of business acumen was desirable, for St. Jane Frémiot de Chantal wrote that "there should also be one who is civil, intelligent and prudent, to know how to purchase the stuffs and necessary provisions, to go on messages, and return proper answers; in short they must be chosen according to the places and employment assigned them."[7]

Upon entrance into the monastery, even before entering the novitiate, the out-sisters were required to undergo a six week period of probation and trial, during which the duties of their state of life were explained to the candidates.[8] Only then were they to be received in the same manner as the other sisters, being subjected to the regular postulancy and a two-year novitiate. At the end of the novitiate, they made profession of the simple vow of obedience and oblation.[9]

5 "La Congrégation recevra le moins qu'elle pourra, des Soeurs Tourières; et semble bien que deux ou trois seront également et necessaires et suffisantes pour tout ce qui est requis au service de la Maison."—*Ibid.*, p. 293.

6 "Or, la Supérieure prendra garde que celles qu'elle prendra soient de bon corps de bon coeur, de bonne complexion et de bon naturel, ..."—*Ibid.*, pp. 293-294.

7 *Answers of the Blessed Mother Jane Frances Frémiot*, translated from *Reponces de Notre Sainte Mère Jeanne-Francoise Frémiot de Chantal* by B. Rayment, 1817 (Georgetown, D.C., 1834), p. 170. (Hereafter cited as *Answers*).

8 "One les éprouvera donc six semaines durant, pendant lequel temps on leur proposera les articles du service et de l'obéissance qu'elles auront à rendre, la soumission de leur propre volonté en toutes choses, avec le reste de l'observance de la Règle."—*Const.*, XLII, p. 294.

9 "Après quoi, on les recevra les mèmes conditions et considérations que les autres Soeurs. . . . Elles demeureront deux années novices, passées lesquelles elles seront établies en la Congrégation par le voeu simple d'obéissance et l'oblation, comme il sera dit."—*Ibid.*, pp. 294-296; cf. *ibid.*, XLIII, XLIV, XLV.

Some have maintained that this profession involved the taking of vows which were strictly private and temporary, so that the out-sisters were no more than unprofessed oblates who were nevertheless accorded the privilege of being accounted members of the community.[10] However, the Constitutions speak not of a private vow, but rather of a simple vow.[11] It is true that the attitude of the Church towards the taking of simple vows was, at this time, unfavorable; nevertheless, new institutes of simple vows continued to be founded by episcopal authority and tolerated by the Holy See. During the eighteenth century, the Holy See began to approve such societies, not recognizing them as true religious institutes, but regarding them as a new form of the life of perfection.[12] In this case, the simple vows were not only tolerated by the Apostolic See, but were actually prescribed in the Constitutions approved by Pope Urban VIII.[13] Moreover, there was a definite liturgical rite prescribed for the public ceremony accompanying the taking of these vows.[14] If one wishes to label such vows "private" in order to distinguish them from the solemn vows which alone were recognized as true religious vows, the foregoing status of these vows must nevertheless be recognized; moreover, it scarcely seems cor-

[10] "Si fides sit *Monitore Ecclesiastico*, 1931, p. 331, originem ducunt a S. Francisco Salesio, qui, ut per Moniales a Visitatione, operosam erga proximum caritatem exercere posset, unicuique monasterio sui Ordinis coniunxit parvos coetus "Soeurs Tourières," sine clausura, solis votis privatis et temporariis astrictarum, ut simplices Oblatae, non professae, quae tamen ipso titulo dicebantur *a Visitatione*."—A. Vermeersch, *op. cit.*, p. 44.

[11] Cf. *supra*, p. 39.

[12] Ledwolorz, *Epitome Iuris Religiosorum* (2 vols., Romae, pro manuscripto, Pont. Athenaeum Antonianum), I, 51-52.

[13] *Const.*, XLII, p. 295.

[14] Quand les Soeurs tourières feront leurs voeux le Célébrant viendra à la grille pour les recevoir, et après qu'elles les auront prononcés, il leur mettra la Croix au col, et leur donnera un cierge, disant les paroles convenables à ces cérémonies, selon qu'elles sont ci-des-sus."—*Coutumier et Directoire pour les Soeurs Religieuses de la Visitation Sainte-Marie* (Annecy, 1850), p. 68. (Hereafter cited as *Coutumier*); *Answers*, p. 172.

rect to equate the out-sisters with non-professed oblates. Nor does it seem correct to speak of this profession as the taking of only temporary vows, when the formula of profession prescribed for the *Soeurs Tourières* specifically mentions *perpetual* vows of obedience and oblation of self to the service of the monastery.[15] True, the vows were conditioned on the perseverance of the sister in the monastery, and a dispensation could be granted by a prelate or by the spiritual father of the monastery for a just and grave reason, e.g., if the sister gave scandal or became incorrigible and obstinate in some serious matter.[16] But *per se* the vows were taken for life. The renewal of vows prescribed each year on the Feast of the Presentation of the Blessed Virgin was not at all a renewal of temporary vows which had expired, but a devotional renewal.[17]

The out-sisters did not change their mode of dress, but dressed in accordance with the custom of the place in which the community happened to be established. Their clothing consisted of a simple black dress without any trimmings; they wore a silver cross suspended about the neck.[18] They observed the fasts just as the other sisters, and were bound to the performance of certain regular devotional exercises. Their office seems to have consisted of the Rosary. In general, they were to conform themselves to the regular program of the monastery insofar as this was permitted by the occupations to which they were assigned.[19]

In the performance of their duties, they were under the

[15] "Je N. offre, dédie, et consacre mon coeur et mon corps à Dieu, en l'honneur de la glorieuse Vierge Marie Notre Dame, et du bienheureux saint Augustin, pour servier à jamais à la divine Majesté en la Congregation de céans; faisant, à cet effet, voeu de perpétualle obéissance et oblation de ma personne, selon la Règle et Constitutions d'icelle Congrégation."—*Coutumier*, p. 68.

[16] *Loc. cit.; Answers*, p. 172; La Puma, *op. cit.*, p. 427.

[17] *Coutumier*, p. 183; La Puma, *op. cit.*, p. 426.

[18] *Const.*, XLII, p. 295; *Answers*, p. 171.

[19] "Bref, autant que les occupations auxquelles elles sont destinées le permettront, on les rendra conformes en moeurs, en exercices et en affection aux Soeurs de la Congregation."—*Const.*, XLII, p. 296.

direction of the superior and the procurator, as well as that of the sister appointed to instruct them in spiritual matters. The superior was admonished to command them in charity, and all the sisters were required to call them sisters, despite the fact they were employed in exterior and domestic duties.[20] They lived outside the cloister, but were allowed to enter it for the necessary services of the monastery, and this by permission of the ordinary, which was obtained by the superioress at the beginning of each year. In grave illnesses, provided these were not contagious, they were cared for just as the cloistered sisters, in the community infirmary. Moreover, on certain great feasts and for certain special religious exercises, they entered the cloister as full members of the community.[21] When actually outside the monastery to procure provisions, they were to conduct themselves in an edifying manner. They were not permitted to eat outside the monastery, nor to enter any house without the consent of the superior, except in a case of necessity. Even engaging in public conversations on the streets was forbidden; it was only to the superior that they might bring any news, messages or recommendations which they might have received.[22]

Section II
Spread of the Institution

Providing, as it did, an ideal solution to the needs of cloistered monasteries, the institution of extern sisters spread to other religious institutes. Thus, there soon existed among the Ursulines of the Observance of Paris an arrangement similar to that found among the Visitation Sisters. With the permission of the bishop, these convents had extern sisters who wore a form of religious habit. After a novitiate of one year, they professed simple vows of obedience and chastity for the period of their service in the monastery.[23]

[20] *Ibid.*, pp. 296-298; *Answers*, pp. 170-171.

[21] *Const.*, XLII, p. 298; *Answers*, pp. 171-172; La Puma, *op. cit.*, pp. 426-427.

[22] *Const.*, XLII, pp. 299-300.

[23] Ähnlich lagen die Verhältnisse bei den *Ursulinen von der Ob-*

A slightly different situation existed among the *donatae* of the Premonstratensian nuns. According to their statutes, which were approved by the General Chapter of 1630, the *donatae* made a novitiate of one year, during which they remained clothed in modest secular garb. After the year of novitiate, they made the espousal and dedication (*sponsio et donatio*), by which they gave themselves to the service of the cloister, promising the conversion of their lives in the observance of poverty, chastity and obedience for the length of their service to the convent.[24] Under the terms of this profession, the *donatae* obliged themselves not to leave the service of the monastery of their own volition; on the other hand, if dismissed legitimately, they promised not to oppose this move.[25] The statutes specifically mentioned that they were destined for work outside the enclosure and the monastery, which had always been performed by lay sisters (*conversae*) who were not bound to the observance of the enclosure. These *donatae* were forbidden to enter the enclosure at all; even their instruction in the spiritual life had to be given in the parlor.[26]

Among the Benedictines, there existed a group of extern oblates who took the vows of obedience and stability; these vows could be dissolved either by the monastic authorities, or by the oblates themselves. In case of illness, the oblates were to be cared for inside the enclosure; they were likewise

servanz von Paris, bei denen man sog. Torschwestern hatte, die mit Erlaubnis des Bischofs ein entsprechendes Ordenskleid trugen und nach bestandenem Probejahr die einfachen Gelübde des Gehorsams und der Keuschheit für die Dauer ihres Aufenthalts im Kloster ablegten."—Hofmeister, *op. cit.,* p. 429.

24 *Ibid.,* p. 430.

25 "Ausserdem verpflichteten sie sich noch, den Klosterverband nicht freiwillig zu verlassen und, wenn sie "ob demerita vel ob causas in Statutis expressas" entlassen würden, auch wirklich weg-zugehen und dieser Massregel keineswegs Widerstand leisten zu wollen."—*Loc. cit.*

26 *Loc. cit.*

permitted to enter it for the performance of certain services as determined by the common law.[27]

In certain areas, where the declarations on the papal cloister had never been received in practice, there was followed the old custom whereby lay sisters were permitted to leave the enclosure with the permission of the superioress. Thus, at Aachen in 1631, there existed a set of statutes based on the Statutes of the Third Order of St. Francis, which permitted sisters with solemn vows (*sorores egredientes*) to go out of the enclosure to perform the outside service. It was not long, however, before these sisters were made to become cloistered lay sisters.[28]

The growing progress of the status of simple profession in institutes of women brought changes and improvement in the status of the extern sisters. Most of the development began in the latter part of the nineteenth century. In 1800, only among the Benedictine nuns of the Holy Hearts of Jesus and Mary were there extern sisters who professed the three vows of poverty, chastity and obedience;[29] but by the end of the century such externs with the three religious vows were far more common.

In 1888, the abbesses of the Poor Clare monasteries at Romans, Valence and Crest petitioned the Holy See to permit the extern sisters in these monasteries to take the three simple vows of poverty, chastity and obedience, to be observed according to the Rule of the Third Order of St. Francis which had been approved in 1521 by Pope Leo X in the Bull *Inter cetera*.[30] This Rule was adapted to the extern sisters by means of certain declarations and explanations appended to each chapter. Moreover, the petition requested that the extern sisters share in the indulgences and spiritual favors granted to the monastery in which they served.[31] Pope Leo

[27] *Loc. cit.*

[28] *Ibid*, pp. 430-431.

[29] *Ibid*, p. 431.

[30] Bulla Leonis X, "Inter cetera," 20 ian. 1521—*Bull. Rom.*, V, 764-767.

[31] "... humillime postulant, ut Sorores externae praefatorum Mona-

XIII approved this request on May 8, 1888, and it was made public by the Sacred Congregation of Bishops and Regulars on May 18, 1888.[32] Not only was the permission granted for the three monasteries which had entered the request, but it was conceded that all monasteries of Poor Clares subject to the jurisdiction of the bishops might, with the permission of the ordinary, adopt this Rule with its accommodations to the extern sisters. Moreover, they were allowed to retain their own proper statutes and legitimate customs, provided they were not contrary to the provisions appended to the Rule.[33]

In treating of the reception of extern sisters to the novitiate, the adaptations and explanations appended to the first chapter of the Rule summarized briefly the past status of externs in the Order. Referring to the old custom of employing lay brothers in the quest, the explanation stated that it had been the recent practice to employ only women for such services. These women had professed the Rule of the Third Order Secular, adding a simple vow to keep the Ten Commandments. Moreover, promises of poverty, chastity and obedience were made to the abbess.[34]

steriorum, Tourières nuncupatae, emittant in posterum tria vota simplicia Paupertatis, Obedientiae et Castitatis iuxta Regulam Tertii Ordinis B. Patris Francisci de Poenitentia a S. M. Leone PP. X approbatam, Bulla "Inter cetera" 20 Januarii 1521 cum declarationibus tamen et explanationibus inferius relatis, quibus praedicta Regula pro iisdem Sororibus externo servitio addictis aptatur, cum participatione indulgentiarum et gratiarum spiritualium Monasterio, cui inserviunt, concessis."—*Acta Ordinis Minorum,* VII (1888), 82.

[32] *Ibid.,* p. 87.

[33] "Omnibus Clarissarum Monasteriis, Episcoporum iurisdictioni subiectis, fas sit praedictam Regulam Tertii Ordinis S. Francisci, Sororibus externis accommodatam, acceptare, praevia Ordinarii licentia; eisdem tamen liceat propria servare statuta ac legitimas consuetudines, quae praefatae Regulae adnexisque animadversionibus non adversantur."—*Loc. cit.;* La Puma, *op. cit.,* p. 427; D'Ambrosio, "Sorores externae monasteriorum monialium," *Apollinaris,* IV (1931), 399.

[34] "Notandum tamen de *Fratribus* nullo modo esse quaestionem. Licet enim in transactis saeculis multa Secundi Ordinis Seraphici

According to the declarations of 1888, authority to receive externs rested with the abbess and her council, the ordinary or his delegate possessing a right of confirmation. Before their investiture, these sisters were to make a postulancy of one year, during which they were clad in secular garb. Only then might they be invested in a habit, the style of which was determined by the customs or approved constitutions of each monastery. At the conclusion of the novitiate, the extern sisters were admitted to the profession of the simple vows of poverty, chastity and obedience for a period of ten years. Then, at the discretion of the abbess and her council, they could be admitted to the profession of simple perpetual vows.[35]

It was prescribed that these extern sisters recite not the regular Office of the nuns, but one composed of the *Pater noster*. The rigorous fasting of the Order was somewhat mitigated in their favor, since the abbess was empowered to dispense them from fasts of the Rule, and they were not required to observe fasts of the Rule at all on days when they went out on the quest. Their duties were assigned by the abbess and her council; in addition, they were subject to one of the externs called the elder sister (*soror maior*) who was appointed for three years by the abbess and her council. The others were to be subject to this one as to an older sister, but she was not regarded as a superioress.[36] In addition to these forms of supervision, the externs were required to have a spiritual conference with the abbess at least once within a period of fifteen days.[37]

The conversation and general relationship of the extern

Monasteria ad quaestuationem aliaque externa munera obeunda, Fratres Laicos habuerint, mos tamen hodie ubique invaluit pias tantummodo mulieres ad huiusmodi servitia admittendi. Quae quidem mulieres Tertii Ordinis saecularis Regulam ordinarie profitebantur, superaddito simplici voto servandi Decalogi praecepta promissisque Matri Abbatissae obedientia, castitate ac paupertate."—*Acta Ordinis Minorum*, VII (1888), 83.

[35] *Ibid.*, p. 84.

[36] *Ibid.*, pp. 84-85.

[37] *Ibid.*, p. 85.

sisters with both secular persons and the nuns of the monastery were determined by the statutes of each particular convent. Thus the specific services and instances for which the externs might enter the cloister were left to local determination. The declarations on the seventh chapter of the Rule, however, specifically provided that, where the number of extern sisters was too small to minister to a sick sister, she might, with the previous permission of the ordinary, be admitted to the enclosure by the abbess with her council.[38]

With this general adoption of extern sisters among the Poor Clares, still other monasteries and institutes, including congregations of simple vows, adopted the institution, some by particular rescripts of the Apostolic See, others by its inclusion in the text of their constitutions, and still others by legitimate custom.[39] The statutes approved for the externs in these monasteries partly coincided with the Constitutions of St. Francis de Sales and the declarations approved for the Poor Clares; on the other hand, some notable differences were to be found in them, depending on the situation in each monastery adopting the institution.[40]

Worthy of special mention in the evolution of extern sisters are the Constitutions of the Congregation of Sisters of the Good Shepherd, which were submitted to and corrected by the Congregation of Bishops and Regulars in 1897.[41] These particular Constitutions fundamentally conserve the Constitutions of the nuns of Our Lady of Charity, which, in their turn, were taken from those of St. Francis de Sales.[42] The

[38] "Ingravescente morbo, si propter exiguum numerum Sororum externarum, infirmae ministrare difficile fuerit, tunc praevia Ordinarii licentia, Obbatissa cum suo Discretorio infirmam intra septa clausurae admittere potest, ut diligentius curetur, ac ad recipienda Sacramenta facilius disponatur."—*Ibid.*, p. 86.

[39] La Puma, *op. cit.*, p. 428.

[40] "Normae autem regiminis apud haec Monasteria partim coincidunt cum Constitutionibus S. Francisci Salesii, et cum declarationibus pro Clarissis approbatis, partim ab eis plus minusve differunt."—*Loc. cit.*

[41] "Constitutiones pro Sororibus externis Boni Pastoris (Andegaven.)"—*Loc. cit.*

[42] "Congregatio enim Boni Pastoris fundamentaliter conservat Con-

corrections made by the Sacred Congregation on the text submitted by the religious are a good indication of the changed attitude of the Holy See towards the taking of simple vows, and the status to be accorded to extern sisters. The proposed constitutions merely permitted the entrance of the extern sisters into the religious state, and proposed that they be permitted to take a vow of poverty at the discretion of the superioress. The Sacred Congregation simply bypassed these restrictions, and ordered that the extern sisters, after two years of novitiate and eight years of temporary vows, be allowed to profess perpetual vows of poverty, chastity and obedience.[43]

Although the Sisters of the Good Shepherd were a congregation whose members took only simple vows, they had been permitted in 1897 to introduce extern sisters as a true third class of members of the institute. In 1901, however, the development of extern sisters among congregations of simple vows was arrested by the publication of new norms for the approval of institutes of simple vows.[44] The members of such institutes could be divided into no more than two categories, the first for the government of the congregation and the development and culture of the letters and arts, the other for the domestic and manual labor.[45] Likewise such institutes could not aggregate to themselves any group similar to a Third Order. However, for the external service of the convents, they might make use of certain pious women for

stitutiones Monialium Nostrae Dominae a Charitate quae sunt ex Constitutionibus S. Francisci Salesii desumptae."—*Loc cit.*

[43] *Loc. cit.*

[44] *Normae secundum quas S. Congr. Episcoporum et Regularium procedere solet in Approbandis Novis Institutis Votorum Simplicium* (Romae, 1901).

[45] "Membra omnia Instituti aut unam tantum categoriam constituant aut in duas non autem in plures distribuantur . . . si in duas, ad primam pertinent praecipua munera gubernationis, directionis, institutionis in religione, litteris et artibus etc.; altera vero domestics et manualibus operibus praecipue incumbit."—*Ibid.*, p. 14, n. 48.

whom a rule of life could be prescribed, and who could be permitted to share in the merits of the institute.[46]

Among monasteries of nuns, the institution of extern sisters experienced great and rapid growth during the twentieth century. Many of the reasons which had led the Poor Clares to seek and receive the Rule and declarations of 1888 existed also among the Carmelites. In 1921, the Procurator General of the Order of Discalced Carmelites, moved by the inconveniences and necessities which existed in convents of Carmelite nuns throughout the world because of the absence of extern sisters, petitioned the Holy See to approve a set of statutes which would establish the institution in the Carmelite monasteries and alleviate the needs.[47] The matter was not finally settled until April 28, 1925, when the Sacred Congregation of Religious declared that these *Tourières* were to be considered members of the religious community, were to be admitted to profession of simple vows, and were to live in conformity with the statutes included in the decree of the Sacred Congregation. This arrangement was approved for a period of seven years as an experiment.[48]

A number of other institutes and monasteries now compiled statutes for externs, which were somewhat related to the Carmelite Statutes, but with certain omissions and improvements. Thus there were statutes for the Benedictine

[46] "Congregationibus votorum simplicium non permittitur sibi aggregare tertium quemdam coetum habentem speciem Tertii Ordinis. Nihil tamen obstat, quominus pro exterioribus domus negotiis . . . Congregationes Sororum pias foeminas sibi addicant, quibus certam vivendi formam praescribant, et meritorum proprii Instituti participationem concedant."—*Ibid.*, n. 51.

[47] La Puma, *op. cit.*, p. 429.

[48] "Sacra enim Congregatio Religiosorum per decretum diei 28 aprilis 1925 edixit Summum Pontificem Pium XI in audientia sub eadem die concessa Eminentissimo Card. Praefecto benigne concessisse externas monialium Carmelitarum Sorores, "Tourières appellatas," considerari exinde tamquam membra religiosae communitatis, ad vota simplicia nuncupanda admitti atque vivere debere in conformitatem statutorum exhibitorum et per Sedem Apostolicam ad septennale experimentum adprobatorum."—D'Ambrosio, *op. cit.*, p. 399.

monastery at Dourgne, and a set for the Benedictine convent at Ferrara. The Benedictine Congregations of Beuron and Solesmes each drafted and submitted statutes, as well as the Benedictine Adorers of the Most Blessed Sacrament. Statutes existed for the Canonesses of B. Peter Fourier, the Poor Clares' Protomonastery of *San Damiano* in Assisi, and the Dominican Nuns of the United States.[49] Yet, despite all this activity, there existed many other extern sisters whose juridic condition was still uncertain, and who were deprived of the spiritual benefits to which they were entitled.[50]

This was the situation existing when the Sacred Congregation of Religious, desiring to bring some degree of unity into the situation, caused to be drawn up special statutes which were to be observed by all extern sisters already in existence, or by those who might in the future devote themselves to such a life. Pius XI first approved these statutes on June 24, 1929, but the ultimate approval and affirmation by the Sacred Congregation came in the decree *Conditio plurimorum monasteriorum,* of July 16, 1931.[51]

[49] La Puma, *op. cit.*, p. 429; Hofmeister, *op. cit.*, p. 431.

[50] "Hisce tamen non obstantibus quae ab Apostolica Sede speciatim constituta fuerant in favorem praefatorum monasteriorum, quam plures adhuc apud caetera monasteria sive in Italia sive in exteris regionibus aderant externae sorores quarum iuridica condicio admodum incerta erat et minimis suffulta spiritualibus emolumentis."—D'Ambrosio, *op. cit.*, p. 399.

[51] *AAS*, XXIII (1931), 380; Bouscaren, *The Canon Law Digest*, (Milwaukee: Bruce and Co., 1934-1958), II, 170-172; Hofmeister, *op. cit.*, p. 431; La Puma, *op. cit.*, p. 429; D'Ambrosio, *op. cit.*, pp. 399-400.

CHAPTER VII

THE STATUTES OF 1931

Faced by the definite need for uniform legislation in regard to extern sisters, the Sacred Congregation of Religious, on July 16, 1931, issued a set of statutes for these religious, approving and affirming these norms in the decree *Conditio plurimorum monasteriorum*.[1] A proper understanding of these Statutes of 1931 is essential before one can adequately grasp and appreciate the present law for extern sisters which is embodied in the Statutes of 1961.[2] Hence, the purpose of this chapter is to evaluate the juridic effects of the Statutes for Extern Sisters which were approved in 1931, and to comment upon the norms which they introduced for the guidance and control of this relatively new canonical institution within the Church.

SECTION I

AN ANALYSIS OF THE DECREE "*Conditio plurimorum monasteriorum*"

ARTICLE 1

THE CONCEPT OF EXTERN SISTERS

According to the wording of the Decree, the extern sisters

[1] Only the following notice of approbation actually appeared in the *AAS*, together with the notice that the Statutes themselves were on file at the Sacred Congregation of Religious, scil.: "Ssmus. Dnus. Noster Pius divina Providentia Pp. XI decreto Sacrae Congregationis Negotiis Religiosorum praepositae, dato die 16 Iulii 1931, Statuta pro Sororibus externis monasteriorum Monialium cuiuscumque Ordinis, approbavit. Statuta haec, Typis Polyglottis Vaticanis nuper edita, apud ipsam Sacram Congregationis [sic] de Religiosis asservantur; ad quam proinde recurrere possunt antistitae illorum monasteriorum, in quibus ad servitium externum adhibentur Sorores a votis simplicibus, quae vulgo Tourières vel alio nomine vocantur."—*AAS*, XXIII (1931), 380; complete text of the Decree and 128 Statutes in La Puma, *op. cit.*, XII (1931), 409-425, also in Hilling, "Die neuen Normalstatuten für die externen Schwestern der Nonnenklöster," *Archiv für katholisches Kirchenrecht*, CXIII (1933), 441-462.

[2] *AAS*, LIII (1961), 371-380.

were to profess the same rule as the nuns; together with the nuns they constituted one and the same religious family, obeying the same superioress.[3] After describing the similarities between the extern sisters and the nuns, the Decree next went on to point out certain differences between the two groups. Although the nuns made profession of solemn vows, the extern sisters could profess only simple vows; these were at first temporary, but afterwards were to become perpetual. In view of the purpose the extern sisters were to serve, the Decree proceeded to prescribe a mitigated form of the enclosure for them, stating that "they do not observe the enclosure so severely and strictly as do the nuns, for the reason that, in order to transact external affairs, they have to go outside the limits of the house to which they belong."[4]

ARTICLE 2

THE NATURE OF THE STATUTES

The Decree stated that it seemed advisable to issue a single text of statutes to be observed by extern sisters, in order that this institution, in those places where it was necessary, might become better established without any spiritual detriment to the sisters. For this reason, the Sacred Congregation of Religious caused such a set of statutes to be drawn up, and decided that they should be observed as a norm of religious life by those sisters who, by special indult of the Holy See, were already, or might in the future be, devoted to the external service of monasteries of nuns.[5] This brief

[3] "Huiusmodi porro Sorores eamdem Regulam profitentur et unam eamdemque religiosam familiam constituunt cum Monialibus internis, atque eidem Antistitae obediunt."—Decretum *Conditio plurimorum monasteriorum*, citatum apud La Puma, *op. cit.*, XII (1931), 63, nota 1.

[4] Attamen vota tantum simplicia emittunt, primum quidem temporaria, postea vero perpetua; et non ita severe et stricte, sicut Moniales internae, clausuram observant, eo quod ipsis ad explenda externa negotia etiam extra septa domus eis destinatae exeundum est."—*Loc. cit.*

[5] "Iamvero, ad hoc ut talis institutio, ubi necessaria est, absque spirituali ipsarum Sororum detrimento, magis ac magis firmior evadat, opportunum visum est ut unicus Statutorum textus ederetur, ab iisdem externis Sororibus servandus. Quam ob rem haec S. Congregatio Reli-

paragraph of the Decree raised some important questions, which may well be treated at this point.

A. *The Permission Necessary to Introduce Extern Sisters*

As noted above, the Decree spoke of sisters who, by special indult of the Holy See, were already or might in the future be devoted to the external service of monasteries of nuns.[6] Moreover, the very first article of the statutes applied those norms to extern sisters in the monasteries to which the Apostolic See had granted the special faculty of introducing such sisters.[7] Does the use of such language mean that, even after the promulgation of the Statutes of 1931, it was still necessary to obtain the special permission of the Holy See to introduce extern sisters into a given monastery?

A glance at the history of the development of extern sisters will be of assistance in answering this question. In the long period before the introduction of the Statutes of 1931, an indult of the Holy See was certainly required to have sisters serving outside the monastery, since this constituted a situation which, to all appearances, fitted in poorly with the strict enclosure and discipline of nuns. In each case such a concession was a more or less particular provision and grant.[8] It is this situation, before the promulgation of the

giosorum Sodalium negotiis praeposita, specialia Statuta ex officio redigenda curavit, atque re mature perpensa, censuit ut ea ad religiosae vitae formam servarentur a praefatis Sororibus, quae, ex speciali indulto Sanctae Sedis, servitio externo monasteriorum Monialium iam nunc addictae sunt vel in posterum addicentur."—*Loc. cit.*

[6] *Loc. cit.*

[7] "Sorores externae monasteriorum Monialium cuiuscumque Ordinis, quibus Apostolica Sedes specialem facultatem ad illas instituendas concesserit, regi et gubernari debent ad normam Statutorum, quae sequuntur."—*Statuta a sororibus externis Monasteriorum Monialium cuiusque Ordinis servanda*, Art. 1, cit. apud La Puma, ut *supra*, p. 51, nota 1 (hereafter cited as *Statuta, 1931*).

[8] "Conditio plurimorum monasteriorum Monialium, quae defectu laborant personarum saecularium ad negotia externa obeunda, necessarium fecit ut, annuente in singulis casibus Sede Apostolica, ipsarum rerum externarum expeditio quibusdam sororibus, quae 'externae' vocantur, non raro committeretur."—Decretum *Conditio plurimorum monastariorum;* cf. *supra*, pp. 44-50.

Statutes of 1931, to which the Decree and Article 1 of the Statutes referred when treating of the special permission given by the Apostolic See for the introduction of extern sisters.[9] True, the individual monasteries, even after the promulgation of the Statutes of 1931, had no obligation to introduce extern Sisters.[10] But if a monastery wished to begin employing extern sisters, faithfully following the prescriptions of the Statutes of 1931 in all things, there existed no need to seek a special indult, since the necessary faculty was already granted in the general form and promulgation of the Decree. Only in cases where it was desired to introduce extern sisters governed in a manner differing somewhat from the prescriptions of the Statutes was it necessary to obtain an indult from the Holy See; such different norms would indeed have overstepped the general permission given by the Apostolic See in the Decree *Conditio plurimorum monasteriorum.*[11]

Thus, although the wording of the Decree itself, referring to sisters who were already, or who might in the future, be engaged in the external service of monasteries of nuns, was

[9] Cf. La Puma, *op. cit.*, XIII (1932), 248.

[10] *Loc. cit.;* Vermeersch, *op. cit.*, p. 47.

[11] "Legitime Sorores externas habent, nec novum indultum tales habendi postulare debent."—*Ibid.*, p. 50; "Osserviamo anzitutto che tali 'Sorores externae' non possono più aversi senza l'indulto pontificio: trattasi infatti non di avere delle *fattoresse*, ma delle vere religiose, del proprio Ordine e della propria Regola, ma di professione diversa e senza clausure: è dunque una nuova istituzione religiosa, per quanto sussidiaria, che va autorizzata in modo speciale dalla Santa Sede. Ciò si conferma da quanto è detto appresso, che, a differenza di quel che si riteneva e praticava fin qui, le dette 'Sorores externae' d'ora in poi costituiscono 'unam eamdemque religiosam familiam cum monialibus internis' il che, attesa la differenza gravissima nei voti e nell'obbligo di clausura, solo la Santa Sede può concedere: e infatti lo concede nel modo più ampio, stabiliendosi, nel. n. 4 degli Statuti che 'Quali membri della stessa Communità alla quale servono, le Suore esterne sono partecipi degli stessi beni spirituali che le monache, godono delle indulgenze e di tutti i privilegi, di cui sono capaci.' "—*Il Monitore Ecclesiastico,* Anno LVI, Serie V, Vol. III, Fasc. XI (Nov., 1931), 333; cf. La Puma, *op. cit.*, XIII (1932), 248.

not very clear and left room for doubt, the meaning of the law was restricted to those permissions which had been given by the Holy See in the past. Subsequent practice of the Holy See amply demonstrated the correctness of this view. Vincent La Puma, then Secretary and later Cardinal Prefect of the Sacred Congregation of Religious, testified that, once it was known that these Statutes had been developed and were on file at the Sacred Congregation, many monasteries and bishops asked for copies of them. However, none of the monasteries or bishops requested, nor did the Sacred Congregation grant, any new faculties to introduce extern sisters. The very nature and purpose of the Statutes of 1931 simply made such indults useless and unnecessary.[12]

B. *Effect of the Statutes of 1931 on Various Classes of Externs*

1. Ones not Bound to Observe the Statutes

As has been shown, the Statutes of 1931 were intended only for extern sisters who, by special indult of the Holy See, were engaged in the external service of monasteries of nuns.[13] On this basis, there existed several classifications of women, engaged in the external service of monasteries of nuns, who were, nevertheless, not bound to the observance of the new Statutes which were promulgated in 1931.

Some externs were merely pious lay women, perhaps members of some Third Order Secular, who were employed by the monasteries to work for a salary.[14] The Statutes stated

[12] "Insuper nobis constat hucusque satis multa Monasteria et plures Episcopos exemplaria requisisse a S. Congregatione Statutorum pro Sororibus externis; sed neque Episcopos vel Monasteria, neque S. Congregationem concedendam novam facultatem ad assumendas Sorores externas. Natura ipsa quam Apost. Sedes determinat pro Sororibus externis et statutis specialibus locupletat, inutile reddit novum indultum."—La Puma, *op. cit.*, XIII (1932), 248.

[13] Cf. *supra*. pp. 52-53.

[14] "Sic dictae 'Tourières' sunt quandoque honestae famulae laicae, pro modico pretio servitiis externis monasterii addictae. Hae possunt etiam ut singulae esse cuiuspiam Ordinis Tertiariae."—Vermeersch, *op. cit.*, p. 45.

that they were only for *Sorores,* i.e., for women religious of simple vows. In no sense did they attempt to include these lay persons, nor did the Statutes forbid monasteries to employ such lay persons for external service.[15] Hence, the members of this classification were surely not bound to observe the Statutes of 1931.

Still other women engaged in the external service of monasteries of nuns were members of pious sodalities, approved and erected by local ordinaries. The members of these sodalities were without vows, or took at most private vows.[16] It seems quite obvious that these women were not included under the Statutes of 1931, since they could by no means be classed as *sorores.*[17] Even in the case where, on the authority of the local ordinary after consulting the Holy See, a group of externs was erected into a diocesan religious community with public vows, it does not seem that these sisters were bound to observe the Statutes of 1931. The Statutes were clearly intended only for those who engaged in such service by special indult of the Holy See, hence, not for those who did so under episcopal authorization.[18]

A final class of extern sisters who were not bound by the

[15] Cf. Decretum *Conditio plurimorum monasteriorum* et *Statuta, 1931;* "Praesentia statuta minime prohibent quin monasteria committere pergant praestanda servitia externa piis personis saecularibus, probante Ordinario loci, sive sint Tertiariae, sive non sint. Statuta enim spectant *Sorores;* laicae personae seu famulae, hoc nomine non veniunt: id est manifestum."—Vermeersch, *op. cit.,* p. 47.

[16] " 'Tourières' possunt quoque conflari in pium sodalicium ab Ordinario loci cum votis privatis vel sine votis approbatum et erectum." —*Ibid.,* p. 45.

[17] "Neque spectant sodalicium huiusmodi famularum quod Ordinarius etiam cum votis approbarit, dummodo agatur de votis privatis: neque hae sunt *Sorores.*"—*Ibid.,* p. 47.

[18] "Restant iam 'Tourières' quae, auctoritate Episcopi, in communitatem vere religiosam, sed dioecesanam coaluerunt. Cum nova Statuta bis, tum in art. 1 tum in Decreto quo confirmantur, servanda dicantur a Sororibus quae ex *speciali S. Sedis facultate vel indulto* externo Monasteriorum servitio addictae sunt vel addicentur, censemus ... Dioecesanas Congregationes Sororum externarum, istis Statutis minime affici."—*Ibid.,* p. 50.

Statutes of 1931 were those who belonged to a separate and distinct religious institute, and who performed the external services in a monastery of nuns, just as they might have been employed at such work in a seminary or in any Catholic school.[19] The Statutes were intended only for those extern sisters who in some way pertained to the same monastery as the nuns and, moreover, were governed by the same superioress.[20] Sisters belonging to the communities under consideration, however, were members of a completely different religious institute, and were canonically subject to their own internal superiors. The superioress of the monastery of nuns had at most only a domestic power over them.[21]

2. Third Order Extern Sisters Pertaining to the Monastery

In the monasteries of several Orders of nuns, the extern sisters were members of a Third Order Regular; however, they were, even before the Statutes of 1931, in some way attached to the community of nuns and were governed by the same superioress.[22] In some of these cases there was relatively little difficulty involved in determining whether or not these particular extern sisters were bound to observe the Statutes of 1931. For instance, special Statutes for Carmelite extern sisters had been approved by the Sacred Congregation of Religious in 1925.[23] The general Statutes were promulgated by the Holy See on September 1, 1931, and went into effect in December of that same year. In the few intervening months until the Carmelite Statutes expired in

[19] " 'Tourières' pertinere possunt ad Institutum religiosum, cuius sodales non aliter quam in pluribus collegiis vel seminariis servitia externa monasterii curanda assumunt."—*Ibid.*, p. 46.

[20] Decretum *Conditio plurimorum monasteriorum;* cf. *supra.* p. 52.

[21] "Statuta enim agunt de Sororibus quae ad eandem familiam religiosam cuius sunt Moniales pertineant, ac Superiorissae Monialium ut religiosae subsint, dum praefatae Sorores in aliud Institutum cooptatae sunt nec subsunt nisi domesticae potestati Superiorissae Monialium." —Vermeersch, *op. cit.*, p. 48.

[22] " 'Tourières' inter se componunt Congregationem Tertii Ordinis, quae, ut annexa communitati Monialium, ab ipsa Abbatissa seu Superiorissa regitur."—*Ibid.*, p. 46.

[23] Cf. *supra*, p. 49.

April of 1932, it was an easy matter for the Holy See to expressly or tacitly allow these extern sisters to continue to follow their own proper norms. Then, upon expiration of the Carmelite Statutes, a clear-cut decision on the part of the Sacred Congregation of Religious could determine whether or not a given monastery of Carmelites should begin to observe the common Statutes or continue to abide by the proper Carmelite legislation.[24]

Among the nuns of the Order of St. Clare and the Poor Clare Colettines, however, the situation was far from evident. Most of these extern sisters were observing the Third Order Rule of 1521, to which certain declarations and explanations had been appended, the whole being approved by Pope Leo XIII in 1888. The origin and nature of this Rule and the declarations of 1888 have already been described in detail.[25] It suffices here to note the important fact that the Decree of Approbation provided for the sisters to make profession "according to the Third Rule of St. Francis approved by Pope Leo X, and also according to the declarations and explanations given above, which His Holiness has benignly deigned to approve and confirm as they are contained in this copy."[26]

[24] "Rursus autem Statuta generalia de Sororibus externis promulgata in fasciculo 1 sept. 1931, cum leges novae per tres menses vacent, tantum a 2 die decembris vim suam exserere coeperunt. ... Ut per sex reliquos menses Carmelitanae Sorores proprio suo iure uti pergant, id, ni fallimur, ipsa S. Sedes expresse vel tacite facile concedet. Elapso autem hoc temporis spatio, ipsa S. Congregatio, ad quam pro innovando vel confirmando isto iure recurri debebit, decernet utrum an non externae Sorores Carmelitanae communi regimini obnoxiae esse debeant." —Vermeersch, *op. cit.*, pp. 49-50.

[25] Cf. *supra*, pp. 44-47.

[26] "Sanctissimus D. N. Leo PP. XIII ... indulsit ut Sorores externo servitio eorumdem Monasteriorum addictae, 'Tourières' nuncupatae, rite expleto Novitiatu, consueta tria vota simplicia Paupertatis, Castitatis et Obedientiae prius ad tempus, dein in perpetuum emittant, iuxta Tertiam Regulam S. Francisci a S. M. Leone PP. X approbatam, nec non declarationes et explanationes supra relatas, quas Sanctitas sua, ut in hoc exemplari continentur, cuius autographum in Archivio praelaudatae S. Congregationis asservatur, benigne approbare et confirmare dignata est."—*Acta Ordinis Minorum*, VII (1888), 87.

Then, in the year 1927, the Rule of 1521, to which the declarations and explanations of 1888 had been appended, was abrogated by Pope Pius XI in favor of a new Rule of the Third Order Regular. According to the introduction to the new Rule of Pius XI, many things which had been decreed by Leo X had, in the course of time, become obsolete, and were out of harmony with the prescriptions of the Code of Canon Law. Therefore, in order that members of the Third Order Regular and other institutes of simple vows which followed this Rule might progress the more in Christian perfection, this Rule of 1927 was intended to accommodate the Rule of Leo X to modern times and the recent legislation of the Church.[27] In approving and confirming the new Rule, Pius XI completely abrogated the old law of Leo X, adding the hope that this Rule of 1927 would aid not only members of the Third Order Regular, but all other Franciscan religious who did not, *ex instituto*, have solemn vows, to become shining examples of Christian perfection for the other Tertiaries who remained in the world.[28] Moreover, Pius XI annulled and invalidated anything done con-

[27] "Atqui, ut in humanis rebus contingit, plura quidem, decursu temporum, quae a Leone PP. X decreta fuerant, prorsus obsolevere vel cum quibusdam C. I. C. praescriptis non omnino consentiunt. Quamobrem necesse fuit ut illa Leonis X lex ad nostra haec tempora itemque ad recentiora Ecclesiae decreta accommodaretur, ut Tertiarii Regulares, aliaeque multiplices votorum simplicium religiosae familiae quae, cum in suum ipsarum institutum Francisci spiritum induxerint et franciscali nomine utantur, Franciscum Patrem quodam modo habent, novum inde incrementum capientes, alacritate vel maiore optime de christiana civilique re mereri pergerent."—*AAS*, XIX (1927), 362.

[28] "Nos quidem, veterem Legem Leonis PP. X prorsus abrogantes, libenter, saeculo a Francisci obitu septimo exeunte, hanc Regulam Tertii Ordinis Regularis Seraphici Patris S. Francisci apostolica auctoritate Nostra approbamus et confirmamus; id fore plane confisi ut Tertiarii Regulares, iique omnes qui, etsi vota sollemnia ex instituto non habent, religiosam tamen vitam, duce Francisco, agunt, spiritu novae Legis roborati, quemadmodum egregie scribebat Decessor Noster Benedictus PP. XV, ceteris sodalibus Tertiariis, qui mundi negotiis curisque impliciti remaneant, in christiana perfectione colenda sint exemplo, eisque tamquam duces ad sempiternam salutem quaerendam praeire pergant."—*Ibid.*, pp. 366-367.

trary to the Decree of Approbation, by whomsoever it might be done or on whatsoever authority. This was to hold, all things to the contrary notwithstanding, even though they be worthy of special and individual mention.[29]

Considering this historical background, it is not surprising that the appearance of the Statutes of 1931 gave rise to much legal discussion concerning the Rule to which the Poor Clare extern sisters were bound. Moreover, on a practical level, a good deal of doubt and confusion resulted among both the Poor Clare Colettines and the members of the Order of St. Clare. These canonical problems and the practical difficulties to which they gave rise are important in order to understand the situation which developed among the extern sisters in the thirty years immediately preceding the promulgation of the present Statutes of 1961.

a. *Canonical Problems*—According to one line of reasoning, the Rule of the Third Order as approved in 1927 not only completely suppressed the old law of Leo X, but also the declarations and explanations of 1888 along with it. In this view, the declarations and explanations were so completely dependent upon and bound up with the old Leonine Rule that the abrogation of that Rule left the Poor Clare extern sisters without a form of life.[30] Although authors do not mention the alternative, it seems to the writer that, if the Rule of 1927 did actually abrogate the Rule and declarations of 1888, those Poor Clare extern sisters who were following this Rule of 1888 would have been bound to observe the Rule of 1927, which replaced their old form of life. It

[29] "Sicque rite iudicandum esse ac definiendum, irritumque ex nunc et inane fieri, si quidquam secus super his, a quovis, auctoritate qualibet, scienter vel ignoranter attentari contigerit. Non obstantibus contrariis quibuslibet, etiam speciali atque individua mentione dignis."—*Ibid.*, p. 367.

[30] "Valetne hoc ratiocinium: SS. D. N. Pius PP. XI, nova Regula Tertii Ordinis 'veterem legem Leonis X prorsus' abrogavit. Ergo, suppressa lege, declarationes et explanationes simul sunt suppressae. Ergo, 'Tourières' quae apud Clarissas Congregationem Tertii Ordinis constituunt ab anno 1927 omni approbata regula distituuntur."—Vermeersch, *op. cit.*, p. 48.

seems repugnant to maintain that the Holy See meant to leave any group of religious without any form of life at all. As will be subsequently shown, this view is substantiated by the practice of the Sacred Congregation of Religious during the years immediately following the promulgation of the Statutes of 1931.[31]

However, potent objections can be offered to the very idea that the Rule of 1927 had any effect whatsoever upon the Rule and declarations of 1888. The new Rule of 1927 was completely silent concerning the declarations and explanations which, as has been shown above, were explicitly approved by Pope Leo XIII in 1888.[32] Therefore, it is certain that the declarations and explanations of 1888 were not expressly abrogated as such in 1927. Moreover, these declarations and explanations, together with the Rule of 1521 to which they were appended, formed a rule of life which the Poor Clare extern sisters observed from 1888 on. Even after the Rule of 1927 had abrogated the Rule of Leo X as such, these extern sisters continued to peacefully observe the same form of life of 1888. Therefore, there is no reason why at least the declarations and explanations should not have continued to subsist *per se,* and it is reasonable to conclude that they did not perish along with the suppressed Rule of 1521.[33]

Another and even stronger argument against the suppression of the Rule and declarations of 1888 by the Rule of 1927 is based upon the principle embodied in canon 22: "A subsequent law, enacted by competent authority, repeals a former law if it entirely revises the whole subject matter of the former law."[34] Now, when Pope Leo XIII, in 1888, appended the explanations and declarations to the old Rule of Leo X as approved in 1521, he intended to completely

[31] Cf. *infra,* p. 72.

[32] *AAS,* XIX (1927), 362-367; cf. *supra,* pp. 44-45; Vermeersch, *op. cit.,* p. 48.

[33] *Loc. cit.*

[34] "Lex posterior, a competenti auctoritate lata, obrogat priori, si ... totam de integra ordinet legis prioris materiam; ..."—Canon 22.

revise and rearrange the material of that former Rule, adapting it to the life of the extern sisters.[35] The conclusion follows that when, in 1888, Leo XIII permitted the extern sisters to make profession according to the Rule which had previously been approved by Leo X, at the same time approving and confirming the declarations and explanations appended to that Rule, he in effect abrogated the old Rule of Leo X as such, insofar as it pertained to Poor Clare extern sisters. In its stead, he created and approved for them a new body of legislation based on that same Rule of Leo X, modified by the declarations and explanations of 1888. This new body of legislation, possessing its own specific approval, continued in effect after 1927, although the old Rule of 1521 as such was definitely abrogated.

Thus, after the promulgation of the new Rule of the Third Order Regular of St. Francis in 1927, there were divergent views concerning the status of those Poor Clare extern sisters who had been following the Rule and accommodations of 1888. According to one view, the form of life of 1888 was completely abrogated, and these sisters were left without a form of life. A modification of this opinion held that the form of life of 1888 was indeed abrogated, but that the sisters were then bound to observe the Rule of 1927. According to the third view of the matter, the Rule of Leo X with the declarations and explanations of 1888 continued in force and provided a form of life for these extern sisters even after 1927.[36] Obviously, the revocation of the law of 1888 in all its parts was a matter of doubt, and it is imperative to remember at this point the principle of canon 23: "In case of doubt, the revocation of a pre-existing law is not presumed, but subsequent laws should be adapted to prior laws and, as far as possible, made to harmonize with them."[37]

[35] "Iam vero quid Leo XIII intendit, quando declarationes et explanationes regulae Leonis X ad usum 'Tourières' accommodavit? Quid, inquam, intendit, nisi regimen sororum externarum apud Clarissas ordinare?"—Vermeersch, *op. cit.*, p. 48.

[36] Cf. *supra*, pp. 60-62.

[37] "In dubio revocatio legis praeexsistentis non praesumitur, sed leges

Not only is it repugnant to conclude that these sisters were left without any form of life at all, but it is necessary to remember that the correction of law is an odious thing, and does not enjoy the favor of law. If it is not certain that the legislator intended to correct the former law, both laws should be given their effect.[38] In view of these considerations, it is the opinion of the present writer that, even after 1927, the extern sisters of the Order of St. Clare and the Poor Clare Colettines were justified in continuing to follow the Rule and declarations of 1888.

In the light of the foregoing discussion, it is possible to understand the canonical questions which were raised in regard to Poor Clare extern sisters when the Statutes for Extern Sisters made their appearance in 1931. Obviously, if one adopts the opinion that the Rule of the Third Order approved by Pius XI in 1927 completely abrogated the Rule and declarations of 1888, and grants that this abrogation left these extern sisters without any rule of life at all, there is no difficulty. The extern sisters, left without a Rule and form of life, would simply have been bound to follow the Statutes of 1931. But if it is maintained that these extern sisters were bound to observe the Rule of 1927 after its promulgation, or that they were justified in continuing to observe the Rule and declarations of 1888 even after 1927, it becomes necessary to ask the further questions: What was the effect of the Decree and Statutes of 1931 upon the Rule of 1927, or upon the Rule and declarations of 1888?

From even a superficial glance at the Decree and Statutes of 1931, it is apparent that, by means of this new legislation, the Holy See intended to completely revise and reorder the form of life of the extern sisters. Therefore, in virtue of the principle embodied in canon 22 and cited above,[39] the Statutes of 1931, revising as they did the whole subject matter

posteriores ad priores trahendae sunt et his, quantum fieri possit, conciliandae."—Canon 23.

[38] Abbo-Hannan, *The Sacred Canons* (2 vols., 2nd rev. ed., St. Louis: Herder, 1960), II, 47.

[39] Cf. *supra*, p. 61.

of any particular set of norms for extern sisters, effected the repeal of those particular norms. This means that any group of Poor Clare extern sisters who had begun to observe the Rule of 1927 would have been bound to adopt the Statutes of 1931, which effected the abrogation of the Rule of 1927 insofar as these extern sisters were concerned. It also means that those monasteries where the extern sisters had continued to observe the Rule of 1521, together with the declarations and explanations of 1888, were bound to follow the Statutes of 1931, which abrogated that Rule, together with the declarations and explanations.[40]

An objection is offered to this conclusion, based upon that section of canon 22 which states: "General laws shall not derogate from particular laws governing specified territories or definite moral persons, unless the general law contains an express provision to this effect."[41] The objection states that the new Statutes of 1931 were a general law; the law of 1888 and the law of 1927 were special particular law observed by the extern sisters of the Order of St. Clare and the Poor Clare Colettines. Therefore, in this view of matters, if either the Rule of 1927, or the Rule and declarations of 1888, was validly in force before the promulgation of the Statutes of 1931, it continued to hold even after these Statutes became law. However, this interpretation neglects to give due weight to the final words of canon 22: ". . . unless the general law contains an express provision to this effect." As a matter of fact, the Decree accompanying the Statutes indicated that they were approved and affirmed, "all things to the contrary notwithstanding."[42] According to most authors, this formula definitely revokes particular law contrary to the general law.[43] Thus, it is very highly probable that

[40] Cf. Vermeersch, *op. cit.*, p. 49.

[41] ". . . lex generalis nullatenus derogat locorum specialium et personarum singularium statutis, nisi aliud in ipsa expresse caveatur." —Canon 22.

[42] ". . . contrariis quibuscumque non obstantibus."—Decretum *Conditio plurimorum monasteriorum.*

[43] Michiels, *Normae Generales Iuris Canonici* (2 vols., ed. altera,

the Statutes of 1931 actually did abrogate the Rule and declarations of 1888, as well as the Rule of 1927, or indeed any other particular rule of life followed by extern sisters prior to the promulgation of the general Statutes of 1931.

In spite of this strong evidence, some expressed a further doubt concerning the applicability of the Statutes of 1931 to those extern sisters who had been observing the Rule and declarations of 1888, or the Rule of 1927. This doubt was based on the fact that the Decree *Conditio plurimorum monasteriorum* mentioned that the extern sisters professed the same Rule as the nuns. Proponents of this opinion maintained, however, that, in the case of the Poor Clares, the extern sisters were subject not to the same rule as the nuns, but to a different form of life, namely the Rule of the Third Order Regular. Thus, they maintained that there was strong doubt that the Decree and Statutes of 1931 were meant for these sisters.[44]

This conclusion, however, seems to completely overlook the fact that it was the precise intention of the Holy See in issuing the Statutes of 1931 to change the situation whereby extern sisters professed a different rule than the nuns, and even belonged to a different Order. To the mind of the present writer, when the Decree *Conditio plurimorum monasteriorum,* and Article 2 of the Statutes, treated of the extern sisters professing the same Rule and belonging to the same religious family as the nuns, they were describing the situation *as it was to be under the Statutes of 1931,* not as it had been under the particular law for extern sisters in various institutes. This opinion, which would exclude the Poor Clare extern sisters from the 1931 Statutes simply because they

Tornaci: Desclée, 1949), I, 664; Beste, *Introductio in Codicem* (ed. altera, Collegeville, Minn.: St. John's Abbey Press, 1944), p. 87.

[44] "Etenim, in Decreto quo nova Statuta confirmantur, Sorores dicuntur, 'eandem Regulam profiteri' quam Moniales internae observant. Sed istud est minime generale. Non raro Sorores externae alii regulae obnoxiae sunt. Ita apud Clarissas, Sorores externae profitebantur regulam Tertii Ordinis regularis, dum Moniales ad secundum Ordinem pertinent. Inde quispiam dubitare possit num nova statuta huiusmodi Sorores externas spectent."—Vermeersch, *op. cit.,* pp. 50-51.

had been observing the Rule of the Third Order Regular, has its entire foundation in a situation which the Holy See explicitly set out to reform.[45] This consideration, coupled with the foregoing discussion of the abrogating effect of the new Statutes of 1931 on particular statutes, leads to the well-founded conclusion that extern sisters who may have been observing another rule, e.g., the Rule and declarations of 1888, were very much included under the Statutes of 1931. The effect of this in the case of extern sisters in the Order of St. Clare and the Poor Clare Colettines was to remove them from the Third Order Regular and make them full members of the Second Order, the same Order to which the nuns belonged.[46]

This change of the discipline to which the extern sisters were subject created a further canonical problem not only for the Poor Clares, but also for the other institutes in which a similar change took place. What was the status of a novice whose probation had taken place under the old law to which the extern sisters were subject before 1931? Was such a novitiate valid for profession under the new Statutes? Was temporary profession made under the old discipline valid for perpetual profession to be made under the Statutes of 1931? Vermeersch gives assurance, based on private authority, that the Sacred Congregation of Religious, as far as any such new institute or change of regime is concerned, gives full credit to acts placed under the old regime. This meant, for example, that a Poor Clare extern sister who had made her novitiate either entirely or in part according to the Rule and declarations of 1888, would not have to repeat it in order to make valid profession in the Second Order, under the Statutes of 1931. A sister whose temporary vows had been made under the Rule and declarations of 1888 would not have to renew them under the Statutes of 1931; rather these tem-

[45] Cf. Decretum *Conditio plurimorum monasteriorum: Statuta, 1931*, Art. 2.

[46] "Vis novi regiminis haec est, ut in posterum istae 'Tourières' non iam ad Tertium Ordinem pertinebunt sed classem constituent secundi Ordinis . . ."—Vermeersch, *op. cit.*, p. 51.

porary vows were given full credit just as if they had been made under the new discipline. In the change of these sisters from the Third to the Second Order, the Sacred Congregation saw not so much a transfer to another institute, but rather a subjection to a new form of regime in their own institute.[47]

A final canonical question concerns the status of those extern sisters who had, before 1931, made profession under the old law of their institute, e.g., the Rule and declarations of 1888. Were they still bound by the obligations and possessed of the rights acquired by their profession under the former discipline? Were they, on the other hand, required to accommodate themselves to the new form of life demanded under the Statutes of 1931, or did they perhaps enjoy the liberty to choose in this matter for themselves? According to the testimony of Vermeersch, when a new regime is introduced into a religious institute, the Holy See ordinarily grants to those already professed in that institute the option of continuing to follow the old law, or of adopting the new. Hence, unless the Sacred Congregation of Religious determined otherwise in some particular instance, extern sisters who were professed before the Statutes of 1931 became obligatory could continue to observe the old discipline under which they had made profession. Or, if they preferred, they could adopt the new discipline prescribed according to the Statutes of 1931.[48] This policy is in accord with the prin-

[47] "Ut liquet, condicio Sororum 'Tourières' quae in incepto perseverare cupiunt a S. Congregatione definiri debebit. Ut nobis, privatim tamen, relatum est, S. Congregatio sibi proposuit ut pro Instituto nunc condito valerent quaecumque hactenus sub anteriore regimine legitime acta erant. Quare nec noviciatus ex toto vel ex parte, nec temporaria professio repetenda erunt, sed plenam utilitatem servabunt quasi iam secundum nova statuta facta sint. Hoc ceterum cum ipsa rerum natura satis congruit: Sorores enim istae, potius quam alterum Institutum transeant, novo proprii Instituti regimini, secundum S. Sedis voluntaem, subduntur."—*Loc. cit.*

[48] "Quae nunc iam professae sunt regimine quo hactenus usae sunt uti pergere possunt, nisi aliter a S. Congregatione statuatur. ... S. Sedes professis concedere solet quandam optionem pristini et novi regiminis, si quod inducatur."—Vermeersch, *op. cit.*, p. 50.

ciple of canon 4, so that the right acquired by profession under the old system of discipline for extern sisters remains intact, unless there should be an express revocation of it.[49] It also fits in well with the principle of law expressed in canon 10: "Laws affect the future, not the past, unless express mention is made of the past."[50] Thus, for example, among the Order of St. Clare and the Poor Clare Colettines, an individual professed extern sister who was observing the Rule and declarations of 1888 before 1931 could, if she so desired, continue to observe the norms of 1888 even after the promulgation of the Statutes of 1931, remaining a member of the Third Order Regular. She could also, if she preferred, begin to observe the Statutes of 1931 in place of the former discipline of 1888, becoming a member of the Second Order. For the monastery as such, however, there was no such choice. Of course, with the permission of the local ordinary, an individual monastery could cease to have extern sisters and hire lay persons. But if a monastery intended to continue recruiting extern novices, it was necessary, in line with a supposed repeal of the Rule and declarations of 1888, to adopt the new Statutes in regard to these novices.[51]

b. *Practical Difficulties.*—In order to obtain some idea of the concrete situation which resulted from the previously discussed legal problems, the writer sent a special letter to each of twenty-five monasteries of the Order of St. Clare and the Poor Clare Colettines in the United States and Canada.[52] In this letter, the monasteries were asked to send a reply to two separate questions:

> 1) Was the reception, profession, manner of life of the extern sisters of your monastery regulated

[49] "Iura aliis quaesita . . . integra manent, nisi huius Codicis canonibus expresse revocentur."—Canon 4.

[50] "Leges respiciunt futura, non praeterita, nisi nominatim in eis de praeteritis caveatur."—Canon 10.

[51] "Singulis monasteriis integrum est Sororibus externis in futurum renuntiare, et, annuente Ordinario loci, laicas personas assumere. Si autem maluerint Novicias pro servitiis externis cooptare, oportet ut regimen novorum statutorum adoptent."—Vermeersch, *op. cit.*, p. 50.

[52] Letter of June 17, 1962.

by the Rule and declarations of 1888, and, if so, until what years?
2) Was the reception, profession, manner of life of the extern sisters of your monastery regulated by the Statutes of 1931, and, if so, just when did this begin?

Eighteen of the monasteries contacted responded with information upon which the following summary is based.

Six of these monasteries ceased to observe the Rule and declarations of 1888 when the new Statutes were promulgated in 1931. Three of these six communities simply adopted the Statutes of 1931 immediately, or very soon after their promulgation, transferring their extern sisters from the Third Order Regular to the Second Order. One monastery adopted the Statutes partially in 1931, but did not admit the extern sisters to the Second Order until 1950; after 1950, this particular monastery did not follow the Statutes of 1931 at all, but the extern sisters observed the Rule and Constitutions of the Second Order. Still another of these six monasteries partially followed the Statutes of 1931 from the time they were promulgated, but this particular monastery did not admit the extern sisters to the Second Order until 1952. The last of these monasteries, although it indeed ceased observing the law of 1888 in 1931, did not adopt a modified form of the Statutes of 1931 until the year 1935; it was not until 1950 that the extern sisters of this particular community were permitted to become members of the Second Order.

In the year 1933, two more convents ceased to observe the Rule and declarations of 1888. One of them simply adopted the Statutes of 1931 in their entirety, admitting the extern sisters to the Second Order at once. The other adopted a modified form of the Statutes of 1931, and did not admit the extern sisters to the Second Order until 1943.

One monastery observed the Rule and declarations of 1888 until the year 1940. Although the Franciscan Provinical to whom this particular convent was subject had urged the observance of the Statutes of 1931 at the time of their promulgation, it was only gradually that the conversion from the law of 1888 was made, being complete and final only in 1940 with the admission of the extern sisters to the Second Order. Then, in 1943, another monastery abandoned the observance of the Rule and declarations of 1888, immediately adopting the Statutes of 1931 in their entirety, and making the transfer from the Third to the Second Order.

At the direction of its Minister Provincial, another monastery ceased observing the Rule and declarations of 1888 in 1952, at which time it admitted the extern sisters to the Second Order. However, this particular convent did not adopt the Statutes of 1931, and the extern sisters followed the Rule and Constitutions of the Second Order instead. In another case, a monastery observed the Rule and declarations of 1888 until 1962; in that year this monastery adopted the Statutes of 1931, one year after they had been abrogated by the Statutes of 1961.

There are two monasteries which, although they were in existence long before 1931, never observed the Rule and declarations of 1888. One of these followed the Rule of the Third Order Sisters of St. Francis for its extern sisters, a practice which continued even after 1931. The other had its own and completely special book of rules for extern sisters. An attempt was made to inaugurate the observance of the Statutes of 1931 among the older extern sisters who were already long professed under the old Rules of life. These preferred to remain members of the Third Order and to continue to observe their former Rules, rather than make the change to the Second Order and the Statutes of 1931. Finally, four other monasteries which were founded after 1931 adopted the Statutes of 1931 from the time of their founding, placing the extern sisters in the Second Order.

This great diversity of practice in an area where a reasonable amount of uniformity might have been expected prompts one to inquire further into the concrete causes which produced such conflicting situations. In order to discover these causes, the writer asked and obtained the permission of one of the eighteen monasteries to examine its complete file of correspondence relating to the extern sisters. The concrete case history of this Monastery X in Diocese Y serves admirably well to bring out the reasons which resulted in so much confusion among the Poor Clares.

It was not long after the appearance of the Statutes of 1931 that the doubt and confusion waxed strong. This is well illustrated by the following excerpt from a letter to the Abbess of Monastery X from a Belgian Poor Clare Abbess, July 20, 1932:

> As to the question of the Statutes of the Out-Door Sisters, it is still to be known whether or not they are intended for our extern sisters. Have the latter been approved by the Holy See? The Statutes say positively that they are only for the sisters who have been instituted by the Monasteries of nuns to whom the Holy See has given the special faculty of founding them. The question: Is it the Holy See which has given us this faculty or the Bishops? If we have the permission of the Bishops, it appears that the Statutes are not intended for us. Others say that we may only have Sisters of the III Order, obedient to an Abbess of the II Order. We have placed the question at Rome and await a reply.

This doubt was apparently not shared among the authorities at the Franciscan General Curia in Rome; for already on January 17, 1932, one of the Definitors General of the Order had written to the Abbess of Monastery X: "They (the Statutes of 1931) are prescribed for all the Monasteries which have Extern Sisters."

On January 5, 1934, the Abbess of the above mentioned Belgian monastery of Poor Clares addressed an important letter to the Abbess of Monastery X. Although the Statutes of 1931 required that the canonical year of novitiate be made by extern sisters within the enclosure, this Belgian monastery had, in late 1933, obtained an indult, for a period of three years, that the extern novices might continue to make their entire novitiate outside the papal enclosure. This same letter contained the information that, in two other Belgian monasteries, the extern sisters had remained in the Third

Order, and were observing the Rule of Pius XI as approved in 1927. Since this Rule contained nothing on fast and abstinence, on the duration of the postulancy and the novitiate, or on the duration of the temporary vows, these points, together with certain other prescriptions taken from the Rule of the Extern Sisters in a French Canadian monastery, along with certain excerpts from the Code, were added to the Constitutions for Extern Sisters in the Belgian monasteries by a Canadian priest. The Abbess announced her intention to submit this entire compilation for diocesan approval. This same letter of the Belgian Abbess states that the Sacred Congregation of Religious was also questioned concerning the status of the extern sisters in monasteries of France, America and England. She cites the following reply of Fr. Vermeersch of the Sacred Congregation of Religious:

> I will now come to the question of the Extern Sisters, which I have today discussed with the S. Secretary, then with two officials of the Sacred Congregation. We have all four agreed upon the following conclusion. In order that the Colettines may be able to have their extern sisters as foreseen by the new Statutes, Externs who will become members of the Second Order, it will be necessary that each Monastery petition this of the Sacred Congregation. When this has been granted them, then the dispensation permitting the Novitiate to be made outside of the enclosure will have to be obtained. If the Monastery does not make this petition, it is at liberty to keep the Tertiary Extern Sisters that it already has. Consequently, the Monasteries which are content with their present usage will have nothing to ask from Rome.

The Belgian Abbess cites the following letter of Fr. Vermeersch, concerning observance of the Rule of 1927:

> If the extern sisters remain in their present condition, the Rule of the Third Order will be that of Pope Pius XI, which His Holiness promulgated suppressing at the same time all preceding Rules. If the extern sisters pass into the Second Order, they would have to receive all their Rule books just like the interns.

Although this Rule of 1927 was accepted in some European monasteries, as is evidenced in the reported correspondence, it does not seem to have been observed in the United States. Perhaps the reason for this may be found in the following communication of the same Father Vermeersch to an American Franciscan Provincial. Although the letter contains many of the same ideas as that to the Belgian Abbess cited above, it also provides that the extern sisters may continue to follow the same Tertiary Rule they have been observing, making no mention of the Rule of 1927. Consequently, many American Poor Clares simply continued to follow the Rule and declarations of 1888. Here are the pertinent excerpts:

> That question of the *Tourières* has given much trouble. The discussion we had, the Secretary and Officials (two officials) has given us this conclusion: a) to adopt the Statutes of the Extern Sisters the Poor Clares Colettines *need* an *Indult* of the Holy See. If they desire to have such Sisters, *then* they must ask dispensation for that Novitiate *intra claustra.*
> b) If they are satisfied with the present state they have now, the Extern Sisters may remain as they are without any obligation of recurring to Rome. Indeed, who are the present Extern Sisters? They are members of the Third Order of St. Francis, and are not at all Sisters of the Second Order. Nothing obliges them to change a point of the Rule given by the actual Pope to the Tertian Sisters of the Poor Clare Monasteries. That seems to me very practical. The Belgian Poor Clares have not made use of the dispensation given them by the Cardinal. They remain Tertiary Sisters.

Further correspondence in the files of Monastery X indicates that, after receipt of the foregoing reply of Fr. Vermeersch, a set of Statutes for the Extern Sisters of that monastery was drawn up, providing for the manner of life of these sisters, who were to continue as members of the Third Order Regular, making their canonical novitiate in the dwelling of the extern Sisters. These Statutes were approved by the local ordinary of Diocese Y, and forwarded to Rome for approval of the Holy See on February 11, 1936. Not until early 1938 was a reply received from the Sacred Congregation of Religious, which completely reversed the answer which had been received from the Sacred Congregation four years earlier. The Sacred Congregation refused to approve the Statutes submitted by the monastery, which called for the extern sisters to remain in the Third Order; instead, these sisters were told to follow the official Statutes of 1931, which required that they become members of the Second Order. So strongly did the Holy See desire that these extern sisters become members of the Second Order that it granted them the special privilege of becoming cloistered lay nuns if they so desired, even apart from the making of a new novitiate.[53]

Despite this clear expression of the will of the Sacred Congregation, the nuns of Monastery X, because of what was later described as a misunderstanding, continued to follow their own particular Statutes for the extern sisters, who remained in the Third Order. Apparently, some uncertainty arose concerning this matter in the Chancery Office of Diocese Y, since the local ordinary advised that the extern sisters continue to make profession in the Third Order, pending a definitive solution of the problem.[54] Finally, on February 13, 1940, the ordinary of Diocese Y wrote a lengthy letter to Vincent Cardinal La Puma, who was then the Prefect of the Sacred Congregation for Religious. In this letter, the ordinary set out the entire case, including all the facts narrated above as well as other practical problems which had

[53] "The official Statutes for Extern Sisters, however, published and translated by the S. C. of Religious, are to be observed by your Extern Sisters. The S. C. of Religious also calls attention in its recent rescript, no. 7271/36, to the privilege which your Extern Sisters have of becoming cloistered lay Sisters of the Second Order if they were received as Novices prior to the promulgation of the Statutes for Extern Sisters."—Letter from the Vicar for Religious of Diocese Y, Feb. 18, 1938.

[54] Letters of March 8, 1939 and January 5, 1940, from Monastery X to Chancery of Diocese Y.

arisen as a result of the uncertainty. A clarification of the situation was asked, along with any indults or sanations which might be necessary because of the confusion which had reigned for so many years. Unfortunately, no reply was ever received to this letter, and the situation continued as before, with the extern sisters belonging to the Third Order and observing their own special Statutes. Then, in 1946, the Vicar for Religious of Diocese Y, hoping to put an end to the difficulty, wrote to the Abbess of Monastery X: "It is my opinion now that your Extern Sisters do not and cannot belong to the Third Order Regular. That question was decided by the Holy See with regard to your monastery."[55] At length, on May 18, 1950, the extern sisters of Monastery X were admitted to the Second Order and the Statutes of 1931 were adopted as the norms for the extern sisters of the monastery.

It is interesting to note that this transfer of the extern sisters of Monastery X from the Third Order to the Second Order was made without any formal rescript of the Sacred Congregation of Religious, beyond the simple directive, in 1938, that the extern sisters should observe the Statutes of 1931.[56] However, in 1954, Monastery A entered a formal petition to the Holy See, asking that its extern sisters might become members of the Order of St. Clare, with simple perpetual vows, excluding that of enclosure. On October 20, 1954, the Holy See formally granted this petition.[57] From the information received in his survey, the writer concludes that, in some cases, monasteries simply went ahead and made the change from the Third to the Second Order without any formal and individual permission from the Holy See; in other cases, an individual indult was sought, granting permission for the monastery to make the change.

To conclude the summary of conditions in Monastery X, once the extern sisters had been formally transferred to the Second Order, doubt arose concerning the validity of novi-

[55] Letter of December 6, 1946.

[56] Cf. *supra*, p. 74.

[57] S. C. de Rel., Prot. n. 7846/54.

tiates and professions which had been made after 1931 in the Third Order. Accordingly, in 1951, a petition was made to the Holy See for the sanation *ad cautelam* of these novitiates and professions. No answer was received to this petition, which was at length resubmitted in 1955. On December 1 of that year, the requested sanations were finally granted, bringing to an end a period of doubt and confusion which had persisted through almost a quarter of a century.

c. *Summary and Conclusions*—The previous discussion of the legal problems and practical difficulties which followed the promulgation of the Statutes of 1931, as well as still further information gleaned from private correspondence with individual monasteries, leads the writer to the following evaluation of the situation of the extern sisters among the Poor Clares. Indications are that the confusion which existed over the Statutes of 1931 was not limited to the Poor Clares themselves. The officials of the Sacred Congregation of Religious itself were not at all certain just how this legislation of 1931 affected the Poor Clares and the status of their extern sisters. The first opinions emanating from the Holy See after the publication of the new Statutes held that the Poor Clares needed an indult to adopt the Statutes, and that, consequently, their extern sisters could remain members of the Third Order. This same opinion recommended that these sisters adopt the Rule of 1927 given by Pope Pius XI.[58] This accounts for the fact that, throughout the world, some monasteries followed the Rule of 1927 for their extern sisters; others, unaware of this opinion, continued to observe the Rule and declarations of 1888; still others proceeded to adopt the Statutes of 1931.

However, only a few years after the earlier opinion was tendered by the Congregation, the practice of Rome began to swing towards another opinion. For, despite the fact that the earlier view had held that the Poor Clares were not bound to the Statutes of 1931, the Holy See refused to approve Statutes for individual monasteries of the Order if

[58] Cf. *supra*, p. 72.

they were contrary to the Statutes of 1931. Thus, monasteries which petitioned approval for statutes which called for a novitiate of the extern sisters entirely outside the papal enclosure, and for the extern sisters to remain in the Third Order, were not approved by the Holy See. Moreover, the monasteries which had submitted these statutes contrary to the legislation of 1931 were told to observe the official Statutes, and to have their ordinaries approve particular modifications which were not contrary to those Statutes.[59]

By 1940, the practice of the Sacred Congregation of Religious and the opinion of most bishops and provincials in the United States showed beyond doubt that the Holy See wished all monasteries of the Order of St. Clare and the Poor Clare Colettines to follow the Statutes of 1931 and all Poor Clare extern sisters to be members of the Second Order. Nevertheless, some monasteries still desired to keep the extern sisters as members of the Third Order and to avoid following the Statutes of 1931, even though the overwhelming practice of the Holy See was now against such an interpretation. Unfortunately, no official general statement on the matter ever came from Rome; hence, many monasteries had no way of knowing how strongly the Sacred Congregation of Religious was urging the adoption of the Statutes of 1931. Looking back over all that has transpired, it is relatively clear that these monasteries should simply have adopted the Statutes of 1931; but amid the uncertainty and confusion of the actual events themselves, it is easy to see just why matters became so very unsure.

Among those monasteries in which the nuns felt reasonably sure of themselves in adopting the Statutes of 1931 and in admitting the extern sisters to the Second Order, some asked the Holy See for sanations of novitiates and professions which had been made in the Third Order after the Statutes of 1931 had taken effect. Some petitioned the Holy See for permission to observe the Statutes of 1931, others for permission to transfer the extern sisters from the Third

[59] Cf. *supra*, p. 74.

Order to the Second Order. The ordinaries of some of these monasteries felt that these sanations and indults were necessary; still other ordinaries felt that they were not, but obtained provisional indults in order to be on the safe side. Although these indults were granted by the Holy See in most cases,[60] this, in the opinion of the writer, does not mean that the Sacred Congregation of Religious thereby indicated that they were in all cases necessary. Since no authentic general interpretation of the binding force of the Statutes of 1931 had ever been made, but this binding force became evident by the practice of the Sacred Congregation over a number of years, the officials of the Congregation itself were in no position to state whether such documents were required or not. Rather, they issued them in order to remove all possibility of invalid novitiates and professions, to quiet the consciences of the sisters, and to make sure of the juridic standing of the extern sisters in question.

ARTICLE 3

APPROBATION AND CONFIRMATION OF THE STATUTES

The third section of the Decree consisted simply of the approval and confirmation of the Statutes, which were granted by the Holy Father, all things to the contrary notwithstanding.[61] In addition to the papal approval of the Statutes, this part of the Decree endowed ordinaries, both local and religious, with further authority in this matter. These ordinaries were entitled to approve even more detailed regulations for extern sisters, according to the customs of individual monasteries, provided these further regulations were not contrary to the Code of Canon Law nor to the Statutes for Extern Sisters.[62]

[60] Cf. *supra*, pp. 75-76.

[61] Cf. *supra*, p. 64.

[62] "Porro Sanctissimus Dominus noster divina Providentia Pius Pp. XI, in audientia die 24 Iunii 1929 Exlmo. P. Dno. Secretario S. Congregationis de Religiosis concessa, praefata Statuta, ut continentur in hoc exemplari, cuius autographum in Tabulario eiusdem S. Congregationis asservatur, benigne adprobare et confirmare dignatus est, prout

SECTION II
BENEFITS OF THE STATUTES OF 1931 FOR EXTERN SISTERS

A comparison of the condition of extern sisters before the Statutes of 1931 with their new situation after the promulgation of these Statutes shows what a great benefit the new legislation conferred upon these sisters. With the exception of the extern sisters of the Poor Clares and the Discalced Carmelites, externs in monasteries of nuns were sometimes bound only by a simple promise of obedience or fidelity, or at most by some type of temporary vows. Even among the Visitation Sisters, who made a kind of perpetual profession, the vows made were those of obedience and oblation to the service of the monastery, not poverty, chastity and obedience.[63] These extern sisters were governed by statutes drawn up by the proper ordinaries of each individual monastery, and had little in common with the religious family which they served, except the fact that they were subject to the same superioress. Indeed, they were placed in an inferior condition, receiving no share in the spiritual favors, privileges, papal blessings and suffrages proper to the monasteries they served.[64]

As has been shown above, extern sisters among the Poor Clares and the Discalced Carmelites were in a somewhat better condition.[65] These were ruled by papally approved

vi huius Decreti eadem adprobantur atque confirmantur: salvo iure Ordinariorum adprobandi minutiores dispositiones de ratione vitae, iuxta monasteriorum consuctudines, ipsis Sororibus externis propriae, dummodo tamen Sacris Canonibus aut praesentibus Statutis minime opponantur. Contrariis quibuscumque non obstantibus."—Decretum *Conditio plurimorum monasteriorum.*

[63] Cf. *supra,* pp. 38-42; D'Ambrosio, *op. cit.,* p. 407.

[64] "Particularibus normis communiter a proprio cuiusque Ordinario adprobatis regebantur, nihilque commune cum familiis seu communitatibus Monasteriorum habebant quibus addicebantur praeter Superiorissam cui erant subiectae; imo in gradu inferioritatis prae Communitatibus Monasteriorum versabantur quibus erant addictae, uti patet, et nulla proinde illis aderat participatio gratiarum spiritualium, privilegiorum, benedictionum papalium, suffragiorum quae cuique monasterio erant propria."—*Loc. cit.*

[65] Cf. *supra,* pp. 44-47, 49.

norms of their own, and, after the completion of a canonical novitiate, professed the three temporary vows of poverty, chastity and obedience, later being admitted even to perpetual profession. Moreover, they shared in all the spiritual favors, indulgences and privileges of the monasteries in which they served. However, despite these favors, the extern sisters in these Orders were considered merely to be aggregated to the monasteries they served. They were placed in a position which was considered inferior to that of the nuns who professed the Rule of the Second Order of St. Francis or of Carmel, which Rule was held in higher standing than the Rule professed by the extern sisters, since it conferred special rights and privileges, benefits which the profession of the externs did not entail.[66]

However, in virtue of the Statutes of 1931, the condition of all extern sisters who came under their provisions, regardless of their previous status, was greatly improved. No longer were they in a greatly inferior condition, or considered as merely aggregated to the monasteries they served. Instead, by the Apostolic authority itself, they were incorporated into and made full members of the communities they served, with the single exception that they had no active or passive voice in the Order. To this end, the extern sisters were ordered to make profession not only of the Statutes of 1931, but of the same Rule professed by the nuns in the monastery. This meant that they were true members of the same Order to which the cloistered nuns belonged. Therefore, they had the same rights and benefits as the other members of the monastic community, since they were no longer united to that community by aggregation, which implies a certain disparity or difference, but by full affiliation, which implies equality.[67]

[66] "Tamen in gradu inferioritatis constitutae erant prae Monialibus et earumdem communitatibus, quippe moniales regulam profitebantur secundi Ordinis respective Franciscalis aut Carmelitae, cui maior est gradus et specialia sunt nativa iura et emolumenta."—D'Ambrosio, *op. cit.*, p. 407.

[67] "E contra, vi recentiorum statutorum, iuridica omnium Sororum

Consideration of the foregoing juridic status of extern sisters shows that, in promulgating the 1931 Statutes for Extern Sisters, the Holy See in effect set up a new canonical institution, the members of which participated in the condition of both monastic nuns and sisters of simple vows. The extern sisters formed a sort of middle ground between the cloistered nuns, and the sisters whose lives were spent in the active apostolate. These Statutes of 1931 thus definitely pointed out the fact that the vocation of the extern sister was entirely unique, a special calling combining elements of both the cloistered and the active life, yet distinct from each.[68]

SECTION III
COMMENTARY ON THE STATUTES OF 1931

ARTICLE 1
GENERAL COMMENTARY

It is of interest to note, first of all, just why the regula-

externarum condicio admodum evecta est; quippe Monialibus ipsis monasteriorum, quibus sunt addictae, non iam aggregantur sed aequiparantur earumque communitatibus Apostolica auctoritate veluti incorporantur, quum eadem regula, praeter statuta illis profitenda imponatur unde membra communitatis monasteriorum praedictorum ipsae exinde evadunt. Ideoque eisdem eadem sunt iura et beneficia non vi aggregationis, quae disparitatem subaudit, sed vi filiationis, uti dici solet, quae paritatem importat."—D'Ambrosio, *op. cit.*, pp. 407-408; "Vis novi regiminis haec est, ut in posterum istae 'Tourières' non iam ad Tertium Ordinem pertinebunt sed classem constituent secundi Ordinis vel Ordinis simpliciter talis, si, ut in religione S. Benedicti, non sit nisi unus Ordo."—Vermeersch, *op. cit.*, p. 51; "Intanto si vede già come queste suore hanno, si può dire, la stessa condizione canonica delle monache in quanto non è modificata dalla necessitá di vivere fuori della clausura claustrale."—*Il Monitore Ecclesiastico*, Anno LVI, Serie V, Vol. III, Fasc. XI (Nov. 1931), pp. 333-334.

[68] "Dalle provvide e illuminate cure che a tale necessità ha dedicato la Sacra Congregazione dei Religiosi, è derivato così un vero novello istituto canonico, che partecipa sapientemente della duplice condizione di monache e di suore, quasi cumulandone esteriormente i vantaggi, e

tions for extern sisters published in 1931 were called Statutes. In the first drafts of these norms, they were referred to as Constitutions, but this name was purposely changed in order to avoid confusion with the general Constitutions of monasteries. Besides, the term *Statutes* conformed better to the practice of the Roman Curia and to the accepted historical use of the word in canonical terminology, since the norms to which it referred concerned only one particular class of persons.[69]

The Statutes of 1931 formed a complete body of law for extern sisters, covering the whole substance of their life in all its circumstances.[70] They were far superior to previous Statutes approved by the Holy See, whether as a part of the constitutions of some institute, or as a separate set of norms for the extern sisters of an institute. The Statutes of 1931 were accurate and complete, providing a precise definition of the canonical status of these sisters, outlining the more important features of their religious life and their place in the life of the monastery. Preceding statutes had either introduced these sisters almost timidly, or merely improved upon the institution in certain limited respects where it had already been in existence. The new discipline of 1931, however, was a polished and mature body of law, canonizing the

formando un *quid medium* tra l'uno e l'altro, che può ben ragionevolmente allettare in guisa nuova aspiranti alla vita religiosa, favorendo insieme le vocazioni, l'incremento degli Ordini monastici e la loro opera sociale d'apostolato. Sono le *Sorores externae.*"—*Ibid.*, p. 332.

[69] "Revera, in primis huius documenti schematibus, loco *Statutorum* hae normae dicebantur *Constitutiones.* Mutatum fuit e proposito nomen, ne confusio fieret cum Constitutionibus generalibus Monasteriorum. Ceterum melius et aptius, attentis stylo Curiae et vocum historia, hae normae, quae classem particularem tantum respiciunt, nomine Statutorum quam Constitutionum designantur."—La Puma, *op. cit.*, XIII (1932), 340.

[70] "Memorata Statuta . . . generalium normarum corpus completum exhibent; omnia enim quae ad substantiam vitae Sororum externarum pertinent, practice et opportune, relatione scilicet generatim habita ad circumstantias tum temporis tum personarum tum destinationis, omnino considerant et moderantur."—D'Ambrosio, *op. cit.*, p. 400.

institution of extern sisters as a permanent feature in the Church.[71]

ARTICLE 2
SPECIAL COMMENTARY

Since the Statutes of 1931 played so important a part in the recent history and development of extern sisters, and since they contributed so prominently to the evolution of the situation which prompted the present Statutes of 1961, the writer has considered it worth while to present an outline of the norms of 1931, together with a commentary on the more important points therein contained.

A. *Chapter One: The Purpose and Status of Extern Sisters*

The Statutes of 1931 were intended to govern the extern sisters in monasteries of nuns of every Order to which the Apostolic See had granted the special faculty of introducing such sisters.[72] The binding force of these Statutes was the exact equivalent of that obligation imposed by Constitutions which had been approved by the Holy See.[73] As a matter of fact, these Statutes of 1931 actually took the place, in regard to the extern sisters, of the Constitutions of the Order or monastery to which they belonged. This is evident from Article 2 of the Statutes, which stated that the extern sisters were to strive for their sanctification by observance of the three simple vows, the Rule of their monastery, and the Statutes themselves, no mention being made of the Constitutions of the Order or monastery.[74] However, al-

[71] Cf. La Puma, *op. cit.*, XIII (1932), 342.

[72] "Sorores externae monasteriorum Monialium cuiuscumque Ordinis, quibus Apostolica Sedes specialem facultatem ad illas instituendas concesserit, regi et gubernari debent ad norman Statutorum, quae sequuntur."—*Statuta, 1931,* Art. 1.

[73] "Obligatio Statutorum ... prorsus illi aequiparatur qua Constitutiones a S. Sede approbatae obligant."—La Puma, *op. cit.,* XIII (1932), 343.

[74] Sorores illae externae finem generalem intendunt propriae sanctificationis consequendae per exactam observantiam trium votorum simplicium religionis, necnon Regulae sui cuiusque monasterii et praesentium Statutorum."—*Statuta, 1931,* Art. 2.

though the extern sisters were not directly bound to observe the Constitutions of their institute, it was possible that certain elements of the Constitutions might indirectly affect them. In this regard it suffices to remember that the ordinary of the monastery was empowered by the Decree *Conditio plurimorum monasteriorum* to approve more detailed regulations for extern sisters, provided they were not contrary either to canon law or to the Statutes of 1931.[75] Some of these regulations may well have been taken from the Constitutions. Moreover, according to Article 9 of the Statutes, the training and formation of the extern sisters was largely in the hands of the superioress of the monastery; it was her task to integrate them smoothly into the life of the monastery which was regulated by the very Constitutions to which the extern sisters were not directly subject.[76] In this way there was, of necessity, a strong indirect influence of the Constitutions on the extern sisters. As will be shown later, the existence within a monastery of a class of sisters who, although members of the Order, were not bound to its Constitutions, was a fundamental weakness of the Statutes of 1931.[77]

According to the Statutes, the special purpose of the extern sisters was to serve the monastery and the church connected with it in all those external tasks which it was permissible and fitting for them to perform.[78] This expression of purpose was very broad in scope, and, in practice, was always so understood and interpreted. Thus, extern sisters have been assigned not only to those tasks which strictly must be done outside the enclosure, but also to such work which could conveniently be done within the cloister by the nuns, or outside of it by the extern sisters.

[75] Cf. *supra*, p. 78.

[76] *Statuta, 1931*, Art. 9.

[77] Cf. *infra.*, pp. 106-107.

[78] "Finis autem illarum specialis est suo quaeque [sic] monasterio et adnexae ecclesiae pro quibusvis externis muniis ac necessitatibus inservire, quae ipsis liceant atque conveniant; . . ."—*Statuta, 1931*, Art. 3.

In practice, the only limitation placed by the Statutes on the work to which the extern sisters might be assigned was that which contemplated tasks which were unbecoming, dangerous, or foreign to the religious state.[79]

The extern sisters were forbidden to enter the papal enclosure, except on occasions when their assistance within the cloister was considered necessary. Then they were permitted to enter for as brief a time as possible, with at least the previous habitual approval of the local ordinary.[80] No presumed or interpretative permission beyond this rather strict norm of the Statutes was allowed, although where broader faculties for entrance of the extern sisters into the cloister of the nuns were required the Sacred Congregation of Religious was disposed to grant them.[81] Through private correspondence with the American monasteries of the Order of St. Clare and the Poor Clare Colettines, the writer was able to obtain information concerning a number of such indults. In a good many cases, the extern sisters received outright permission to dwell within the papal enclosure, thus sharing completely in the community life of the nuns.[82] In

[79] La Puma, *op. cit.*, XIII (1932), 345.

[80] "... non autem ad interiora monasterii, nisi interdum et ad tempus quo fieri poterit brevius, earum opera censeatur ibi necessaria, impetrata prius saltem habituali approbatione ab ordinario loci."—*Statuta, 1931*, Art. 3.

[81] La Puma, *op. cit.*, XIII (1932), 346.

[82] Information was received concerning the following indults issued by the Sacred Congregation of Religious: Prot. n. 7846/54, granted for three years in 1954 and renewed for five years in 1957, permitted the extern sisters to dwell within the papal enclosure, leaving at the discretion of the abbess or her vicaress; Prot. n. 11012/57 granted, *in perpetuum*, permission for the extern sisters to dwell in the papal enclosure, and demanded that there be a fitting separation between them and the nuns; Prot. n. 12429/57 granted the extern sisters permission to live in the enclosure and to perform the exercises of the common life with the nuns, for a period of five years; Prot. nn. 4577/58, 6487/58 and 4369/60, all covering periods of five years, permitted the extern sisters, novices and postulants to enter the cloister of the nuns for meals, recreation, work, instructions and spiritual exercises, to sleep within the enclosure, to remain therein during sickness

other instances, although no permission was received for the extern sisters to dwell more or less permanently within the papal cloister, various extensions of the limited permission to enter the enclosure were granted by the Sacred Congregation of Religious. Indults permitted entrance of the extern sisters for work, recreation, special occasions and the like.[83] As is evident from the dates of some of these indults, they were still in effect at the time the Statutes of 1931 were abrogated by the Statutes of 1961; the canonical effects of

or infirmity, and, finally, to admit travelling Poor Clare extern sisters from other monasteries into the enclosure.

[83] Information was received concerning the following indults issued by the Sacred Congregation of Religious: Prot. n. 12825/52, which was granted in 1953 for five years, permitted extern sisters and postulants, even those who belonged to other monasteries of the same federation, to enter the enclosure, as often as the abbess deemed it necessary, for funerals and for recreation; in 1958, this same monastery received an indult, Prot. n. 5654/58, which, for a period of five years, allowed the extern sisters, novices and postulants to enter the enclosure for exercises of piety and recreation. Prot. n. 6551/53 granted permission for the extern sisters to enter the enclosure for exposition of the Blessed Sacrament, meals, recreation, processions, extra work, as well as to enter the garden and the garage which were located within the limits of the cloister; this particular indult was granted for three years in 1953, and renewed in 1956 and 1961, each time for five years. Faculties based on Prot. n. 11003/55 were used by the diocesan Chancery to allow extern sisters and postulants, even those who visited the monastery, to enter the enclosure occasionally (approximately once a month) for recreation, as well as to permit them to enter the enclosure on the occasion of a funeral; this was granted for five years in 1955, and *in perpetuum* in 1960, increasing the frequency of entrance to approximately once a week. Prot. n. 11291/55, which was granted *in perpetuum* in the year 1955, provided that the abbess, with the consent of her discretorium, could admit sick extern sisters to the monastery infirmary, and could likewise allow the extern sisters to have common recreation with the nuns. Prot. n. 11897/58, which was granted in 1958 for five years, granted permission for the extern postulants to enter the enclosure for instructions in Christian doctrine and the spiritual life, and for the extern sisters, novices and postulants to enter for special recreations at the pleasure of the abbess. Prot. n. 10378/61, granted in 1961 for a period of three years, allowed the extern sisters to enter the enclosure for special occasions determined by the abbess and discreets.

this fact will be discussed at the proper place in the consideration of the Statutes of 1961.[84] Article 4, treating of matters which have already been discussed,[85] declared that the extern sisters, as true members of the community they served, were sharers in the same spiritual benefits as the nuns of the monastery, enjoyed the same indulgences, and all the privileges of which they were capable.[86] Finally, since the extern sisters were constituted members of the same Order as the nuns, Article 5 required that they become imbued with the spirit of their particular Order, and profess the Rule of that Order. However, the Sacred Congregation, considering the special role of these sisters, prescribed that the Statutes of 1931 were to prevail even over the Rule of the Order, should a conflict arise.[87]

According to La Puma, who was intimately connected with the drawing up of these Statutes of 1931, the Sacred Congregation of Religious definitely realized many of the difficulties involved in setting up the status of the extern sisters as described in the First Chapter of the Statutes. Especially, it did not seem fitting to recognize as full members of the community and the Order these sisters who were bound to the Rule only insofar as it did not conflict with the Statutes of 1931, who were in no way directly bound to the Constitutions, and who ordinarily lived outside the papal enclosure. Nevertheless, after carefully weighing these matters, and taking special votes concerning them,

[84] Cf. *infra*, pp. 218-219.

[85] Cf. *supra*, pp. 52, 80.

[86] "Utpote membra Communitatis cui inserviunt, Sorores externae eorundem ac Moniales spiritualium bonorum sunt participes, iisdemque gaudent indulgentiis ac privilegiis omnibus, quorum sint capaces."—*Statuta, 1931*, Art. 4.

[87] "Satagant autem Sorores, ut eodem quoque peculiari Ordinis spiritu apprime imbuantur, atque ipsius Regulam profiteantur et exacte observent in omnibus quae hisce Statutis non adversentur."—*Ibid.*, Art. 5; "Die externen Schwestern legen die Profess auf dieselbe Ordensregel ab wie die internen Nonnen, bilden mit diesen eine und dieselbe Klosterfamilie und unterstehen derselben Oberin."—Hilling, *op. cit.*, p. 442.

the Holy See decided to set up the arrangement described above.[88]

B. *Chapter Two: The Living Quarters and Government of the Sisters*

The dwelling of the extern sisters was to be annexed to the monastery. Part of this extern dwelling was to be so reserved to the sisters that no member of the other sex could be admitted except according to the judgment of the superioress, for a just and reasonable cause.[89] Because of practical considerations, e.g., ease in communicating between the extern sisters and the cloistered nuns, it was considered better if the quarters of the extern sisters were connected immediately with that part of the monastery where the nuns lived. However, such immediate union and continuity were not demanded.[90] That portion of the dwelling of the extern sisters which was reserved exclusively to the sisters constituted a type of enclosure which was fundamentally the same as the enclosure observed in houses of Congregations, described in canon 604, § 1, and which is commonly referred to as the episcopal enclosure.[91] Since this dwelling

[88] "Sane, aliquantulum videbatur inelegans uti vera membra Monasterii agnoscere simul cum *Monialibus,* Sorores votorum simplicium quae, non nisi *iuxta modum* Regulae ligabantur, quae nullo modo Constitutionibus obstringebantur, quae extra clausuram inhabitare debebant, etc. His omnibus non difficulter respondetur: ceterum omnia accurate perpensa sunt et prae oculis habita imo, speciale super his Votum redactum fuit in quo quaestio diligenter pertractatur. Aliqua attigerunt D'Ambrosio, p. 14-16; *Il Monitore Eccl.,* 1931, p. 333."—La Puma, *op. cit.,* XIII (1932), p. 347, nota 17.

[89] "Sorores externae suam habeant domum monasterii adnexam, cuius pars ita ipsis reservetur, ut in eam nemo alterius sexus admittatur, nisi ii quos ex iustis et rationabilibus causis Antistita monasterii admitti posse censuerit."—*Statuta, 1931,* Art. 6.

[90] "Haec adnexio melius intelligitur de vera *unione,* ita ut *intra domum propriam* inveniantur Sorores, cum ad crates habentur instructiones de quibus in Art. 9. Tamen *abstracte loquendo* unio seu continuitas non imponitur."—La Puma, *op. cit.,* XIII (1932), 348.

[91] Cf. can. 604, § 1; "Mithin unterstehen die Wohnräume der externen Schwestern bloss der sogen. bischöflichen Klausur, von der in Canon 604 des kirchlichen Gesetzbuches die Rede ist."—Hilling, *op. cit.,* p. 442.

was located outside the confines of the papal enclosure, the superioress and the other nuns, contrary to the concessions of certain previous Statutes, were not, *per se*, allowed to enter this portion of the house, even for the purposes of visitation or inspection.[92] However, in some cases indults were granted to permit the nuns to leave the enclosure to perform necessary work in the quarters of the extern sisters, and also to permit the superioress to go into this section to supervise the work of the sisters.[93] Moreover, as has been pointed out above, numerous indults were granted by the Sacred Congregation of Religious to permit the extern sisters to dwell habitually within the confines of the papal enclosure, thus completely superseding the prescriptions of Article 6.[94]

It will be noted that the earliest such indult among the group reported to the present writer was issued in 1954; after that date there were granted a number of others that allowed the extern sisters to live habitually within the enclosure.[95] However, information is available which suggests that the Sacred Congregation of Religious was not always so well disposed towards granting such favors. Thus, in 1936, the Cardinal Archbishop of Genoa in writing to the Sacred Congregation asked whether approval could be given to the immemorial custom or to the provisions of the *Consuetudinarium* or ancient books of a monastery which permitted extern sisters to reside in the cloister, notwithstanding the prescriptions of the Statutes of 1931 that they reside in external places annexed to the monastery.[96] The

[92] La Puma, *op. cit.*, XIII (1932), 348.

[93] S. Cong. of Religious, Prot. nn. 11291/55 and 10378/61.

[94] Cf. *supra*, p. 85.

[95] *Loc. cit.*

[96] "Se si poteva approvare la consuetudine *ab immemorabili* o le direttive dei Costumieri o antichi libri dei Monasteri di voti solenni di far dimorare le Suore esterne dentro la Clausura, nonostante le disposizioni degli Statuti di questa S.C. del 16 luglio 1931 che prescrivono la loro abitazione in locali esterni annessi ai Monasteri stessi." —Ex *Rivista Diocesana di Genova,* 1936, p. 215, cit. apud *Commentarium pro Religiosis,* XVII (1936), 209.

Sacred Congregation replied that the Statutes of 1931 had abrogated all customs and provisions of ancient books or directories. Those monasteries which had suitable places outside the cloister were ordered to conform to the Statutes at once; those which did not were allowed to continue the same practice as before for a period of five years, provided that, in the meantime, they made provisions conformable to the Statutes.[97] Larraona, in his annotations to this response of the Sacred Congregation, stated that the reason for this abrogation of particular contrary customs and prescriptions was the fact that they were in several respects contrary to the law of enclosure, insofar as they permitted the habitual entrance and exit of sisters who, while they lived in the enclosure, were not bound by it. Moreover, such an arrangement was contrary to the Statutes of 1931, especially to Articles 3, 6 and 7.[98]

It is apparent, then, that there was a change in the attitude of the Holy See, which led the Sacred Congregation of Religious to take a more liberal attitude towards the habitual dwelling of extern sisters in the enclosure, as well as towards more frequent entrance of those whose habitation was located outside the cloister. One good reason for this was very likely the large number of complaints which reached the Holy See concerning these regulations of the Statutes. As Larraona mentioned in his annotations to the above mentioned Decree of the Sacred Congregation, some

[97] "Questa S. Congregazione in proposito retiene che gli Statuti del 16 luglio 1931 hanno abolito qualsiasi consuetudine o direttiva di antichi libri o costumieri. Pertanto quei Monasteri che hanno i locali adatti sono tenuti ad osservare gli Statuti anzidetti. Per quelli che difettano di detti locali, questo S. Dicastero concede che per un quinquennio possano continuare come hanno fatto sin qui, *dummodo interim provideatur* a norma dei precitati Statuti."—*Loc. cit.*

[98] "Responsum evidens est: praedictae consuetudines ac praescripta de quibus agitur e regione contraria sub diversis respectibus *legi clausurae* videntur, cum ingressum et egressum habitualem exigant sororum quae, quin clausura teneantur, intra ipsam tamen vivunt et praeterea textui Statutorum (cfr. Art. 3, 6, 7, etc.) directo contradicunt."—*Ibid.*, pp. 211-212.

Orders did not wish to admit extern sisters to the cloister even for their novitiate; others, though they had living quarters for extern sisters outside the enclosure, were accustomed to admit the extern sisters to the enclosure on greater feasts.[99] In the writer's opinion, these complaints and frequent petitions to the Holy See brought about a greater regard on the part of the Sacred Congregation of Religious for the customs and usages of individual monasteries. This greater consideration for particular usages was a key factor in drafting the Statutes of 1961, which are most liberal in regard to the entrance and dwelling of extern sisters within the papal enclosure.[100]

Article 7 spelled out exactly the cases when, according to the Statutes, the extern sisters were permitted to enter the enclosure of the nuns. Such entrance was allowed only in order to make their first or canonical year of novitiate, in case of necessity according to the norm of Article 3, and in case of infirmity which could not be cared for adequately in the extern dwelling, according to the norm of Article 107. Under no circumstances were postulants to enter the enclosure at all.[101] In this matter of extern sisters entering the enclosure, the Statutes of 1931 steered a middle course between certain former statutes which were more lenient, and others which forbade entrance altogether.[102] Moreover, as has been pointed out above, the Sacred Congregation of Religious granted numerous indults which permitted the extern sisters to enter the papal enclosure for other reasons as well as those enumerated in the Statutes.[103]

Both the religious discipline of the extern sisters, and the service they rendered to the monastery were under the

[99] *Ibid.*, p. 211.

[100] Cf. *infra*, p. 135, note 32.

[101] "Non licet Sororibus externis clausuram ingredi monasterii, nisi ad novitiatum canonicum ibi peragendum et in casibus praevisis sub articulis 3 et 107 horum Statutorum. Postulantes autem nunquam clausuram ingrediantur."—*Statuta, 1931,* Art. 7; cf. *supra*, Art. 3, p. 85; Hilling, *op. cit.*, p. 443.

[102] La Puma, *op. cit.*, XIII (1932), 349.

[103] Cf. *supra*, p. 86.

direction of the superioress of the house, to whom they owed religious obedience.[104] This superioress was to prescribe the daily order of exercises for the extern sisters, and train them in the way of perfection and the spiritual life.[105] In addition, the superioress was directed by the Statutes to appoint a prudent and mature sister, who had made perpetual profession, to supervise and direct the others, and to keep the superioress informed of conditions outside the enclosure.[106]

The last article of Chapter Two vindicated the right and duty of the ordinaries, both local and religious, either personally or through a delegate, to conduct canonical visitation of the extern sisters and their dwelling place whenever they made the canonical visitation of the monastery.[107]

C. *Chapter Three: Admission, Probation and Profession of Extern Sisters*

1. Requirements for Admission

This section of the Statutes dealt with requirements for admission to the class of the extern sisters. After restating canon 538, which determines who may be admitted to the religious life,[108] the Statutes proceeded to list the requisites for valid and licit entrance into the novitiate, as taken from canon 542, no mention being made of those which had no application to the extern sisters.[109] It is noteworthy that, although canon 542 makes mention of the fact that the Constitutions of each institute are to retain their force in this connection, mention of this reservation was omitted from the Statutes of 1931.[110] This omission was occasioned by the

[104] *Statuta, 1931,* Art. 8.

[105] *Ibid.,* Art. 9.

[106] *Ibid.,* Art. 10.

[107] "Ordinarii ius est et officium per se vel per alium Sorores quoque externas earumque domum visitandi, quoties canonicam monasterii visitationem instituit."—*Ibid.,* Art. 11; La Puma, *op. cit.,* XIV (1933), 352.

[108] *Ibid.,* Art. 12.

[109] *Ibid.,* Art. 13-14.

[110] "Firmo praescripto can. 539-541, aliisque in propriis cuiusque religionis constitutionibus: . . ."—Canon 542.

fact that the extern sisters, according to the Statutes of 1931, did not observe the Constitutions of their institute, but the Statutes which took the place of these Constitutions.[111] Article 13a, moreover, incorporated an interpretation which was given by the Code Commission in 1919, concerning the first invalidating impediment to entrance into the novitiate. Canon 542, 1°, simply excludes those who have adhered to a non-Catholic sect; the Statutes, reflecting the decision of the Commission, limited this restriction to those who had fallen away from the Church and joined a non-Catholic sect. Hence, converts were not affected by this impediment.[112]

Although canon 555, § 1, 1°, demands an age of only fifteen years complete for valid entrance into the novitiate, the Statutes raised the age required for a valid entrance into the novitiate among extern sisters to eighteen years complete.[113] Articles 16-18 then proceeded to outline the qualities of those to be received as extern aspirants, and to prescribe that each candidate present certain documents and testimonial letters.

According to the Statutes, the right to admit candidates to the postulancy of the extern sisters, as well as to the novitiate and the annual renewals of vows, belonged to the superioress of the monastery with the consent of her Council. The right to admit them to both first temporary profession and perpetual profession was assigned to the same superioress, with the consent of the regular superior, in case the monastery happened to be subject to Regulars. Moreover, the monastic Chapter was entitled to a vote in this matter of first temporary or perpetual profession; this vote was deliberative indeed in the former case, but simply consultative

[111] "Constitutiones praeterea, reservandae non erant, quia haec Statuta locum obtinent Constitutionum."—La Puma, *op. cit.*, XIV (1933), 32.

[112] Comm. Pont., 16 oct. 1919—*AAS*, XI (1919), 477: "Invalide ad novitiatum admittuntur quae, a catholica fide deficientes, sectae acatholicae adhaeserunt."—*Statuta, 1931*, Art. 13, a.

[113] "Pro valida admissione ad novitiatum inter Sorores externas monasteriorum requiritur ut postulans octodecimum aetatis annum compleverit."—*Ibid.*, Art. 15.

in the case of perpetual profession.[114] Since he was not an internal superior of the Order, the consent of the local ordinary was not required for the admission of a candidate to first temporary or perpetual profession, even though the monastery might be subject to him. Article 19 mentioned such consent only on the part of the religious superior, if there happened to be one.[115] However, in virtue of canon 552 and Article 20 of the Statutes, the superioress was required to notify the local ordinary at least two months before each admission to the novitiate or to the profession of temporary or perpetual vows, in order that he or his delegate might conduct the canonical examination of the candidate.

2. The Postulancy

The Statutes, altering the law of canon 553, § 1, demanded that the postulancy last a full year. Moreover, after hearing her Council, the superioress was authorized to extend the postulancy, but not beyond six months.[116] The prescriptions of canon 540, § 3, which states that postulants in monasteries of nuns are bound by the law of enclosure, did not apply to these extern postulants, who were forbidden in Article 7 of the Statutes ever to enter the enclosure, and ordered in Article 22 to make their postulancy in the dwelling of the extern sisters. This section of the Statutes also provided norms and regulations concerning the garb, training and preparation for the novitiate of the postulants.[117]

3. The Novitiate

The novitiate was to begin with the reception of the habit, according to the rite of investiture approved for the nuns of the Order. Proper alterations, approved by either the

[114] *Ibid.*, Art. 19.

[115] La Puma, *op. cit.*, XIV (1933), 35-36.

[116] "Omnes adspirantes, antequam ad novitiatum admittantur, postulatum ad annum integrum peragant; quod tempus Superiorissa, audito suo Consilio, potest prorogare, non tamen ultra semestre."—*Statuta, 1931*, Art. 21.

[117] *Ibid.*, Art. 22-24.

local or religious ordinary, were to be made in this rite for adaptation to extern sisters. The habit of the novices was that of the lay sisters (*conversae*) of the monastery, with appropriate adaptations to the needs of extern sisters.[118]

The novitiate was to last for a period of two years. The first year was to be strictly canonical and, in order to be valid, had to be completed within the enclosure.[119] Private correspondence of the writer with various monasteries of the Order of St. Clare and the Poor Clare Colettines indicates that, in many cases, it was not realized that a novitiate, the first year of which was made outside the enclosure, was not valid. In several cases sanations were later obtained for such novitiates.

Article 28 of the Statutes applied canon 558 to the case of the extern sisters, and stated that a novitiate which was made for the extern sisters was not valid for the nuns, either choir nuns or lay sisters (*conversae*). Nor was a novitiate made for either of these classes valid for the extern sisters. Thus, it is evident that, under the Statutes of 1931, the extern sisters constituted a true and distinct class of sisters belonging to the monastery, a class completely distinct from the choir nuns and the lay sisters (*conversae*).[120]

After treating of the purpose of the novitiate and the weekly instructions in Christian doctrine which the novices were to receive,[121] the Statutes repeated the prescription that the canonical year of the novitiate be spent in the cloister, namely in the portion reserved to the lay sister novices.[122] The formation of the novices was in the hands of the novice

[118] *Ibid.*, Art. 25-26.

[119] "Novitiatus duos annos durabit, quorum primus erit stricte canonicus. Hic, ut valeat, debet esse integer et continuus, intra claustra monasterii peragendus."—*Ibid.*, Art. 27.

[120] "Novitiatus pro Sororibus externis peractus, pro Monialibus tum choristis tum conversis non valet, neque e contrario valet pro Sororibus externis novitiatus peractus pro Monialibus."—*Ibid.*, Art. 28; cf. Hilling, *op. cit.*, p. 444.

[121] *Statuta, 1931,* Art. 29-30.

[122] *Ibid.*, Art. 31.

mistress, to whom they were subject.[123] During the year of the canonical novitiate, the Statutes allowed the novices to perform only those tasks of the lay sisters which did not interfere with the duties of the novitiate.[124]

According to Article 34, the second year of the novitiate was to be spent in the dwelling place of the extern sisters, under the special guidance of a sister appointed for this purpose. The mistress of novices was to impart instructions and corrections to these novices at the parlor grille.[125] Although Article 35, in accordance with the practice of the Sacred Congregation of Religious, permitted the novices of the second year to perform some services outside the house, the cultivation of the spiritual life had to remain the prime purpose of this second year. Such external service was to be done prudently and moderately, and the novices were always supposed to be under the guidance of a professed sister.[126] However two months before profession, the novices, according to Article 36, were to refrain from all outside work and retire within the enclosure in order to prepare themselves for profession.[127]

123 *Ibid.*, Art. 32.

124 *Ibid.*, Art. 33.

125 *Ibid.*, Art. 34.

126 "Quoties igitur constitutiones praescribant secundum novitiatus annum in eoque sinant novitios in operibus propriis Instituti se exercere, hoc liceat, salvis fundamentalibus novitatus legibus. Ideoque prae oculis habendum est novitiatum esse institutum ad novitiorum animos informandos.... Quamobrem mandat haec Sacra Congregatio ut, etiam secundo novitiatus anno perdurante, ante omnia quaelibet munia, disciplina spiritualis vitae apprime curetur. Fas tamen esto, secundo novitiatus anno, novitio vel novitiae Instituti operibus vacare si id ferant constitutiones; verum prudenter et moderate id fiat, tantummodo ad novitiorum instructionem;... operibus ipsis vacent sub directione et vigilantia gravis religiosi, vel religiosae, qui verbo doceat exemploque praecurrat."—Instr. S. C. de Rel., 3 nov. 1921—*AAS*, XIII (1921), 539-540.

127 "Duobus ante professionem mensibus ab omni opere externo abstineant, si extra novitiatum fuerint, ad illum revocentur, ut per integrum bimestre ad professionem emittendam, in spiritu suae vocationis firmati, se praeparent."—*Ibid.*, p. 540.

The Statutes granted to the extern novices full participation in the indulgences and suffrages of their Order, as well as the privilege of making profession in danger of death. Any renunciation of goods made during the novitiate was invalid.[128] The novice might be dismissed for any just cause by the monastic Chapter or by the superioress with the consent of her Council, according to the Constitutions of the monastery. When the time of the novitiate expired, the superioress, after consulting her Council, was permitted to extend it by as much as six months.[129] Finally, Article 42 prescribed a retreat of eight full days before the first temporary profession and the perpetual profession, and a three-day retreat before each annual renewal of vows.

4. Profession

The Statutes adapted the requirements of canon 572, which treats of the conditions for valid profession, to the case of the extern sisters. Thus, the age for the first temporary profession was twenty years, that for the perpetual profession, twenty-six.[130] It was required for the validity of the profession that it be received either by the superioress of the monastery herself, or by another female religious delegated by the superioress.[131] The profession made by the extern sisters after the novitiate consisted of six years of temporary vows, which had to be renewed annually. Moreover, after the six years of temporary vows were completed, the superioress, after hearing her Council, was authorized by the Statutes to prolong the time of the temporary vows, but not beyond another six months.[132] This extension beyond the

[128] *Statuta, 1931,* Art. 37-39.

[129] *Ibid.,* Art. 40-41.

[130] "Ad validitatem cuiusvis religiosae professionis requiritur ut quae eam emissura est, legitimam aetatem habeat, scilicet viginti saltem annos compleverit pro prima professione, viginti et sex pro professione perpetua."—*Ibid.,* Art. 43, a.

[131] "Ad validitatem cuiusvis religiosae professionis requiritur ut ab Antistita monasterii per se vel per aliam religiosam recipiatur."—*Ibid.,* Art. 43, h.

[132] "Quaelibet novitia post expletum novitiatum, apud ipsum monasterium debet votis perpetuis praemittere votorum simplicium profes-

six years of temporary profession granted by canon 574 is of special interest, since it was something ordinarily not granted by the Holy See.[133]

When an extern sister's temporary vows expired, she was either to renew the temporary profession, make her perpetual profession, or return to the world. The Statutes made provision for the anticipation of the renewal of temporary vows, and demanded that the superioress consult her Council before permitting this. The rite the externs were to observe in making profession was to be the rite in use for the nuns of the monastery, with the necessary adaptations to the case of the extern sisters. Since the extern sisters were to spend the last two months of their novitiate within the enclosure, their first profession was permitted to be made in the cloister, but this was not demanded. The profession had to be made in the quality of a sister destined for the external service of the monastery. The sister was to promise to live according to the Rule of that monastery and the Statutes approved by the Apostolic See.[134] Finally, Article 48 prescribed that, for each profession or renewal of profession, there be a document or record signed by the sister making profession, by the person receiving the vows, and by the mistress of novices.

The extern sisters in temporary vows were accorded the same spiritual favors as the ones in perpetual vows, and were bound by the same obligation to observe the Rule and the Statutes. Not even the extern sisters in perpetual vows could ever acquire active or passive voice with regard to the external or internal offices of the monastery. Concluding the section on profession was a directive that devotional

sionem per sex annos, quovis tamen anno renovandam. Superiorissa monasterii potest, ob iustas ac rationabiles causas, auditoque suo Consilio, hoc tempus prorogare, renovata a Sorore temporaria professione, non tamen ultra sex menses."—*Ibid.*, Art. 44.

[133] "Post sex annos votorum temporariorum potest adhuc professio prorogari, quod numquam pro religiosis conceditur."—La Puma, *op. cit.*, XIV (1933), 164.

[134] *Statuta, 1931*, Art. 45-47.

renewals of vows, which however had no juridic effects, were to be made according to the custom of each monastery.[135]

5. Cession of Administration, Disposition of Use and Usufruct, the Will.

No dowry was to be demanded from the extern sisters; they were simply required to bring to the monastery with them certain clothing and other items according to the usage of the individual monasteries.[136] Articles 52-54 applied the matter contained in canon 569 to the extern sisters, treating of the cession and disposition of goods, of the cases wherein this cession was not made before profession, and of the will to be made by novices before their temporary profession. Although, according to canon 570, § 1, the Constitutions of an Order or an express agreement may allow something to be asked for the expenses of food and clothing at the time of entrance into the postulancy or the novitiate, the Statutes forbade the superioress to ask anything of the extern sisters even for these ends.[137] Finally, in accord with canon 570, § 2, Article 56 required that those goods which a young lady had brought with her to the monastery and which had not been used up be given back to her at her return to the world.

D. *Chapter Four: The Vows and the Respective Virtues*

1. Obedience

The vow of obedience extended to the commands of a legitimate superior in those matters which, directly or indirectly, pertained to the observance of the vows or the Statutes.[138]

135 *Ibid.*, Art. 49-50.

136 *Ibid.*, Art. 51.

137 "Superiorissa monasterii nihil exigere poterit a postulantibus vel novitiis pro impensis postulatus vel novitiatus."—*Ibid.*, Art. 55; La Puma, *op. cit.*, XIV (1933), 168.

138 "Per votum obedientiae quaecumque Soror obligationem contrahit obediendi praecepto legitimi Superioris in iis quae, directe vel indirecte, ad votorum horumque Statutorum observantiam pertinent."—*Statuta, 1931*, Art. 57.

The Constitutions were not even mentioned as bearing reference to the observance of the vow, since the Statutes occupied the place of these norms in the case of the extern sisters. Although the Rule of the Order was not mentioned at this point, it is evident from the consideration of Articles 2 and 5 that the Rule did constitute matter of the vow, insofar as it was not contrary to the Statutes.[139] The sisters were bound to obey in virtue of the vow of obedience only in the case of commands given by formal precept or the equivalent, which were to be issued only rarely and then before two witnesses or in writing.[140] Finally, Article 60 dealt with the virtue of obedience as it was to be practiced by the extern sisters.

2. Chastity

In three brief articles, the Statutes described the obligations of the vow of chastity, the perfect exercise of this virtue, and the practice of the modesty necessary to preserve chastity.[141]

3. Poverty

The Statutes defined the obligations of the simple vow of poverty taken by the extern sisters, stating also the requirements of the spirit of poverty.[142] According to Article 66, which repeated the norm of canon 580, § 1, the sisters retained the ownership of their goods and the capacity to acquire other goods, but could not retain the administration or enjoy the revenues of such goods. The cession or disposition of goods made by the sisters could be changed with the permission of the local ordinary and the regular superior, if there happened to be one. This change, at least with refer-

[139] Cf. *supra*, pp. 83, 87; "Loco *Constitutionum* ponitur *Statutorum*, quae pro his Sororibus vice Constitutionum funguntur. Ad normam Art. 2 et 5 simul cum Statutis, et in his quae Statutis non adversantur, Regula etiam voti materiam definit."—La Puma, *op. cit.*, XIV (1933), 248.

[140] *Statuta, 1931*, Art. 58-59.

[141] *Ibid.*, Art. 61-63.

[142] *Ibid.*, Art. 64-65.

ence to a notable part of the goods, was not permitted to be in favor of the monastery.[143] Article 68 repeated the norm of canon 580, § 2, specifying that whatever a sister acquired by her work or in view of the monastery was acquired for the monastery. Article 69 contained practically the same norms concerning giving away one's property and changing one's will as are contained in canon 583. It is to be noted, however, that although the Code requires the permission of the major superior to change the will in cases where urgency exists and there is no time to have recourse to the Holy See, Article 69 demanded recourse to the ordinary in such a case. Although the superioress of a monastery of nuns is considered a major superior, she was allowed to grant such permission only if the religious or local ordinary could not be reached.[144] Articles 70 and 71 described the manner in which the sisters were to carry out their vow of poverty in practice.

E. *Chapter Five: Confession and Communion*

The obligation of weekly confession was placed directly upon the individual extern sisters. As members of the monastery, they were to confess to the same ordinary confessor as the nuns, unless for some just cause another priest was appointed. The Statutes applied to the extern sisters the law of the Code concerning special, extraordinary, supplementary and occasional confessors. Moreover, when gravely ill, the extern sisters could call in any priest approved for the confessions of women. The Statutes also referred to the practice of manifestation of conscience as treated in canon 530.[145]

The sisters who were rightly disposed were to have frequent and even daily access to Communion, but the superior-

[143] *Ibid.*, Art. 67.

[144] "Sororibus non licet testamentum conditum ad normam art. 54 mutare sine licentia Sanctae Sedis, vel si res urgeat nec tempus suppetat ad eam recurrendi, sine licentia Ordinarii aut, si nec ille adiri possit, Superiorissae monasterii."—*Ibid.*, Art. 69, b.

[145] *Ibid.*, Art. 72-79.

ess was allowed to forbid a sister who had given grave scandal or committed a grave external fault to receive Communion until she had gone to confession. The final article in this section treated of the preparation and thanksgiving for Holy Communion.[146]

F. *Chapter Six: Other Exercises of Devotion*

This brief Chapter dealt with the various spiritual exercises to be performed by the extern sisters, including attendance at Mass, meditation, and examination of conscience. In place of the Divine Office recited by the nuns, the extern sisters were to recite the same Office as that of the lay sisters of the monastery. Finally, the sisters were required to make a five-day retreat each year.[147]

G. *Chapter Seven: Religious Discipline*

1. The Common Life

The Statutes required that the extern sisters lead a common life with regard to food, clothing and personal effects; moreover, they were to keep no money, being required to turn over to the superioress all donations. Their furniture and appointments were to reflect the poverty they vowed.[148] According to Articles 91 and 92, the spiritual exercises, meals and recreation of the extern sisters were to be in common.

2. Abstinence and Fasting

The sisters were obliged to the fasts of the Church, being permitted to make use of any indults granted by the local Ordinary in this regard. Moreover, they were bound to keep the abstinence and the facts of the monastery in the same manner as the nuns, unless the severity of these was relaxed by the superioress, after consultation with the local ordinary and the religious superior, if there happened to be one.[149]

[146] *Ibid.*, Art. 80-82.
[147] *Ibid.*, Art. 83-87.
[148] *Ibid.*, Art. 88-90.
[149] *Ibid.*, Art. 93-94.

3. Silence and Work

The Articles of this section of the Statutes regulated the time of silence and the manner of work of the sisters. The superioress was admonished to watch especially lest harm come from too frequent conversations with visitors.[150]

4. Leaving the Monastery and Writing of Letters

The extern sisters were allowed to go out of the monastery for the service of the community or for some other reasonable cause. Outside the case of necessity, they were never to go out alone. Only for a serious reason could the superioress permit the sisters to remain outside their own house, and then for as brief a time as possible. For an absence which exceeded a month, permission of the local ordinary was required; for one which exceeded six months, that of the Holy See. Unless excused by a grave reason, the extern sisters were to wear the habit of the Order both inside and outside the monastery.[151]

The superioress was accorded a right of inspection of both incoming and outgoing mail; however, letters to and from the superiors to whom the monastery was subject were immune from this inspection.[152]

5. Mutual Charity

This portion of the Statutes, Articles 104 and 105, contained ascetical matter, exhorting the sisters to mutual charity and good example.

H. *Chapter Eight: The Sick Sisters and the Deceased*

When a sister fell ill, the superioress was to be informed, in order that she could make the necessary provisions. If the gravity and nature of the illness were such that it could not properly be cared for in the quarters of the extern sisters, the sick sister could, with the previous permission of the local ordinary, be taken to the monastery infirmary.

[150] *Ibid.*, Art. 95-98.
[151] *Ibid.*, Art. 99-101.
[152] *Ibid.*, Art. 102-103.

Moreover, old sisters who were no longer able to perform the work of the extern sisters could, with the consent of the local ordinary, be received within the monastery. However, unless in the judgment of the doctor the sisters needed special treatment, they were not to be sent to hospitals or the homes of seculars, even though these were relatives. The sisters were exhorted to bear in the spirit of poverty the lack of any necessity during the time of illness. The spiritual needs of these sick sisters were to be taken care of in due time.[153]

The deceased extern sisters were to receive the same suffrages as a departed nun. The extern sisters, in their turn, were bound to recite the same suffrages as the nuns for a deceased member of the monastic community.[154]

I. *Chapter Nine: Transfer, Departure and Dismissal*

Article 113 of the Statutes forbade the transfer of an extern sister from one independent monastery to another, even of the same Order, without permission of the Holy See.

A sister in temporary vows could freely leave the institute at the expiration of these vows. Likewise, the superioress, with the consent of her Council and after consultation with the local ordinary and the regular superior if there was one, could, for just and reasonable causes, exclude a sister from renewing her temporary profession or from making her perpetual profession. However, this could not be done because of sickness, unless it could certainly be proved that this was deceitfully hidden before profession.[155]

According to Article 115, the granting of indults of exclaustration and secularization to extern sisters was reserved to the Holy See. Should an apostasy occur, the Statutes, in Article 116, placed upon the superioress the obligation of notifying the local ordinary; he, in turn, was to punish the sister according to the gravity of her crime and, if the case

[153] *Ibid.*, Art. 106-110.
[154] *Ibid.*, Art. 111.
[155] *Ibid.*, Art. 114.

warranted, proceed to her dismissal according to the norms of Articles 118 and 119. These two Articles, along with Article 117, treated in some detail of the process to be followed in dismissing extern sisters, both those who were in temporary vows and those who had made perpetual profession. Article 120 treated of the dismissal of a sister in case of grave exterior scandal or grave harm threatened to the community; in such cases the superioress, with the consent of her Council and the local ordinary, could send the sister back to the world at once. Any sister dismissed according to the Statutes was, by that very fact, freed from all religious vows, whether temporary or perpetual.[156]

Sisters who left the monastery at the expiration of temporary vows or after receiving an indult of secularization, or who were dismissed, could seek no renumeration from the monastery for services performed. However, anything such a sister may have brought to the monastery with her and which was not used up was to be returned to her. Those who could not provide for themselves out of their own goods were to be decently supported by the monastery for an equitable time.[157]

J. *Chapter Ten: The Binding Force of the Statutes*

According to Article 124, the extern sisters were not only to observe their vows, but were likewise to order their lives according to the Rule of their Order and the Statutes. Those portions of the Statutes which were taken from the Code of Canon Law or from other laws of the Church were binding upon the consciences of the sisters; other prescriptions of the Statutes were not obligatory in conscience, and any infraction paved the way simply for an application of the penalty imposed for their violation, unless contempt was involved or unless the matter pertained to the vows or to the

[156] "Soror ad normam praecedentium articulorum legitime dimissa, ipso facto solvitur ab omnibus votis religiosis, sive temporariis sive perpetuis."—*Ibid.*, Art. 121.

[157] *Ibid.*, Art. 122-123.

divine law.[158] The superioress had the obligation, according to Article 127, to promote among the extern sisters the knowledge and execution of the decrees of the Holy See which pertained to religious; moreover, she was to see to it that the Statutes were publicly read to the extern sisters at least four times a year. The superioress was not empowered to dispense from the Statutes, except in particular cases and in merely disciplinary matters, and then only for a just and reasonable cause. The last article in the Statutes, Article 128, stated that each sister and novice was to be given a copy of the Statutes to be faithfully observed by her.

SECTION IV
AN APPRAISAL OF THE STATUTES OF 1931

The great benefits which the Statutes of 1931 conferred upon the extern sisters have already been treated at some length.[159] These Statutes actually took the place of the Constitutions of the institute to which the extern sisters belonged.[160] Thus, as is evident from the foregoing summary, they necessarily contained certain prescriptions of the common law which were already contained in the Constitutions of the nuns. Moreover, there was a constant need to accommodate the prescriptions of the Statutes, to which the extern sisters were subject, to the norms of the Constitutions, to which the nuns of the Order were obliged.[161] As has been indicated,[162] this accommodation did not in all cases proceed equitably and smoothly, so that it led to many and widespread difficulties. In the opinion of the writer, the at-

[158] *Ibid.*, Art. 125-126.

[159] Cf. *supra*, pp. 79-81.

[160] Cf. *supra*, p. 83.

[161] "Verum cum experientia hisce sex lustris comparata aperte ostenderit nonnulla in praedictis Statutis anni 1931 perficienda esse... aliqua omittendo praescripta iuris communis, quia in ipsis Monialium Constitutionibus iam continentur, tum denique ea ad Regulas ac Constitutiones Secundi Ordinis ad quem Sorores pertinent arctius accommodando..."—"Instructio et Statuta de Sororibus externo monasteriorum servitio addictis"—*AAS*, LIII (1961), 372.

[162] Cf. *supra*, p. 84.

tempt to substitute the Statutes of 1931 for the Constitutions of the Order to which the extern sisters belonged was the major flaw in this legislation. This contention is amply proved by the fact that the Holy See, in issuing the Statutes of 1961, clearly intended to perfect the legislation for extern sisters by not even mentioning certain prescriptions of the common law which were contained in the Constitutions of the various Orders, and by accommodating to the Constitutions of their Order the law by which the extern sisters were bound.[163] In fact, as will be seen,[164] under the Statutes of 1961, the extern sisters are, for the most part, bound to observe the Constitutions of their Order. In this way the Holy See hopes to alleviate much of the difficulty involved in the integration of the extern sisters into the life of the monastery.

[163] Cf. *supra*, p. 106, nota 161.
[164] Cf. *infra*, p. 118.

PART TWO
CANONICAL COMMENTARY

CHAPTER VIII

THE INSTRUCTION OF 1961

The present law governing extern sisters is contained in the *Statutes Concerning the Sisters Engaged in the External Service of Monasteries of Nuns,* which, together with an Instruction of the Sacred Congregation of Religious, were promulgated in 1961.[1] Following is the text of this Instruction of the Holy See:[2]

> The characteristic condition of nuns living within cloister is such that, in order to safeguard their life of recollection, they need some persons to take care of the business and affairs of the monastery outside the cloister. Accordingly, there have always been pious women, who usually lived outside the cloister and who were not bound by any obligations which, properly appraised, could be called obligations of the religious life. These women were called oblates, mandataries, portresses, or some other such name.
>
> In the course of time, however, these pious women expressed a desire for a more intimate participation in the life of the cloistered nuns; and in various places they were permitted to bind themselves to the external service of the monastery, by making a special resolution, promise, oath, or vow. Moreover, there have been rules, constitutions, and

[1] S. Congr. de Religiosis, "Instructio et Statuta de Sororibus externo monasteriorum servitio addictis"—*AAS,* LIII (1961), 371-380. (Statutes hereafter cited as *Statuta, 1961.*)

[2] The English translation of the Statutes was prepared by the writer, after consultation and comparison of the following translations: "Statutes for Extern Sisters of Monasteries of Nuns," *Review for Religious,* XXI (1962), 1-9; Bouscaren and O'Connor, "Externe Sisters of Monasteries of Nuns," *Canon Law Digest,* Supplement for 1961 (Milwaukee: Bruce, 1962), at canon 600. For the convenience of the reader, the complete text of the Instruction and Statutes as found throughout the body of this dissertation is reproduced in an Appendix, pp. 227-238.

special statutes which were approved by the Holy See and which consecrated as it were, this resolve to live the religious life.

In modern times, the decree of the Sacred Congregation of Religious, *Conditio plurium monasteriorum,* of July 16, 1931, confirmed and duly regulated their status as sisters of simple religious vows. These sisters were declared to be "members of the community they serve and participants in the same spiritual goods as the nuns." (*Statutes for the Extern Sisters of Monasteries of Nuns of Every Order,* no. 4.) Lest, however, the juridical incorporation of the sisters into the community should endanger the contemplative life of the nuns, a general norm was laid down according to which the sisters were to live in a part of the monastery outside of the papal cloister.

The experience of the last thirty years, however, has clearly shown that a number of things in the Statutes of 1931 need to be improved through an adaptation of them to more recent pontifical documents concerning cloistered nuns, through nonmention of certain prescriptions of the common law which are already included in the constitutions of nuns, and through a clear adjustment to the Rules and Constitutions of the Second Order to which the sisters belong. Accordingly, the Sacred Congregation of Religious has decided to make a new and shorter, but nonetheless complete, edition of the aforementioned Statutes, without prejudice, however, to the following points.

1. Those monasteries of nuns which do not have extern sisters, and do not need them, since the external service of the monastery is taken care of by trustworthy secular persons who have been chosen with the consent of the local ordinary and who live outside of the cloister, are not obliged to introduce this class of sisters.

2. Where the Rule or Constitutions of a given Order expressly prescribe and regulate the external service of sisters for a monastery of nuns, the canonical dispositions regulating this service retain their full force, provided they are not contrary ei-

ther to the sacred canons or to the Apostolic Constitution *Sponsa Christi.*

3. If, for the better observance of the spirit of their own foundation and vocation, the nuns of an Order wish to insert into their own constitutions special provisions for the external service of the monastery, they are free to draw up such dispositions. These, however, are to be submitted for the approval of the Sacred Congregation of Religious.

After a similar approval by the same Congregation, provisions of the same sort may also be inserted into the Statutes of those federations erected by the Holy See which observe within the same Order a somewhat diversified practice of regular observance. However, the prescriptions which may be added to the Constitutions or to the Statutes of a federation, according to the nature of the Order, must conform to the following general Statutes.[3]

[3] "Peculiaris Monialium intra claustra degentium condicio ea est, ut, ad earum recollectionis vitam in tuto collocandam, opus requirat aliquarum personarum quae Monasterii extra claustrum negotiis ac rationibus incumbant. Hinc nullo unquam tempore piae defuere mulieres, extra claustra generatim commorantes et vel nullis vel non proprie dictis religiosae vitae vinculis adstrictae, quae oblatarum, Mandatarum, Ostiariarum titulo aliisve nominibus appellatae sunt.

Successu autem temporis, piae huiusmodi mulieres desiderium patefecere Claustralium vitam intimius participandi; variis etiam in locis eis concessum fuit ut, peculiari enuntiato proposito, promissione, iure iurando vel voto, externo Monasterii servitio adstrictae manerent. Nec defuerunt Regulae, Constitutiones vel pecularia Statuta, a Sede Apostolica approbata, quae tale earum religiose vivendi propositum veluti consecrarent.

Nostris vero temporibus, status Sororum cum votis religiosis simplicibus firmus effectus recteque ordinatus est Decreto S. Congregationis Religiosorum 'Conditio plurium Monasteriorum' die 16 Iulii 1931 edito. Sorores membra Communitatis cui inserviunt, eorumdem ac Moniales spiritualium bonorum participes, declaratae sunt (Cfr. 'Statuta a Sororibus externis Monasteriorum Monialium cuiusque Ordinis servanda,' n. 4). Ne autem iuridicam Sororum Communitati incorporationem nocumento contemplativae Claustralium vitae esse contingeret, uti norma generalis statutum est ut Sorores partem aliquam Monasterii extra clausuram papalem inhabitare deberent.

The first three paragraphs of this Instruction, dealing with the history of extern sisters, have already been adequately treated in the first seven chapters of the present writing. At this point, then, it is necessary to comment only upon the remaining paragraphs of the document.

SECTION I
WHAT THE NEW STATUTES ATTEMPT TO DO

As the above cited Instruction plainly states, the experience of thirty years indicated that it was necessary, in order to perfect the Statutes of 1931, to make certain

Verum cum experientia hisce sex lustris comparata aperte ostenderit nonnulla in praedictis Statutis anni 1931 perficienda esse, tum ea recentioribus documentis pontificiis circa Monialium institutum aptando, tum aliqua omittendo praescripta iuris communis, quia in ipsis Monialium Constitutionibus iam continentur, tum denique ea ad Regulas ac Constitutiones Secundi Ordinis ad quem Sorores pertinent arctius accommodando, Sacra Religiosorum Congregatio praedictorum Statutorum novam ac breviorem, integram tamen redactionem perficere sibi proposuit, salvis tamen his quae sequuntur:

1. Illa Monialium Monasteria quae Sorores externo servitio addictas non habent, nec eis opus habere censent eo quod servitio externo Monasterii per personas saeculares probates fidei, de consensu Ordinarii loci adscitas et extra clausuram commorantes, provisum sit, hanc Sororum classem inducere non tenentur.

2. Ubi alicuius Ordinis Regula vel Constitutiones servitium externum Sororum pro Monasterio Monialium expressis verbis praescribunt et ordinant, plenum vigorem servant canonicae dispositiones quibus praedictum servitium regitur, dummodo neque ss. canonibus, neque Constitutioni Apostolicae 'Sponsa Christi' contrariae sint.

3. Si Ordinis alicuius Moniales, ut propriae fundationis et vocationis spiritus aptius servetur, peculiares dispositiones pro servitio externo Monasterii propriis Constitutionibus inserere voluerint, liberum eis esto eas conficere, approbationi utique S. Congregationis de Religiosis subiciendas.

Huiusmodi praescriptiones, approbatione pariter obtenta a S. Congregatione, inseri poterunt Statutis illarum Foederationum a S. Sede erectarum quae regularis observantiae usum, intra eumdem Ordinem, paulo diversum servant. Praescripta, tamen, tam Constitutionibus quam Statutis Foederationis, iuxta Ordinis indolem, adiungenda, conformentur sequentibus Statutis generalibus." —*AAS*, LIII (1961), 371-372.

changes in them. To bring these Statutes of 1931 up to date, the Sacred Congregation of Religious determined to make use of three means: 1) the adaptation of the Statutes to the more recent papal documents concerning the institution of nuns; 2) the non-mention in the Statutes of certain prescriptions of the common law, since they are already contained in the Constitutions of the nuns; 3) the adjustment of the Statutes to the Rules and Constitutions of the Second Order to which the sisters belong.[4]

ARTICLE 1

ADAPTATION TO MORE RECENT PAPAL DOCUMENTS

The Apostolic Constitution *Sponsa Christi,* and the Statutes which accompanied it, made reference to works of the apostolate which might be conducted, even in the monasteries of nuns who profess a purely contemplative life.[5] Now, though the extern sisters are not nuns in the canonical meaning of the term, their lives are nevertheless intimately bound up with the functioning of a monastery of nuns. Accordingly, the Statutes of 1961 include, among the external services which these sisters may perform, certain moderate works of the apostolate to be carried out in connection with the monastery, but outside of the papal enclosure.[6] Moreover, this same Apostolic Constitution *Sponsa Christi,* as also the General Statutes for Nuns, devoted considerable attention to the matter of federations of the monasteries of nuns.[7] This preoccupation of the Holy See

[4] Cf. *supra,* p. 112.

[5] "Quoad vero Monasteria illa quae, sive ex instituto sive ex legitimis S. Sedis praescriptis, vitae contemplativae exercitium quorundam ministeriorum cum ipsa consentaneorum intra monasticas ipsas aedes amice coniungunt, clausura pontificia . . . temperatur."—"Constitutio Apostolica de Sacro Monialium Instituto Promovendo," nov. 21, 1950—*AAS* XLIII (1951), 12; cf. "Statuta Generalia Monialium," Art. IX, *ibid.,* p. 20 .

[6] *Statuta, 1961,* Art. 1, § 2; Art. 6; cf. *infra,* pp. 127-129, 159-160.

[7] *AAS,* XLIII (1951), 13, 18-19.

is reflected in the Statutes of 1961, which contain a number of references to these federations.[8]

Again, in cases where approved statutes did not grant special permission for extern sisters to enter the papal enclosure, the Instruction *Inter cetera* required that application be made to the Holy See for this permission.[9] As a matter of fact, in order to meet some of the more frequent needs, the Statutes of 1961 list a number of cases in which such entrance is allowed without recourse to the Holy See.[10] The same Instruction *Inter cetera* mentions the duty which the cloistered nuns may have to exercise proper vigilance in regard to the quarters of the extern sisters. According to the Instruction, the need or great advantage of being able to leave the enclosure in order to look after this matter may well constitute a just and canonical cause to seek appropriate dispensations from the law of enclosure, or even moderate and carefully defined habitual faculties from the Holy See.[11] The Statutes of 1961 specify this matter by placing the dwelling of the extern sisters under the supervision of the superioress of the monastery and by subjecting it to her visitation.[12]

[8] *Statuta, 1961,* Art. 5; Art. 7, § 2; Art. 9, § 2; Art. 10, § 1; Art. 17; cf. *infra,* pp. 159, 162, 166-167, 169, 204-205.

[9] "Item ad S. Sedem recurrendum est ad obtinendas licentias speciales in favorem Sororum externarum quae in Statutis approbatis non continentur."—"Instructio Circa Monialium Clausuram," mart. 25, 1956—*AAS,* XLVIII (1956), 519, n. 33, b.

[10] *Statuta, 1961,* Art. 3, §§ 2, 3, 4; Art. 9, § 2; Art. 10, §§ 1, 2, 3; Art. 15, § 4; Art. 19, §§ 1, 2; cf. *infra,* pp. 136-149, 166-173, 201-202, 211-213.

[11] "Gravia adiuncta seu absolutae et morales necessitates atque magni momenti utilitates iustas et canonicas causas constituere possunt proportionatas dispensationes et etiam aliquas moderatas et accurate definitas habituales facultates a S. Sede expostulandi.

a) Talia adiuncta sunt:

5) vigilantiam exercere circa agros, fundos, aedificia, vel aedes quas Sorores externae inhabitant."—*AAS,* XLVIII (1956), 516-517, n. 24, a, 5.

[12] *Statuta, 1961,* Art. 5; cf. *infra,* pp. 158-159.

ARTICLE 2
NON-MENTION OF THE COMMON LAW ALREADY INCLUDED IN THE CONSTITUTIONS

Examples of the use of this means are quite numerous.[13] For instance, Article 43 of the Statutes of 1931 treated the requirements for valid profession as an extern sister; this Article was, in substance, a mere repetition of canon 572, with certain adaptations to the extern sisters.[14] However, since this same matter is adequately covered by its inclusion in the Constitutions of the various Orders of nuns,[15] these requirements for valid profession are not spelled out in the Statutes of 1961. Another example of the application of this principle is the prescription concerning the ordinary confessor, which was contained in Article 73 of the Statutes of 1931.[16] This article simply repeated the law of canon 520, § 1, which is also included in the Constitutions of many institutes.[17] Numerous other examples of the application of this principle of non-mention might be adduced. However, a better overall picture of the effect of this type of non-mention is obtained through a consideration of the fact that, by leaving out of the Statutes of 1961 all mention

[13] It is the writer's purpose in the course of this work to present a general commentary on the Statutes of 1961, which will be applicable to all extern sisters who are bound to observe the Statutes. However, in order to clarify and illustrate the general principles, frequent use will be made of examples drawn from the Constitutions of the Order of St. Clare and the Constitutions of the Poor Clare Colettines. The Constitutions of the Order of St. Clare cited herein are the ones approved in 1941: *Regulae et Constitutiones Generales Monialium Ordinis Sanctae Clarae* (Romae: Curia Generalitia O.F.M., 1941). In the course of this work, these Constitutions will be cited as *Const., OSC.* The Constitutions of the Poor Clare Colettines cited herein are the following, which were approved in the year 1931: *Regula S. Clarae et Constitutiones pro Monialibus Clarissis Reformationis a Sancta Coleta* (Romae: Curia Generalitia Ordinis Fratrum Minorum, 1932). In the course of this work, these Constitutions will be cited as *Const., PCC.*

[14] Cf. *supra,* p. 97.

[15] *Const., OSC,* Art. 89; *Const., PCC,* Art. 235.

[16] Cf. *supra,* p. 101 .

[17] *Const., OSC,* Art. 200; *Const., PCC,* Art. 52.

of most of those matters of the common law which are included in the Constitutions of various institutes, a drastic reduction in the length of the Statutes was achieved. The Statutes of 1931 were a lengthy tract of one hundred twenty-eight articles; the Statutes of 1961 contain only nineteen articles. A good share of this reduction was brought about by the application of the principle here under discussion; the remainder of it was the result of omitting from the Statutes of 1961 mention of many matters of *particular* law which were in some way contained in the Constitutions of Second Orders.

ARTICLE 3
CLOSER ADJUSTMENT TO THE RULES AND CONSTITUTIONS OF SECOND ORDERS

The Statutes of 1931 took the place of the Constitutions of the Order insofar as extern sisters were concerned; the effect of this was to produce a group of religious who, although members of the Order, were not bound to observe the Constitutions of that Order.[18] However, the new Statutes of 1961 prescribe that the extern sisters profess the same Rule and Constitutions as the nuns, even though, by reason of their special office, the extern sisters are subject to the Statutes which repeal some prescriptions of the Rule and the Constitutions.[19] Moreover, the Instruction accompanying the Statutes determines that, where the Rules and Constitutions of a given Order expressly prescribe and regulate the external service of sisters for a monastery of nuns, these canonical dispositions retain their full force, provided they are not contrary either to Canon Law or to the Apostolic Constitution *Sponsa Christi*.[20]

As mentioned above,[21] the application of this principle made it possible to eliminate many matters from the Statutes

[18] Cf. *supra*, pp. 83-84, 106-107.
[19] *Statuta, 1961*, Art. 2; cf. *infra*, pp. 132-133.
[20] Cf. *supra*, pp. 114-115; cf. *infra*, pp. 122-123.
[21] Cf. *supra*, pp. 117-118.

for Extern Sisters, thus notably contributing to the shortening of the 1931 version. Where the Statutes of 1931 treated extensively of the admission and training of extern sisters,[22] the Statutes of 1961 merely state that, in the admitting and training of extern sisters, there are to be observed the same conditions that are prescribed in the Constitutions for the nuns of the monastery, with due account taken of the special role of the extern sisters.[23] Again, the Statutes of 1931, in treating of the training of the novices for the religious life, included mention of the manner of giving instructions and conferences to the novices.[24] The Statutes of 1961 prescribe that these instructions and conferences be given in the same way that is set down in the Constitutions for the novitiate of the nuns, with a special care to instruct the extern sisters in the matters for which they are destined.[25] Although Article 13 of the Statutes of 1961 sets up certain prescriptions concerning the cession of administration of property, as well as the disposition of the use and of the revenues of that property, this same Article nevertheless adheres to the ideal of close conformity to the Constitutions of the Order. This is clear from the fact that the Article itself mentions that its norms are without prejudice to the prescriptions of the Constitutions.[26] In the Statutes of 1931, two complete chapters including sixteen articles treated of confession, Communion and spiritual exercises.[27] According to the Statutes of 1961, the extern sisters are simply to conform themselves to the Rule and Constitutions of their Order in these matters, with the exeception of those exercises which are strictly proper to the choir nuns.[28] These examples should serve to illustrate the key principle of

[22] *Statuta, 1931,* Art. 12-41.
[23] *Statuta, 1961,* Art. 8; cf. *infra.* pp. 163-165.
[24] *Statuta, 1931,* Art. 9, 34; cf. *supra,* p. 96.
[25] *Statuta, 1961,* Art. 10, § 4; cf. *infra,* p. 173.
[26] *Statuta, 1961,* Art. 13, § 1; cf. *infra,* pp. 187-188.
[27] *Statuta, 1931,* Art. 72-87; cf. *supra,* pp. 101-102.
[28] *Statuta, 1961,* Art. 15, §§ 1 and 2; cf. *infra,* pp. 195-198.

accommodation of the Statutes for Extern Sisters to the particular legislation of the Order to which they belong. Matters which the Statutes of 1931 spelled out in detail, thus producing difficulty and confusion in many instances because of lack of harmony with the Constitutions of various institutes, were disposed of by the Statutes of 1961 with a simple directive to follow the Rule and Constitutions in the same manner as the other members of the monastery.

SECTION II
ABROGATION OF THE STATUTES OF 1931

After enumerating the three means by which the Statutes of 1931 are to be modernized, the Instruction cited above states that the Sacred Congregation of Religious decided to make a new, shorter, but complete edition of those Statutes.[29] Now, according to the norm of canon 22, a subsequent law, enacted by competent authority, abrogates or repeals a former law if it entirely revises the subject matter of that former law. The case envisioned here concerning the Statutes for Extern Sisters is one in which the new law, the Statutes of 1961, offers a completely fresh treatment of the old law, the Statutes of 1931, the same issue and cases being involved. Therefore, not only the provisions of the Statutes of 1931 which are incompatible with the Statutes of 1961 are abrogated, but even those provisions of the older law which are not specifically altered, and indeed are left unmentioned in the new Statutes. In other words, in virtue of the Statutes of 1961, the Statutes of 1931 are, in their entirety, abrogated.[30]

[29] Cf. *supra.*, p. 112.

[30] "Hisce autem verificatis conditionibus, per legem posteriorem automatice revocantur leges priores, *etiamsi illi non sint contrariae.* Hoc indubitanter constat, *tum* ex ipso canonis contextu: si enim principium canonis attingeret solas leges contrarias, prorsus inutile est, quippe cum leges contrariae jam vi principii immediate praecedentis censeantur revocatae;—*tum* ex ratione in qua fundatur principium a Codice statutum; ratio hujus principii enim est, quia hac nova et integra ordinatione legislator sufficienter demonstrat integram suam

Even though the Statutes of 1931 have been abrogated by the new Statutes of 1961, the older Statutes can still be of some use in helping one to understand the new ones. It is a legal principle that, should the meaning of a law remain obscure after consideration of its text and context, it is a proper means of interpretation to consider the circumstances of that law in order to arrive at its true meaning.[31] These circumstances, extrinsic to the law itself, include such matters as the historical occasion for the promulgation of the legislation, as well as the time of its origin, embracing such items as the former prevailing discipline, teaching, opinions and practice in vogue at the time the new law is made.[32] Now, in the case of the Statutes of 1961, the historical occasion of this legislation was simply the fact that the experience of thirty years indicated a definite need for the modification of the Statutes of 1931.[33] Moreover, at the time the new Statutes of 1961 were enacted, the prevailing legal status and practical situation of extern sisters were, to a great extent, based upon the Statutes of 1931. In other words, the situation which existed at the time of the promulgation of the Statutes of 1961 was largely a product of the application of the Statutes of 1931.[34] Ob-

mentem et voluntatem esse in sola lege posteriore contentam, ideoque in hac sola, non jam in priore lege, sub veteri forma, inquirendam; bono enim communi adversatur, ut idem argumentum duplici ordinationi subsit."—Michiels, *op. cit.*, I, 658; "In this case not only are the provisions in the old law incompatible with the new one repealed, but also, by legitimate presumption, the unaltered or unmentioned sections of the former."—Abbo-Hannan, *op. cit.*, I, 46; cf. *supra*, pp. 61-62.

[31] Cf. canon 18.

[32] "Circumstantiae sunt adiuncta aliquo modo cum actu legislativo coniuncta, quamvis legi ipsi extrinseca. Huiusmodi circumstantiae recenseri possunt: *occasio legis*, nam leges ut plurimum non ex abrupto in esse prosiliunt, sed ex facto historico, sub influxu conditionum socialium, paulatim elaborantur, prout sunt correctio excessuum, eradicatio abusuum, exasperatio vel mitigatio disciplinae vigentis; *tempus et locus originis*, scil. vigens disciplina, opiniones, praxis, mores loci et temporis, in quibus lex orta est."—Beste, *op. cit.*, p. 81.

[33] Cf. *supra*, pp. 112, 114-115.

[34] *Loc. cit.*

viously, then, an understanding of these Statutes of 1931 and the conditions which resulted from the application of them can be of great value for a due appreciation of the background of the Statutes of 1961, and for clearing away any doubts concerning the meaning of the new Statutes.

Section III
General Principles Concerning the Relationship of the Statutes to Particular Law of Institutes

The Instruction next proceeds to point out that the Statutes of 1961 are to be understood in the light of certain principles, which are enumerated under three headings.

The Instruction first considers the case of those monasteries which neither have nor need extern sisters because, with the consent of the local ordinary, the external service is performed by trustworthy secular persons who live outside the enclosure. Such monasteries are not required to introduce extern sisters, but may continue to employ the secular persons, unaffected by the Statutes of 1961.[35]

The Instruction next provides and ordains that, where the Rule or the Constitutions of an Order expressly prescribe and regulate the external service of the sisters for a monastery of nuns, those canonical dispositions of the Rule and the Constitutions by which the external service is ruled retain full force, provided they are not contrary either to the sacred canons or to the Apostolic Constitution *Sponsa Christi.*[36] Thus, the sections of particular Rules and Constitutions which treat expressly of the extern sisters are to be observed, even though they should be contrary to the Statutes of 1961. Such sections of the Rules and the Constitutions, therefore, are an exception to the norm of Article 2 of the Statutes which provides that, although the extern sisters make profession of the Rule and the Constitutions of their institute, they are also subject to the Statutes which repeal some prescriptions of the Rule and

[35] Cf. *supra,* p. 112.

[36] *Loc. cit.*

the Constitutions.[37] Therefore, insofar as the extern sisters are concerned, the Statutes of 1961 take precedence over the Rule and the Constitutions of their Order, except in those matters where the Rule and the Constitutions expressly treat of the service rendered by these sisters. In such cases as the latter, these prescriptions of the Rule and the Constitutions of the institute take precedence over the Statutes of 1961.

Finally, the Instruction permits those Orders of nuns which, for the better observance of the spirit of their institute and vocation, wish to insert special dispositions for the external service of the monastery into their Constitutions, to draw up such insertions to be submitted for the approbation of the Sacred Congregation of Religious. Moreover, federations of the monasteries of nuns may also submit for the approval of the Sacred Congregation of Religious their own special dispositions regarding extern sisters. However, in these cases any prescriptions which are to be inserted into either the Constitutions of an institute or the Statutes of a federation must be in accord with the Statutes of 1961.[38]

[37] *Statuta, 1961,* Art. 2; cf. *infra,* p. 132.
[38] Cf. *supra,* p. 113.

CHAPTER IX

THE STATUTES OF 1961—CHAPTER I: CONCERNING THE DUTIES AND DWELLING PLACE OF THE EXTERN SISTERS

The First Chapter of the Statutes of 1961 contains seven articles, which treat of the duties and the living quarters of the extern sisters.[1]

SECTION I
NATURE AND DUTIES OF EXTERN SISTERS

ARTICLE 1
FIRST ARTICLE OF THE STATUTES: ESTABLISHMENT AND APOSTOLATE OF EXTERN SISTERS

A. *Paragraph One: Establishment of Extern Sisters*

> With the consent of the Chapter and with the approval of the local ordinary, as well as that of the regular superior if they are subject to one, monasteries of nuns may introduce extern sisters, whose principal duty is to serve the monastery by attending to external business which cannot be done by the cloistered nuns.[2]

This paragraph clearly describes the legal formalities which are requisite for introducing the institution of extern sisters into a monastery where these religious have previously not existed. The law demands that, in order to introduce extern sisters into a given monastery, the consent of the Chapter of that particular monastery be obtained, as well as

[1] *Statuta, 1961, Caput I,* "De Sororum Servitio Externo Addictarum Muneribus et Habitatione."

[2] "Monialium Monasteria possunt, consentiente Capitulo et accedente beneplacito Ordinarii loci necnon, si eidem sint subiectae, Superioris regularis, Sorores servitio externo addictas instituere, quarum speciale munus sit Monasterio inservire in obeundis externis negotiis quae a Claustralibus geri nequeunt."—*Statuta, 1961,* Art. 1, § 1.

the approval of the local ordinary where the convent is located. Moreover, should the monastery be subject to a regular superior, his permission must also be obtained.

Although the Statutes themselves are quite clear on this point, the matter is sometimes complicated by the provisions of Constitutions which prescribe other formalities for introducing the institution of extern sisters into a given monastery. Since such Constitutions treat expressly of the service of the extern sisters, they are, in accordance with the principles of the Instruction which accompanies the Statutes of 1961, to take precedence over the requirements of the Statutes themselves.[3] For example, the Constitutions of the Order of St. Clare provide that a monastery may have extern sisters, provided the Discretorium deems it advisable, and provided the approval of either the local ordinary or the religious ordinary is obtained.[4] Thus, although the Statutes of 1961, in the Article under consideration, demand the consent of the monastic Chapter for introducing extern sisters into the convent, the Constitutions of the Order of St. Clare specify the consent of the Discretorium or Council of the abbess. The Statutes demand the permission of the local ordinary in any case where extern sisters are to be introduced; if the monastery is subject to a religious superior, his consent is demanded in addition to that of the local ordinary. The Constitutions of the Order of St. Clare permit the introduction of extern sisters with the approval of *either* the local ordinary *or* the religious ordinary. Here is a clear case where the Constitutions of an institute legislate expressly for extern sisters and are, therefore, to be given preference over the norms of the Statutes of 1961. Monasteries of the Order of St. Clare which desire to introduce extern sisters for the first time are to observe the prescriptions of their own Constitutions, and not the norm of Article 1, § 1, of the Statutes.

[3] Cf. *supra*, pp. 122-123.

[4] "Ad mentem sanctae Regulae quodlibet Monasterium, si Discretorio bene visum fuerit, Ordinario loci vel Regulari probante, habere poterit necessarias Sorores servientes extra Monasterium."—*Const.*, *OSC*, Art. 396.

A slightly different problem is presented by the Constitutions of the Poor Clare Colettines which, legislating expressly concerning the introduction of extern sisters into the monastery, permit this to be done, provided the permission of the Apostolic See is first obtained for each monastery. The Constitutions likewise make mention of the fact that the extern sisters are to be established and governed according to the special Statutes properly approved by the Apostolic See;[5] for the present, therefore, the establishment and government of these sisters will proceed according to the Statutes of 1961. However, it is in virtue of these very Statutes of 1961 and the accompanying Instruction that express provisions of the Constitutions concerning the introduction of extern sisters retain their force.[6] Hence, the requirement of the Colettine Constitutions that the permission of the Apostolic See be obtained for introducing extern sisters into each monastery still retains its force. Moreover, analysis of the above cited Article 73 of the Constitutions indicates that the permission of the Holy See which is required for each monastery is merely a permission to introduce extern sisters into a given community; once this permission of the Holy See to have these sisters attached to a monastery has been granted, then the institute of extern sisters is to be set up or established and governed according to the norms of the Statutes for Extern Sisters. At any rate, some permission of the Apostolic See is clearly called for in virtue of the Constitutions.

But must this permission be asked individually of the Holy See for each particular monastery? In the opinion of the writer, such individual requests are not at all required. It seems, rather, that once the formalities of Article 1, § 1, of the Statutes of 1961 have been performed by an individual monastery, i.e., once the consent of the monastic Chapter and

[5] "Nihil vero impedit quominus, obtenta prius pro singulis Monasteriis licentia Sedis Apostolicae, habeantur Sorores votorum simplicium, externo servitio Monasterii addictae; quae institui et gubernari debeant juxta specialia Statuta ab ipsa Apostolica Sede rite approbata."—*Const., PCC,* Art. 73.

[6] Cf. *supra,* pp. 122-123.

the permission of the local ordinary, as well as that of the religious ordinary if there be one, have been obtained, the permission of the Holy See for introducing extern sisters is simply granted implicitly in virtue of the Statutes for Extern Sisters. This view is in conformity with the interpretation which was placed upon the Statutes of 1931. The Decree *Conditio plurimorum monasteriorum* applied the Statutes of 1931 to those sisters who, by special indult of the Holy See, were already or might in the future be engaged in the external service of monasteries of nuns. Yet, as has been shown, the Sacred Congregation of Religious regarded as sufficient the mere fact that a monastery legitimately wished to introduce extern sisters in accord with the Statutes of 1931; no further approbation of the Holy See was considered necessary.[7] This same solution seems applicable in the case at hand, especially in view of the fact that the Constitutions of the Poor Clare Colettines demand only that permission of the Holy See be *obtained* for the introduction of extern sisters into each monastery; these Constitutions do not state that such permission must be *asked* individually in each case.[8] Thus, the permission of the Apostolic See is indeed obtained for introducing extern sisters into the monastery; however, this permission is granted, not in virtue of a specific petition submitted to the Sacred Congregation of Religious, but in virtue of the Statutes of 1961 themselves, once the formalities of Article 1, § 1, have been fulfilled.

B. *Paragraph Two: Apostolate of Extern Sisters*

> Moderate works of the apostolate connected with the monastery but performed outside the papal cloister may be considered as included in the external service to which the sisters are destined.[9]

[7] Cf. *supra*, pp. 53-55.

[8] "... *obtenta* prius pro singulis Monasteriis licentia Sedis Apostolicae ..."—*Const., PCC*, Art. 73; cf. *supra*, p. 126.

[9] "Uti servitium externum, cui huiusmodi Sorores addicuntur, haberi possunt quaedam moderata opera apostolatus Monasterio adnexa, extra tamen clausuram papalem peragenda."—*Statuta, 1961*, Art. 1, § 2.

The Statutes do not list any specific works of the apostolate which may be performed by the extern sisters; rather it is merely stated that such works must be moderate, and performed in connection with the monastery, but outside the papal enclosure. However, the Instruction on the cloister of nuns, *Inter cetera,* does enumerate certain specific works which may be harmoniously associated with the contemplative life of communities where the minor papal cloister is in force. This situation of the minor papal enclosure bears a definite similarity to the case of extern sisters who would engage in works of the apostolate; therefore, those works which nuns bound by the minor papal cloister may, according to the Instruction, perform, might also be fittingly carried out by extern sisters. Thus, extern sisters might engage in the teaching of Christian doctrine or in giving religious instruction. They could undertake the education of boys and girls in certain instances, as well as conduct retreats or exercises like days of recollection for women. They could help in preparing children for the reception of their first Communion, or they might engage in works of charity for the relief of the sick and the poor.[10] This matter of works of the apostolate performed by the extern sisters will be taken up again in the commentary on Article 6 of the Statutes, which treats of the permission necessary for conducting such works and the norms according to which they must be done.[11]

ARTICLE 2

SECOND ARTICLE OF THE STATUTES: JURIDIC STATUS AND PRECEDENCE OF EXTERN SISTERS

> The extern sisters are members of the community of their monastery, and, in the order of precedence, come after the choir nuns and the lay sisters (*conversae*); they profess the same Rule and Constitutions as their sister religious, the nuns, but in virtue of their proper office they are subject to the present

[10] "Instructio circa Monialium Clausuram," mart. 25, 1956—*AAS*, XLVIII (1956), 520, n. 41, a, c.

[11] Cf. *infra*, pp. 159-160.

Statutes, which repeal some prescriptions of the Rule and Constitutions.[12]

A. *Status of the Extern Sisters*

This Article clearly reiterates the principle, already firmly established by the Statutes of 1931, that the extern sisters are truly members of the community of the monastery where they serve.[13] As the order of precedence indicated in this article shows, the Statutes of 1961 continue the arrangement set up by the Statutes of 1931, whereby Orders of nuns served by extern sisters include three classes of members, scil., choir nuns, lay sisters (*conversae*), and extern sisters.[14] The members of all three of these classes belong to one and the same Order.

At no time in the history of the extern sisters, not even in the privileged position accorded them by the Statutes of 1931, did these sisters have an active or passive voice in the government of the monastery or the election of its officials.[15] Nor do the Statutes of 1961, despite the fact that they confirm the extern sisters as members of the monastery and Order which they serve, grant them either active or passive voice. Since the Statutes are silent on this matter, the extern sisters, in virtue of this Article, simply follow the Constitutions of their respective Orders with regard to the determination of their rights in this regard. In accord with long-standing tradition, the Constitutions of the various Orders reserve active and passive voice in elections to the choir nuns, who have made profession of solemn vows. Thus, neither the cloistered lay

[12] "Sorores servitio externo addictae membra sunt Communitatis sui cuiusque Monasterii et ordine praecedentiae post Moniales choristas et conversas veniunt; eamdem Regulam et Constitutiones profitentur ac consorores Moniales, sed ratione officii hisce Statutis obnoxiae sunt, quorum vi praescriptis quibusdam ipsius Regulae et Constitutionum derogatur."—*Statuta, 1961,* Art. 2.

[13] "Les Soeurs Tourières sont de vraies religieuses, membres de la communauté composee, à l'intérieur de la clôture, de religieuses choristes et de converses."—Bergh, "Actes du Saint-Siège," *Nouvelle Revue Théologique*, LXXXIII (1961), 1095; cf. *supra*, pp. 52, 80, 112.

[14] *Statuta, 1931,* Art. 28; cf. *supra*, p. 95.

[15] Cf. *supra*, p. 80.

sisters, nor the extern sisters, participate in the government of the monastery.[16]

The Statutes explicitly assign to the extern sisters a place of precedence after the choir nuns and the lay sisters (*conversae*), in other words, after the cloistered sisters. However, one question is left unanswered by the Statutes: Do the professed extern sisters come before or after the choir nun and lay sister novices in the order of precedence? The Constitutions of most institutes provide no answer to the problem, since, unlike the Statutes of 1961, they simply do not envision the extern sisters entering the papal enclosure for religious exercises, meals, recreation and even permanent residence. In fact, despite the directive of the Statutes of 1931 that the extern sisters were to be members of the same Order as the nuns, Constitutions approved subsequent to the promulgation of those Statutes often do not clearly recognize this status of the extern sisters.[17] Consequently they make no provision for the determination of their precedence within the Order. Nevertheless there are certain canonical considerations which will lead to a practical norm in this matter.

Canon 106, 5°, states that, among the members of a collegiate body, precedence is determined by legitimate Constitutions, otherwise by lawful custom; if no such custom exists, then the determination is to be made according to the prescription of the common law.[18] In the case at hand, the Constitutions do not make any determination of the proper order of precedence. Therefore, if in a given monastery there exists a legitimate custom in this matter, that custom is to prevail, and the precedence among the professed extern sisters and the cloistered novices will be governed by it. Should no such custom exist in a monastery, then a third determining factor,

[16] "Jus eligendi Abbatissam et Discretas competit omnibus et solis Sororibus Choristis sollemniter professis."—*Const., PCC*, Art. 87; the Constitutions of the Order of St. Clare, at Article 223, likewise limit participation in these elections to the solemnly professed choir nuns.

[17] Cf. *Const., OSC*, Art. 396-398, *Const., PCC*, Art. 73.

[18] "Inter sodales vero alicuius collegii, ius praecedentiae determinetur ex propriis legitimis constitutionibus; secus ex legitima consuetudine; qua deficiente, ex praescripto iuris communis."—Canon 106, 5°.

namely the common law, will decide the proper order to be followed. The applicable norm of the common law is contained in canon 106, 3°, which ordains that, among various ecclesiastical persons, none of whom has authority over the others, those who pertain to the higher rank precede those who are of inferior rank.[19] This, however, does little more than restate the original problem, since it is still necessary to determine which group, the professed extern sisters or the cloistered novices, is of higher rank.

One method of determination is based upon the Constitutions of the Order of St. Clare. These Constitutions consider the lay sisters who have made profession as belonging to a higher rank than the choir novices who have not made any profession; accordingly, they assign to the professed lay sisters a place in precedence ahead of the choir novices.[20] According to the norm followed by these Constitutions, the fact that a religious has made profession in any class places her in a higher rank than a novice who has made no profession at all, despite the fact that the novice may be destined for a higher rank in the Order than the professed sister has attained. On this basis, the conclusion follows that the professed extern sisters take precedence over the cloistered novices.

Another method of determination follows from the consideration of the General Constitutions of the Order of Friars Minor. These Constitutions consider the clerical novices, even though they have made no profession whatsoever, as belonging to a higher rank than the solemnly professed lay brothers, despite the fact that these latter have already made profession of solemn vows. Accordingly, they assign to the clerical novices a place in precedence ahead of the solemnly professed lay brothers.[21] According to the norm followed by

[19] "Inter diversas personas ecclesiasticas quarum nulla habeat in alias auctoritatem: qui ad gradum potiorem pertinent, praecedunt eis qui sunt inferioris gradus."—Canon 106, 3°.

[20] *Const., OSC,* Art. 124.

[21] *Regula et Constitutiones Generales Ordinis Fratrum Minorum* (Romae: Curia Generalis Ordinis, 1953), Art. 538, § 4.

these Constitutions, the fact that a novice is called to and destined for a higher state permits him to share in the privileges of that rank, despite the fact that he has made no religious profession at all; it places him, therefore, in a higher rank than a religious who, although he has pronounced solemn vows, is not destined for this higher state. On this basis the conclusion follows that the choir nun and lay sister novices take precedence over the professed extern sisters, since the former are destined for a state which is, according to Article 2 of the Statutes of 1961, of higher rank.

Obviously, the order of precedence between the professed extern sisters and the cloistered novices will depend on which of these two norms one adopts. The norm followed by the Constitutions of the Order of St. Clare, and that adopted by the Constitutions of the Order of Friars Minor, lead to exactly opposite conclusions. In the opinion of the writer, either of these two norms may be reasonably and safely adopted in practice. Thus, each monastery where there exists no norm of the Constitutions and no legitimate custom in the matter may set up its own policy in determining the precedence of the two groups under consideration.

B. *Norms Governing the Extern Sisters*

Since, according to the present Article, the extern sisters profess the same Rule and Constitutions as the cloistered nuns, they are bound to observe the norms of these laws of their Order in essentially the same manner as the nuns themselves. However, Article 2 provides that, by reason of their special office, the extern sisters are also subject to the Statutes of 1961, which repeal some of the prescriptions of the Rule and Constitutions. Thus, wherever the norms of the Rule and the Constitutions of an Order are contrary to the provisions of the Statutes of 1961, the extern sisters are to observe the Statutes and not the paricular law of their Order. The only exceptions to this rule, according to the Instruction accompanying the Statutes, are those norms of the Rule and Constitutions which expressly prescribe and regulate the external service of the monastery. Should a conflict arise between such provisions of the Rule and the Constitutions of an Order and the Statutes of 1961, the particular law of the Order is to be followed in place of the norms of the Statutes.[22]

SECTION II
LIVING QUARTERS OF THE EXTERN SISTERS

ARTICLE 1
THIRD ARTICLE OF THE STATUTES: EXTERN SISTERS DWELLING OUTSIDE THE CLOISTER

A. *Paragraph One: Residence of Extern Sisters and the Common Cloister*

> Without prejudice to Article 4, the extern sisters have a residence which is annexed to the monastery and which is subject to the common cloister (see canon 604 and the Instruction *Inter cetera,* n. 73), though not situated within the limits of the papal cloister of the nuns (see the Instruction *Inter cetera,* n. 11, b; 44, b). Accordingly, they may not enter the part of the monastery reserved for the nuns, except in accordance with the provisions made in these Statutes.[23]

1. The Residence of the Extern Sisters

This first paragraph of Article 3 begins by ruling that its prescriptions are to be understood without prejudice to Article 4, which treats of those monasteries where, by permission of the Holy See, the quarters of the extern sisters are located within the confines of the papal enclosure.[24] In fact, analysis of the other three paragraphs of Article 3 indicates clearly that these paragraphs also are intended to

[22] Cf. *supra,* pp. 112, 122-123.

[23] "Salvo art. 4, Sorores servitio externo addictae habitationem habent Monasterio adnexam et clausurae communi (can. 604; Instr. 'Inter cetera,' n. 73) obnoxiam, non vero intra fines clausurae papalis Monialium positam (Instr. 'Inter cetera,' n. 11, b; 44, b). Quapropter nequeunt partem Monasterii Monialibus reservatam ingredi nisi intra limites his Statutis definitos."—*Statuta, 1961,* Art, 3, § 1.

[24] Cf. *infra,* pp. 149-157.

regulate the entrace into the papal enclosure of extern sisters who habitually dwell outside its limits.[25] Therefore, it may be stated that Article 3 pertains only to those monasteries where the quarters of the extern sisters are located outside the enclosure of the nuns; Article 4 pertains only to those monasteries where the extern sisters habitually dwell within the papal cloister. As the references cited in the text of the paragraph under consideration indicate, the situation envisioned by Article 3 is in strict accord wth the requirements of the Instruction *Inter cetera,* scil., that in monasteries where the major papal enclosure is in force the house where the extern sisters live should be outside the cloister; in monasteries where the minor papal enclosure is established, the places inhabited by the extern sisters are not to be located in that part of the house which is reserved to the nuns after the manner of the major cloister.[26]

Although it is located outside the confines of the papal enclosure, the dwelling place of the extern sisters is nevertheless subject to the cloister established by canon 604, i.e., the common or episcopal enclosure which is observed in houses of religious congregations of both pontifical and diocesan approval. Although the Instruction *Inter cetera* declares that this type of enclosure cannot be recognized for the nuns of the monastery, the Statutes, in the present Article, quite properly adopt this cloister for those extern sisters who habitually live outside the papal enclosure.[27] This arrangement, which was already prescribed for extern sisters by the Statutes of 1931,[28] adequately safeguards the religious life and observance of these sisters who, despite the fact that they are members of an Order, are unable, in virtue of their special station, to observe the papal enclosure usually demanded of women religious who are members of Orders.

By reason of the common enclosure to which the extern

[25] *Statuta, 1961*, Art. 3, §§ 2, 3, 4; cf. *infra*, pp. 136-149.

[26] "Instructio circa Monialium Clausuram," mart. 25, 1956—*AAS*, XLVIII (1956), 514, n. 11, b; 521, n. 44, b.

[27] *Ibid.*, p. 526, n. 73, a.

[28] *Statuta, 1931*, Art. 6; cf. *supra*, pp. 88-89.

sisters are obliged, men are ordinarily not to be admitted to the portions of the monastery reserved strictly for these religious. However, the law is quite lenient in admitting men to this cloister, not only for the reasons mentioned in canons 598, § 2, and 600, but also for other reasons considered by the superiors to be just and reasonable.[29] Moreover, should any part of the monastery outside the papal enclosure be devoted to works of the apostolate, care must be taken that there is also a separate area reserved exclusively for the extern sisters, and subject to the law of episcopal enclosure. In order to admit men even to the sections where the works of the apostolate are carried on, there should be some justifying reason and the permission of the proper superior.[30]

2. Entrance of Extern Sisters into the Papal Enclosure

This first paragraph of Article 3 concludes by stating that the extern sisters are not allowed to enter that part of the monastery which is reserved for the nuns, except in accordance with the provisions of the Statutes. The Statutes of 1931 had been very strict in granting a limited permission for extern sisters to enter the enclosure of the nuns.[31] The Statutes of 1961 are much more liberal in this matter, since there are several different situations in which the present Statutes make provisions for the entrance of extern sisters into the papal enclosure.[32] Each of these instances will be

[29] Cf. canon 604, § 1.

[30] "Praescriptum can. 599 etiam domibus Congregationum religiosarum sive virorum sive mulierum applicetur."—Canon 604, § 2; cf. can. 599, §§ 1 & 2.

[31] *Statuta, 1931,* Art. 3; cf. *supra,* p. 85.

[32] Some of these instances are contained in the remaining three paragraphs of the Article under present consideration. Other instances of permission for extern sisters to enter the enclosure of the nuns are the following: Article 10, § 1, with reference to the canonical year of noivtiate; Article 10, § 2, with reference to the last two months of the second year of novitiate; Article 15, § 4, which treats of religious exercises; Article 19, §§ 1 and 2, which deal with the sick and aged extern sisters. Moreover, as will be shown in the commentary on § 3 of the present Article 3, canon 600, 4°, may very well be used to grant entrance to extern sisters.

treated at its proper place in the commentary. At this point the Statutes are content with the general statement that the entrance of extern sisters into the papal enclosure is to be in accordance with the prescriptions therein contained.

B. *Paragraph Two: Entering the Enclosure for Specified Purposes*

> Without prejudice to the stricter law of individual monasteries, the superioress, with the consent of her Council and with the approval of the local ordinary and of the regular superior if there be one, has the right to permit the extern sisters to meet at times with the nuns inside the cloister of the monastery for purposes of devotion or instruction, as well as for eating and recreating together, care being taken that nothing detrimental follows from this. At these times, the sisters, even if questioned imprudently, should refrain from relating things they have seen or heard outside the monastery; they should especially keep silent about matters which do not set a good example or which can disturb peace and application of mind. The superioress with her councilors should carefully watch over these matters; and, if the entrance of the sisters into the monastery becomes an occasion for abuses, suitable remedies should be applied.[33]

Before proceeding to enumerate certain conditions under which the extern sisters may enter the papal enclosure, this paragraph points out that these conditions are to be

[33] "Salvo strictiore iure singulorum Monasteriorum, ius est Antistitae, de consensu sui Consilii atque probante Ordinario loci et Superiore Regulari, si adsit, permittendi ut Sorores servitio externo addictae interdum intra clausuram Monasterii, pietatis vel instructionis causa, sicuti et ad convescendum et animos recreandos, cum Monialibus conveniant, adhibitis cautelis ne quid exinde incommodi oriatur. Tunc vero Sorores, etsi imprudenter interrogatae, abstineant a referendis iis quae extra Monasterium viderint vel audierint, summopereque sileant de iis quae bono exemplo non sint, vel quae pacem et animi applicationem perturbare possint. His invigilet attente Antistita cum Consiliariis suis, et si ingressus Sororum in Monasterium occasionem praebeat abusibus, opportuna remedia adhibeantur."—*Statuta, 1961,* Art. 3, § 2.

understood without prejudice to the stricter law in force in the individual monasteries. Such stricter law might be found in the Constitutions of an institute or the Statutes approved for some particular monastery. The fact that the norms of individual monasteries are to prevail in such cases as this is in full accord with the principle of the Statutes of 1961, namely that, where the Rule and Constitutions of an institute expressly regulate the service of the extern sisters, these particular norms take precedence over the provisions of the Statutes.[34] For example, such stricter laws might concern the permission required to permit the entrance of the extern sisters, demanding the consent of the monastic Chapter instead of the consent of the Council of the superioress. Such norms might also restrict the frequency or the purposes for which entrance may be granted.[35]

1. Permissions Required for Entrance of Extern Sisters

Under the norms of the present paragraph, the right to admit extern sisters into the papal enclosure is vested in the superioress of the monastery, provided she first obtains the consent of her Council. Moreover, the approval of the local ordinary is necessary, along with that of the regular superior, if the particular monastery is subject to one. Once a given monastery has complied with these requirements for permission, no further indult or grant of any kind is necessary to admit extern sisters to the papal enclosure in the cases covered by the present paragraph. In practice, once the superioress and her Council have decided to avail themselves of the permission granted in this paragraph, the approvals of the local ordinary and the regular superior, once given, suffice for the indefinite use of the right granted. Moreover, the superioress need not seek the consent of her Council on each individual occasion when she desires to permit the extern sisters to enter the

[34] Cf. *supra*, pp. 122-123.

[35] Neither the Constitutions of the Order of St. Clare nor those of the Poor Clare Colettines contain any such stricter norms.

cloister. The consent of the Council, like the approvals of the local ordinary and the regular superior, is given but once. After these formalities are fulfilled, the right to grant entrance into the enclosure in accordance with this paragraph belongs to the superioress in virtue of the Statutes themselves. However, since this right of the superioress must always exist without prejudice to any law of the monastery, and since it is conditioned upon the consent of the Council as well as the approvals of the local ordinary and the religious superior, it seems that her right might well be limited with regard to both the occasions and frequency of entrance. Thus, the Council, in granting its initial consent, and the local ordinary and religious superior, in granting their original approbation, might demand that the superioress present a list of the occasions when entrance would be granted to the extern sisters. The consent and approval given to this list would then confer upon the superioress the habitual right to admit the extern sisters to the cloister of the nuns only on those occasions that are mentioned in the list; her power would be less than that granted by the paragraph under consideration.

2. Reasons for the Entrance of Extern Sisters into the Enclosure

According to the norms of this paragraph, entrance into the enclosure may be granted by the superioress to the extern sisters for the sake of devotion or instruction, as well as for eating and recreating together with the nuns. In regard to the matter of occasions of devotion or piety, the Statutes make provisions in another place for the habitual performance of religious exercises by the extern sisters within the enclosure together with the nuns.[36] At this point there is question of only an occasional admittance of the extern sisters to the papal enclosure. In the view of the writer, the matter of devotion or piety is to be understood in a very broad sense, including such occasions as retreats, conferences on the spiritual life, various religious

[36] *Statuta, 1961*, Art. 15, § 4; cf. *infra*, pp. 201-202.

exercises and, in general, anything which contributes to the spiritual life of the extern sisters.[37] Similarly, it seems that the matter of instruction would include a variety of possible situations. The extern sisters might be allowed to enter the enclosure under the terms of this paragraph to attend an exhortation or a talk given by the superioress to the entire community. Or, there might be question of catechetical instructions, instructions given by the mistress of novices to the junior professed sisters, or to the novices of the second year who are living outside the enclosure.[38]

3. Frequency of Entrance into the Enclosure by Extern Sisters

Just how frequently may entrance to the papal enclosure be granted to the extern sisters under the provisions of this paragraph? The Statutes say that it may be granted *interdum,* i.e., occasionally, at times. It does not seem that the Statutes here mean to grant permission for the extern sisters who live outside the papal enclosure to enter the cloister of the nuns habitually for any reason whatsoever, not even for religious instruction. Such habitual entrance would go beyond the meaning of "occasionally" and could not be permitted under the terms of the present paragraph. Habitual entrance for the performance of religious exercises is granted under the terms of Article 15, § 4, of the Statutes of 1961. Moreover, habitual entrance for religious exercises, meals, recreation, etc., has been granted by various indults of the Holy See, many of which are still in force.[39] But these sources of permission all lie beyond what is conceded by the present paragraph of Article 3.

[37] The Constitutions of the Order of St. Clare list the following as devotional exercises (*exercitia pietatis*): Divine Office, acts of consecration, singing prayers and antiphons, mental prayer, attendance at Mass, examination of conscience, Way of the Cross, Rosary, renewal of vows, retreat, day of recollection, and other similar functions."—*Const., OSC,* Art. 145-177.

[38] Cf. canon 509, § 2, 2°; *Const., PCC,* Art. 221, 261, 2°; *Const., OSC,* Art. 60.

[39] Cf. *supra,* pp. 85-87.

Thus, it is evident that the entrance into the enclosure which is permitted to the extern sisters under the terms of the present paragraph must not be such that it allows these sisters to enter as the common, ordinary and usual procedure. However, it does not seem necessary to set up a certain number as the absolute maximum of times for a week or for a month that the extern sisters may be allowed to enter the enclosure. In a matter of this nature, attended by so many varying circumstances, it is extremely difficult, if not impossible, to set up a hard and fast norm. It is for a similar reason that canonists, discussing the frequency of acts necessary to give rise to a norm of customary law, leave the exact determination to prudent judgment in each case, according to diverse circumstances.[40] *A fortiori*, such prudent judgment based on the circumstances of individual monasteries should be exercised in the case at hand for determining just how frequently the extern sisters may be permitted to enter the enclosure. After all, there is no question here of setting up a norm which will be obligatory upon the community, as in the case of giving rise to a custom; rather, it is a question of applying the objective norms expressed in the written law of the Statutes of 1961.

On this basis, it would seem that the extern sisters may be admitted to the enclosure for the reasons mentioned in this paragraph at the discretion of the superioress of the monastery whenever she prudently judges that such admission does not constitute a habitual manner of acting. At certain times there might be cause for the extern sisters to enter the enclosure of the nuns on four or five days in succession, e.g., for special meals and recreation during the Christmas holidays, for a retreat or special novena. This

[40] "Pluralitatem actuum requisitam vero, quia nulla ratio generalis inveniri potest ad certum numerum definiendum, et jura illam non praescribunt, dicunt esse *relativam*, ideoque *prudenti judicis arbitrio relinquendam;* qui judex 'juxta rerum et factorum diversitatem pensabit, quot actus sint necessarii ac sufficientes, ad ostendendum tale quid fuisse factum frequenter, ipsamque consuetudinem dici posse confirmatam.' (Reiffenstuel, Lib. I, tit. 4, n. 119. Cfr. Suarez, *De leg.*, Lib. VII, c. 10, n. 3.)"—Michiels, *op. cit.*, II, 81.

would not constitute a habitual entrance, since it is not the ordinary, commonplace manner of acting. Indeed, at certain other times there might be no reason for the extern sisters to enter the enclosure for two or three weeks at a time.

Moreover, it appears that the provisions of this paragraph may be used for permitting the extern sisters to enter the papal enclosure on a basis which is *regular,* provided it be not *habitual.* Thus, the extern sisters may be allowed to enter the cloister *regularly* each week for Sunday recreation, for the Chapter of Faults, for a conference, or the like. Such weekly entrance for a certain purpose, although it is indeed a regular happening, does not occur with enough frequency to be classed as the habitual, common ordinary manner of acting. However, it does seem that greater frequency of entrance for some given purpose *on a regular basis,* e.g., three or four recreations week by week, should be viewed as habitual and not included under the cases envisioned by the present paragraph.

As is evident from the preceding discussion, it is not an easy matter to make a definite distinction between occasional entrance and habitual entrance into the enclosure. In fact, it is well-nigh impossible to make an absolute determination in view of the many and varied circumstances of individual monasteries. Therefore, in a concrete, practical situation, should doubt arise in the matter, the determination of what constitutes an occasional entrance and what amounts to a habitual entrance is the right and duty of the local ordinary, who is the official custodian of the papal enclosure.[41] For this reason, should such doubts be envisioned, it would be wise for the monasteries that wish to make use of the permissions granted in this paragraph to include, along with their petition for the approbation of the local ordinary, a list of the occasions when entrance is to be granted to the extern sisters, as well as the frequency of such entrance. If the ordinary grants his approval to this

[41] Clausura monialium, etsi regularibus subiectarum, sub vigilantia est Ordinarii loci, . . ."—Canon 603, § 1.

list, this approval constitutes his determination that the proposed policy is within the limits of this paragraph of the Statutes. The matter need then cause no further concern to the superioress when she grants such permissions.

C. *Paragraph Three: Entering the Enclosure for Work*

> In accordance with the judgment of the superioress and her Council, together with the previous and at least general approval of the local ordinary and of the regular superior if there be one, the sisters living outside the cloister may at times be employed for the internal duties and works of the monastery, care being taken that they do not habitually associate with the nuns.[42]

This paragraph, which regulates the entrance of extern sisters into the papal enclosure for the purpose of work, does not, as does the preceding paragraph, state that its norms are to be understood without prejudice to the stricter law of individual monasteries.[43] However, it is evident that, should such stricter law be expressly regulatory of the service of the extern sisters, that particular law would, in accordance with the general principles of the Instruction of 1961, take precedence over the norms of the Statutes in this regard.[44]

1. Permissions Required for Entrance of Extern Sisters

According to the norms of this paragraph, the extern sisters who live outside the enclosure of the nuns may at times enter that enclosure to perform certain tasks, in accordance with the judgment of the superioress and her Council, and with the approval of the respective ordinaries. Such phrases as "the superioress and her Council" and

[42] "Sorores extra clausuram commorantes possunt, iudicio Antistitae eiusque Consilii, praehabita etiam saltem generali aprrobatione Ordinarii loci et Superioris Regularis, si adsit, internis etiam Monasterii muneribus vel laboribus interdum adhiberi, cauto ne cum Monialibus habitualiter permisceantur."—*Statuta, 1961,* Art. 3, § 3.

[43] Cf. *Statuta, 1961,* Art. 3, § 2.

[44] Cf. *supra*, pp. 122-123, 137.

"the superioress with her Council" appear more than once in the Statutes of 1961.[45] In such cases, is it necessary that the superioress obtain the consent of her Council, or does it suffice if she merely consults the councilors and obtains their opinion in the matter under consideration? According to reliable authors, if, in a given law, there is no clear distinction between the modes of intervention by the superior's councilors, but simply an indication that their intervention is required, their advice only, and not necessarily their consent, must be obtained.[46] Therefore, it is certainly sufficient if the superioress merely consults her Council in those cases where the Statutes employ such expressions as the ones here under consideration. Thus, in the case at hand, the superioress need only ask the advice of her council with a view to admitting the extern sisters to the enclosure for work.

The advice of the Council, as well as the general approbation of the local ordinary and the regular Superior, just as in the case of the permissions required above under paragraph 2,[47] are given but once. Once these formalities are fulfilled, the right to grant entrance into the enclosure in accordance with this paragraph belongs to the superioress in virtue of the Statutes themselves. Since the role of the Council under the terms of this paragraph is merely advisory, it does not seem that this body could in any way limit the power of the superioress in granting admission

[45] Cf. Art. 8; Art. 9, § 2; Art. 10, § 3.

[46] "Locutio 'superior cum suo consilio seu capitulo,' 'superior cum suffragio consilii vel capituli' sensum ambiguum habet, cum significare possit votum tum deliberativum (decisivum), seu consensum, tum consultivum, seu consilium, uti colligitur ex collatione can. 543 cum 575, par. 2. Proinde si res ex textu in casu concreto dirimi nequeat, suffragium requisitum vi can. 11 censendum est mere consultivum. Accedit quod eiusmodi formalitas importat restrictionem liberi exercitii potestatis ex parte superioris, quae ad normam can. 19 subest strictae interpretationi."—Beste, *op. cit.*, p. 162; cf. Abbo-Hannan, *op. cit.*, I, 154-155; Michiels, *Principia Generalia de Personis in Ecclesia* (ed. altera, Tornaci: Desclée, 1955), pp. 497-498.

[47] Cf. *supra*, p. 138.

to the extern sisters for purposes of work within the enclosure. However, since the present paragraph demands at least a general approbation on the part of the local ordinary, and of the regular superior, if there be one, it does seem that these authorities could limit the right of the superioress with regard to the types of work and the frequency of entrance. The local ordinary and the regular superior, in granting their general approbation, might well demand that the superioress present a list of the tasks to be performed within the cloister by the extern sisters, and the frequency of these tasks. The approval given to this list would then confer upon the superioress the right to admit the extern sisters to the papal enclosure only on those occasions which receive mention in the list.[48]

2. Frequency of Entrance into the Enclosure by Extern Sisters

With regard to the frequency with which the extern sisters may be permitted to enter the enclosure under the terms of this paragraph, the Statutes here employ the same term as in the preceding paragraph of this Article 3, i.e., *interdum.* Based on the reasoning presented above in connection with the commentary on the preceding paragraph, one can rightly assume that the extern sisters may be admitted to the papal enclosure for work at the discretion of the superioress of the monastery whenever she prudently judges that such admittance does not constitute a habitual manner of acting. As stated above, this might result in the entrance of the extern sisters to the papal cloister on several days in a row, or once or twice a week on a regular basis. Doubts concerning entrance for work and the frequency of these entrances, just as the doubts which might arise concerning the preceding paragraph, should be submitted to the judgment of the local ordinary.[49]

When there is question of the extern sisters entering the enclosure of the nuns for the purpose of work, as envisioned in the present paragraph, it seems that there is jusification

[48] *Loc. cit.*

[49] Cf. *supra*, pp. 141-142.

for adopting an even more liberal interpretation of what constitutes an occasional entrance. This view is based upon the concluding clause of this paragraph: "... care being taken that they do not habitually associate with the nuns."[50]

This final clause may be viewed as an addition made in order to separate the case under consideration, i.e., entrance of extern sisters who live outside the enclosure, from the case envisioned in Article 4 of the Statutes, which provides for the extern sisters to dwell habitually within the papal enclosure in constant association with the nuns.[51] In this more liberal view, the extern sisters might be allowed to enter the papal cloister for the purpose of work on a regular daily basis under the terms of the present paragraph. Such entrance would still be classed as occasional, since it would not be habitual in the sense that there would be no constant association between the extern sisters and the nuns, as is the case in the situation covered by Article 4, where the sisters live habitually within the enclosure of the nuns. In the writer's opinion, this daily entrance into the cloister could be allowed only for the performance of work in the enclosure, and not for the reasons of devotion, instruction, meals and recreation, as listed in the preceding paragraph. Although paragraph 2 does prescribe that care be taken to prevent any detrimental effects from the entrance of extern sisters into the cloister, it is only paragraph 3 which contains the clause against habitual association of extern sisters with the nuns.[52] This conclusion, moreover, is in harmony with the Statutes themselves, which exhibit even greater liberality when there is question of admitting the extern sisters to the enclosure for work, than when such admittance is granted for other purposes. Thus, paragraph 2 requires that the superioress obtain the *consent* of her Council to admit extern sisters to the enclosure for reasons of devotion,

[50] "... cauto ne cum Monialibus habitualiter permisceantur."—*Statuta, 1961,* Art. 3, § 3.

[51] *Ibid.,* Art. 4, §§ 1 and 2; cf. *supra,* pp. 133-134; cf. *infra.* pp. 149-157.

[52] *Statuta, 1961,* Art. 3, §§ 2 and 3.

instruction, meals and recreation; paragraph 3, however, demands only that she *consult* her Council before taking action to admit the extern sisters for work in the enclosure.[53]

One further question concerns the application of canon 600, 4°, to the extern sisters. According to this norm of the Code, the superioress may, with due precautions, admit to the enclosure physicians, surgeons, and others whose services are needed therein. For this she needs at least the habitual permission of the local ordinary, which may be legally presumed in case of necessity when there is no time to obtain his approval.[54] While the provisions of this law of the Code are quite similar to those of Article 3, § 3, of the Statutes of 1961, there are some differences. Canon 600, 4°, does not demand the approval of the regular superior for admitting persons to the enclosure to perform services, whereas Article 3, § 3, of the Statutes requires the approbation of the regular superior in addition to that of the local ordinary. The norm of the Statutes permits entrance into the enclosure occasionally; canon 600 allows entry whenever necessary, regardless of the frequency. This last point is not of too great importance, however, if the more liberal interpretation of frequency of entrance permitted by Article 3, § 3, of the Statutes be accepted.[55] However, under the terms of canon 600, 4°, it would be legitimate to permit the extern sisters to enter the papal enclosure to perform work therein should a proper case arise, e.g., a situation where the superior would refuse his sanction to such entrance by the extern sisters, thus eliminating the use of Article 3, § 3, of the Statutes. With only the permission of the local ordinary, the extern sisters could, in this situation, be admitted to the enclosure.

It may be objected that canon 600, 4°, can not be applied

[53] *Loc. cit.*

[54] "Antistitae est, adhibitis debitis cautelis, ingressum permittere medicis, chirurgis, aliisque quorum opera sit necessaria, impetrata prius saltem habituali approbatione ab Ordinario loci; si vero necessitas urgeat nec tempus suppetat approbationem petendi, haec iure praesumitur."—Canon 600, 4°.

[55] *Loc. cit.; Statuta, 1961*, Art. 3, § 3; cf. *supra*, pp. 144-145.

in cases where extern sisters are involved, since Article 3, § 1, of the Statutes of 1961 states: "Accordingly, they may not enter the part of the monastery reserved for the nuns except in accordance with the provisions made in these Statutes."[56] However, it must be noted that Article 3, § 1, treats of the quarters of the extern sisters which are subject to the common cloister and are not situated within the limits of the papal enclosure. Thus the prohibition to enter the papal enclosure except in accordance with the provisions of the Statutes is seen to be directly based on the fact that the living quarters of the extern sisters are located outside the cloister of the nuns. The prohibition is laid down "accordingly" ("*quapropter*"), namely, because of this location of the dwelling of the extern sisters outside the papal enclosure.[57] In other words, the prohibition of Article 3, § 1, may be interpreted as referring only to entrance into the papal cloister to dwell there, i.e., to maintain living quarters therein as envisioned in Article 4 of the Statutes. On this basis the prohibition would not at all forbid entrance in accord with canon 600, 4°, in order that the extern sisters might perform some task in the cloister of the nuns. Moreover, the norm of canon 600, 4°, is often incorporated into the Constitutions of various Orders of nuns.[58] The extern sisters, under the law of the Statutes of 1961, are bound to the observance of these Constitutions, except for those prescriptions which are repealed by the Statutes.[59] However, the Statutes of 1961 contain no certain revocation of the right granted in canon 600, 4°, and embodied in the Constitutions of various institutes. Therefore, in accord with the principles of law, no such revocation of the former law of the Code is pre-

[56] "Quapropter nequent partem Monasterii Monialibus reservatam ingredi nisi intra limites his Statutis definitos."—*Statuta, 1961,* Art. 3, § 1; cf. *supra,* pp. 135-136.

[57] "Salvo art. 4, Sorores servitio externo addictae habitationem habent Monasterio adnexam et clausurae communi obnoxiam, non vero intra fines clausurae papalis Monialium positam. Quapropter . . ."—*Statuta, 1961,* Art. 3, § 1.

[58] *Const., OSC,* Art. 424, 4°; *Const., PCC,* Art. 173, 4°.

[59] Cf. *Statuta, 1961,* Art. 2; cf. *supra,* pp. 122-123, 132-133.

sumed; rather, the subsequent law of the Statutes must be adapted to the pre-existing laws of the Code and Constitutions and harmonized with them.[60] No doubtful revocation or limitation of the powers of the superioress to admit extern sisters into the enclosure is enough to deprive her of those powers. Rather, she possesses concurrently the powers granted in the Statutes of 1961 and conceded in the Code of Canon Law and the Constitutions. Quite probably, entrance which is granted to the extern sisters in accordance with canon 600, 4°, and those Constitutions which embody this law, is not at all opposed to the provisions of the Statutes of 1961. It is, on the other hand, quite in accord with the provisions of these Statutes, which themselves enjoin observance of the Constitutions.

D. *Paragraph Four: Entrance of Novices and Postulants into the Cloister*

> What is said in this Article about the entrance of the sisters into the cloister applies also to postulants and to novices of the second year of novitiate.[61]

This paragraph of Article 3 simply applies to the extern postulants and novices of the second year the same rules which govern the entrance of the professed extern sisters into the papal enclosure. According to the norms of the Statutes of 1931, under no circumstances were the extern postulants ever to be admitted into the enclosure of the nuns.[62] This prohibition is completely erased by the Statutes of 1961, and the postulants are permitted to enter the cloister in the same manner as the professed extern sisters. This paragraph mentions only the novices of the second year, since the Statutes provide that the first or canonical year of novitiate is to be made within the cloister of the monas-

[60] Cf. canon 23; cf. *supra*, p. 62.

[61] "Quae in hoc articulo quoad ingressum in clausuram Sororum dicuntur valent etiam pro postulantibus et pro novitiis secundi anni novitiatus."—*Statuta, 1961*, Art. 3, § 4.

[62] *Statuta, 1931*, Art. 7; cf. *supra*, p. 91.

tery.[63] Therefore it would be useless and unnecessary to make provision for their entrance into the papal enclosure.

ARTICLE 2
FOURTH ARTICLE OF THE STATUTES: EXTERN SISTERS DWELLING WITHIN THE CLOISTER

A. *Paragraph One: Conditions for Locating Residence of Extern Sisters in the Enclosure*

> With due regard to the spirit and character of each Order as well as the number of nuns living in the monastery, monasteries, after a previous vote of the Chapter and, in the case of monasteries belonging to a federation, after hearing the Council of the federation, may, with the approval of the Holy See, determine that the extern sisters shall live habitually within the limits of the cloister of the monastery, even though they are not bound by the law of papal cloister. In this case precautions must be taken so that this association of the sisters with the nuns who are bound by the law of enclosure does not harm the spirit of recollection; besides other precautions, a kind of separation should be instituted within the cloister similar to that prescribed for the novitiate (canon 564, § 1), and the sisters should be forbidden to relate to the nuns the things that happen outside of the cloister.[64]

1. Preliminary Considerations

In treating of the conditions under which extern sisters

[63] *Statuta, 1961,* Art. 10, § 1; cf. *infra,* pp. 167-170.

[64] "Attento spiritu et indole cuiusque Ordinis, necnon numero Monialium in ipso Monasterio degentium, praevio voto Capituli et, si agatur de Monasteriis alicui Foederationi adscriptis, audito Consilio Foederationis, Monasteria statuere possunt, approbante S. Sede, ut Sorores servitio externo addictae habitualiter intra clausurae ambitum ipsius Monasterii versari possint, licet lege clausurae papalis non teneantur. Hoc in casu cautelae praescribantur, ne commercium huiusmodi Sororum cum Monialibus clausurae lege obstrictis spiritui recollectionis nocumentum afferat; praeter alia, quaedam separatio statuatur intra ipsam clausuram, ad instar praescripti pro novitiatu (can. 564, § 1) et vetentur Sorores Monialibus referre ea quae extra clausuram accidunt."—*Statuta, 1961,* Art. 4, § 1.

may live habitually within the enclosure of the nuns, this paragraph first requires that consideration be given to the spirit and character of each Order. It must be determined whether the extern sisters may be allowed to have permanent quarters inside the papal enclosure, and to associate frequently with the nuns, without doing violence to the life of the community. In other words, the vote of the Chapter of the monastery and the advice of the Council of the federation which must precede the petition to the Holy See[65] ought to proceed from a mature consideration and judgment that the permanent dwelling of extern sisters within the papal cloister is or is not compatible with the spirit and character of the Order. In the Apostolic Constitution *Sponsa Christi,* Pius XII clearly indicated the fact that a great variation exists among the different Orders of nuns.[66] For this reason the Statutes here direct the attention of the authorities of each monastery and Order to the fact that they have the responsibility to maintain the spirit and character of their institute in whatever arrangement they decide to make.

A second factor influencing the decision whether extern sisters should be permitted to live permanently inside the papal enclosure is the number of nuns living in a given monastery. Where this number of nuns is small, so that the habitual assistance of the extern sisters is required for the performance of the work inside the enclosure, such an arrangement is most practical. A further consideration, not included in the Statutes, but still well worth considering, is the number of extern sisters serving the monastery. Where there is one lone extern sister, or perhaps only two or three, it would be very profitable to have the quarters of the extern sisters located inside the papal enclosure. Such an arrangement would aid greatly in the religious training of these sisters. Moreover, it would give them a greater sense of solidarity with the rest of the community, thus overcoming the very real problem of loneliness which often arises when

[65] Cf. *infra,* p. 151.

[66] *AAS,* XLIII (1951), 8.

one or very few sisters live completely apart from the nuns. Even from a financial viewpoint, the location of the living quarters of the extern sisters inside the cloister of the nuns has advantages, since it eliminates the expensive duplication of many facilities in the monastery. This is especially important when such duplication would be for the accommodation of only one or two sisters.

2. Permissions Necessary to Locate Extern Dwelling within the Enclosure

Any arrangement whereby the extern sisters live permanently within the papal enclosure of the monastery must, according to the norms of the present paragraph, be approved by the previous vote of the Chapter of the monastery. Moreover, should the monastery in question be a member of a federation of monasteries, the advice of the Council of that federation must be sought. Finally, the arrangement must be sanctioned by the approbation of the Holy See. As has been shown above, a number of papal indults permitting extern sisters to dwell habitually within the cloister of the nuns have been granted in the past.[67] It would seem that such indults, provided they have not expired through lapse of the number of years for which they were issued, may still be used under the terms of the present paragraph. There is no need to seek further approval of the Holy See, even though such indults were granted before the promulgation of the Statutes of 1961. Once the formalities required by this paragraph have been completed, the extern sisters may be allowed to take up residence within the limits of the cloister of the monastery, despite the fact that they are not bound by the law of enclosure.

3. Living within the Enclosure

Once the quarters for extern sisters have been established inside the confines of the papal enclosure, the extern sisters are permitted not only to live habitually therein, but also to share in the religious exercises, meals and recreations of

[67] Cf. *supra*, p. 85.

the cloistered nuns. In short, they share quite fully in the daily life and routine of the nuns themselves.[68] The great difference, of course, is the fact that, although the extern sisters live within the confines of the papal enclosure, they are not bound by it.

However, the Statutes demand that certain precautions be established, lest the spirit of recollection be harmed by this close association between the extern sisters and the nuns. Two such precautions are explicitly mentioned in the present paragraph, i.e., the separation between the nuns and the extern sisters, and the prohibition forbidding the extern sisters to relate outside happenings to the nuns. In addition other precautionary measures are ordered by the Statutes. Although the present Article does not mention any other such measures explicitly, it seems that there is room here for an application of the directive of the preceding Article, which states that "the superioress with her councilors should carefully watch over these matters; and, if the entrance of the sisters into the monastery becomes an occasion for abuses, suitable remedies should be applied."[69] This directive, urging vigilance and correction on the part of the authorities of the monastery, seeks to prevent the extern sisters from relating things they have seen or heard outside the monastery, especially matters which do not set a good example, or which can disturb peace and application of mind.[70] Thus, the adoption of this directive is an excellent means of implementing the explicit precaution of the paragraph under consideration, which requires that the extern sisters be forbidden to relate

[68] That the Statutes mean to grant not mere residence within the enclosure, but also a full share in the life of the monastery, is evident from the Latin text of the present paragraph which states that "*Sorores servitio externo addictae habitualiter intra clausurae ambitum ipsius Monasterii versari possint.*" According to reliable authority: "*Versari* means, in the first place, *to be anywhere, frequent any place, stay, abide, remain, live ... associated with ... to keep company or hold intercourse with.*"—Leverett, *Lexicon of the Latin Language,* (Philadelphia: Lippincott, 1895), Latin-English Lexicon, p. 951.

[69] *Statuta, 1961,* Art. 3, § 2.

[70] *Loc. cit.*

to the nuns the things that happen outside the cloister. In a word, such vigilance and correction by the authorities serve as a safeguard for the spirit of recollection, the precise purpose to be achieved according to the present paragraph.

Besides forbidding the extern sisters to relate outside happenings to the nuns, this paragraph explicitly requires one other precaution as a safeguard for the life of recollection in the monastery. The Statutes require the institution of a kind of separation within the cloister similar to that prescribed for novitiate houses in canon 564, § 1. This canon provides that the novitiate shall be separated, as far as possible, from the portion of the house that is inhabited by the professed religious in such a manner that, without a special reason and without the permission of the superior or of the master of novices, the novices have no communication with the professed, nor the professed with the novices.[71] However, it must be noted that the Statutes do not say that the separation between the extern sisters and the nuns is the *same* as that described in canon 564, § 1; rather, the Statutes call for a *similar* arrangement. The separation which is instituted between the two groups of religious must take into consideration the liberal attitude of the present paragraph, which permits the extern sisters to share so completely in the daily life and routine of the nuns.[72] Any such separation must take into consideration the practical fact that the extern sisters and the cloistered nuns are going to be working, recreating and eating together on a daily basis. Consequently, it would be highly unrealistic and impractical to insist that there be no communication between the two groups without special reasons and permissions. It would seem that the separation urged by this paragraph of the Statutes is achieved in practice if the extern sisters reside

[71] "Novitiatus ab ea parte domus, in qua degunt professi, sit, quantum fieri potest, segregatus ita ut, sine speciali causa ac Superioris vel Magistri licentia, novitii nullam habeant communicationem cum professis neque hi cum novitiis."—Canon 564, § 1.

[72] Cf. *supra*, pp. 151-152.

in a special section of the papal enclosure, distinct from that part of the cloister which is inhabited by the cloistered nuns. Ordinarily, the extern sisters should not go into the section of the cloister reserved for the nuns; however, should some special reason arise, with the permission of the superioress they could be allowed to enter this section. In fact, should such a reason demand frequent, even daily, entrance of the extern sisters into the part of the enclosure set aside for the nuns, the superioress could grant a general permission to be used whenever necessary. These special separate sections of the papal cloister would apply only to the living quarters of the religious; both the nuns and the extern sisters would share the same refectory, choir, work and recreation rooms.

B. *Paragraph Two: Leaving the Enclosure*

> Since they are not bound by the law of papal cloister, sisters who habitually live within the cloister may, at the discretion of the superioress, leave the cloister for the service or other external work of the monastery, or for some other just and reasonable cause.
>
> Without prejudice to the discipline and the purpose of the postulancy and the novitiate (canon 565), the same provision holds also for novices even of the first year of the novitiate and for the postulants, if the postulancy, according to the norm of Article 9, § 2, is conducted within the cloister.[73]

1. General Norms for Leaving the Cloister

This paragraph of the Statutes treats of those occasions when the extern sisters whose quarters are located inside the papal enclosure may leave the cloister. This norm should be applied only to those cases where the sisters, although

[73] "Sororibus quae habitualiter intra clausuram degunt, cum lege clausurae papalis non teneantur, pro servitio vel alio opere externo Monasterii vel ob aliam iustam et rationabilem causam, de iudicio Antistitae licet e clausura egredi.

Idem valet pro novitiis etiam primi anni novitiatus et pro postulantibus, si postulatus, ad normam art. 9, par. 2, intra clausuram peragitur, salvis tamen disciplina et fine postulatus et novitiatus (can. 565)."—*Statuta, 1961,* Art. 4, § 2.

they go outside the limits of the papal cloister, do not also depart from the premises of the monastery. This latter case is treated at another point in the Statutes.[74] The present norm makes mention only of leaving the cloister; it says nothing about going out of the monastery itself.

These sisters may be permitted to leave the enclosure to attend to the service of the monastery or other external work. Naturally this would include all tasks required for the proper maintenance of the monastery buildings and grounds. It would also embrace the performance of those works of the apostolate which the extern sisters might carry on in accord with the Statutes.[75] In general, any task connected with the running of the monastery would be included here. Besides these reasons, other just and reasonable causes receive mention, i.e., others not strictly connected with the running of the monastery. Such other causes would include the visiting of relatives in the outside parlors, reasonable recreation, exercise and the like. In view of the generous spirit of the Statutes in matters of this nature, it seems that a liberal interpretation should be adopted in regard to the concession of permissions under the norms of this paragraph. According to these provisions, such permissions are to be granted according to the judgment of the superioress of the monastery. For practical purposes, it would be wise for the superioress simply to grant general permission for the extern sisters to leave the enclosure for those reasons which occur frequently and regularly, e.g., for the daily work. There is nothing in the present norm to prevent such a course of action. Specific permission would then be sought only when the extern sisters desire to leave the enclosure for reasons which are not considered a part of the regular monastic routine.

2. Application to Postulants and Novices

The extern sister novices, even those who are making their first or canonical year of novitiate, as well as the extern

[74] *Statuta, 1961,* Art. 18, § 1; cf. *infra,* pp. 206-208.

[75] Cf. *Statuta, 1961,* Art. 1, § 2; Art. 6.

sister postulants who, according to Article 9, § 2, live habitually within the papal enclosure, may be permitted to leave it under the same conditions and for the same reasons as the professed sisters. In any case, the novices who are making the first year of novitiate will live within the papal enclosure, since this arrangement is demanded by Article 10, § 1, of the Statutes. The novices who are completing their second year of novitiate may live habitually in the papal enclosure for one of several reasons. It may be that the quarters of the extern sisters are located in the enclosure according to Article 4, § 1; since the Statutes call for the second year of novitiate to be made in the proper residence of the extern sisters, the novices who are making this year will quite naturally live in the enclosure.[76] The Statutes also permit the entire second year of novitiate to be made inside the monastic enclosure under certain conditions, even though the residence of the extern sisters is located outside the enclosure of the nuns.[77] In any case, for the final two months of the second year of novitiate, the novices are to dwell inside the papal enclosure.[78] The postulants may live habitually in the papal enclosure for either of two reasons. Since the Statutes require that the postulancy be made within the residence of the extern sisters, the postulants also will live inside the enclosure in those monasteries where the quarters of the extern sisters are located in the cloister of the nuns.[79] Or, even though the dwelling of the extern sisters is located outside the enclosure of the monastery, the postulancy may, under certain conditions, be made inside the cloister.[80]

Since the Statutes state that permission to leave the enclosure may be given to novices *even of the first year*, it is evident that all extern novices, no matter what the precise reason might be for a second year novice to live inside the

[76] *Ibid.*, Art. 10, § 1.
[77] *Ibid.*, §3.
[78] *Ibid.*, § 2.
[79] *Ibid.*, Art. 9, § 2.
[80] *Loc. cit.*

enclosure, may be permitted to leave the cloister under the norms of the present paragraph. This paragraph likewise provides that postulants may be allowed to leave the enclosure if the postulancy, according to the norm of Article 9, § 2, is made within the cloister. Since Article 9, § 2, includes both of the cases in which a postulant may live inside the enclosure, it may be concluded that all extern postulants who habitually dwell in the papal cloister may be allowed to leave it under the provisions of Article 4, § 2.[81]

Finally, the Statutes prescribe that, when postulants and novices are permitted to leave the cloister, this permission must be granted without prejudice to the discipline and purpose of the postulancy and novitiate. Specific mention is made of canon 565, which treats at some length of the spiritual formation and education which are to be imparted during the course of the novitiate. The prescriptions of this canon indeed place certain limitations on the extern novices with regard to leaving the enclosure. Thus, novices are not to be employed in the external works of the institute.[82] For this reason, extern novices could not regularly be permitted to leave the enclosure to participate in works of the apostolate which might be conducted by the extern sisters under the norms of Article 1, § 2, and Article 6 of the Statutes, although they might be allowed to do so occasionally, since this would not constitute regular employment in works of the institute. Although the novices may be permitted to leave the enclosure for the purpose of assisting with other work of the monastery, even on an habitual basis, the frequency of such work and departure from the enclosure must not be such that the purposes of the novitiate outlined in canon 565 are frustrated or seriously impaired. Nor should the extern novices be placed in charge of any of this work, so that they are made primarily responsible for it.[83]

[81] Cf. *infra*, pp. 166-167.

[82] "Anno novitiatus ne destinentur novitii . . . exterioribus religionis muniis."—Canon 565, § 3.

[83] *Loc. cit.*

ARTICLE 3
FIFTH ARTICLE OF THE STATUTES: SUPERVISION OF THE EXTERN RESIDENCE

> The residence and other places outside the limits of the cloister which are destined for the extern sisters are subject, according to the norms of law, to the vigilance and visitation not only of the local ordinary and of the regular superior, if there be one, but also, with all due prescriptions on the matter being observed, to the vigilance and visitation of the superioress of the monastery and of the moderator of the federation, in the case of federated monasteries (see the Instruction *Inter cetera,* n. 24, 5°).[84]

The places destined for the extern sisters, even though they may be located outside the enclosure are, no less than the rest of the monastery, subject to the vigilance and visitation of the local ordinary and the religious ordinary, according to the norms of law.[85] Should a given monastery be subject to no regular superior, but only to the local ordinary, or directly subject to the Apostolic See, the local ordinary has the right to conduct the visitation of the entire monastery, including the residence of the extern sisters.[86] Moreover, even though the monastery may be subject to a regular superior, the local ordinary has the right and duty to exercise vigilance over these areas even outside the time of visitation, since, according to the norms of the Code of Canon Law, it is his responsibility to watch over the proper observance of the episcopal enclosure which is in force in the quarters of the extern sisters.[87]

[84] "Habitatio aliaque loca Sororibus externo servitio Monasterii addictis extra limites clausurae destinata vigilantiae et visitationi subsunt, non modo Ordinarii loci et Superioris Regularis, si adsit, ad normam iuris, sed etiam, servatis servandis, ipsius Antistitae Monasterii necnon Moderatricis Foederationis, si de Monasteriis foederatis agatur (Instr. '*Inter cetera,*' n. 24, 5°).—*Statuta, 1961,* Art. 5.

[85] Cf. canons. 511-513.

[86] "Ordinarius loci per se vel per alium quinto quoque anno visitare debet singula monialium monasteria quae sibi vel Sedi Apostolicae immediate subiecta sunt."—Canon 512, § 1, 1°.

[87] "Episcopus in adiunctis peculiaribus, gravibusque intercedentibus

Moreover, according to the provisions of the present Article, in such monasteries where the quarters of the extern sisters are located outside the limits of the papal enclosure the superioress of the monastery also possesses a right of vigilance and visitation in regard to these areas, with due prescriptions on the matter being observed. These prescriptions, as this Article itself indicates, are to be interpreted in relation to the Instruction *Inter cetera,* which states that the necessity of looking after the house where the extern sisters live is a circumstance of such great importance as to constitute just and canonical cause for asking appropriate dispensations, or even some moderate and carefully defined habitual faculties, from the Holy See.[88] In other words, an indult must be obtained from the Holy See to permit the superioress to leave the papal enclosure to visit and inspect the quarters of the extern sisters; such a permission is not given automatically in virtue of Article 5.

Finally, with the observance of due prescriptions, should the monastery in question belong to a federation, the moderator of that federation likewise has rights of vigilance and visitation over the living quarters of the extern sisters. In this case, the due prescriptions would be found in the Statutes of the federation approved by the Holy See, which are to be observed if they contain legislation on this point.

SECTION III
APOSTOLATE AND CLOTHING OF THE EXTERN SISTERS

ARTICLE 1
SIXTH ARTICLE OF THE STATUTES: WORKS OF THE APOSTOLATE

A. *Paragraph One: Permission to Engage in Apostolic Works*

To engage in works of the apostolate in monasteries

causis, potest hanc clausuram, nisi agatur de religione clericali exempta, censuris munire; semper autem curet ut eadem rite servetur et quidquid in eam irrepat vitii corrigatur."—Canon 604, § 3; cf. *Statuta, 1961,* Art. 3, § 1.

[88] Instructio *Inter cetera,* n. 24, 5°; cf. *supra,* p. 116.

> in a stable manner, according to the norm of Article 1, § 2, besides the previous approval of the local ordinary and of the regular superior, if there be one, the approbation of the Holy See is required.[89]

In order that the extern sisters may carry on the works of the apostolate as described in the commentary on Article 1, § 2,[90] the approbation of the Holy See is required. As this Article indicates, such approval will be given by the Holy See only after the previous permission of the local ordinary and of the religious superior, if there be one, has been obtained for the works in question. It is to be noted, however, that these formalities are not required for any and all participation in apostolic work, but only if the work is to be conducted in a stable manner. In other words, if the work is performed only occasionally and not on a regular basis, none of the above mentioned permissions are required. Only if the work is done on a permanent basis, as a regular labor in which the extern sisters engage, must these formalities be observed. Thus, the prescriptions of this paragraph would have to be observed for the extern sisters to conduct a regularly scheduled weekly or even monthly catechism class, or day of recollection. On the other hand, without the necessity of observing any of these formalities, extern sisters might, on a temporary and extraordinary basis, e.g., sickness of the regular teachers, conduct a catechism class daily until the need ceases.

B. *Paragraph Two: Authority of the Local Ordinary*

> In carrying out the works of the apostolate, the sisters should follow norms set down by the local ordinary.[91]

The norm enunciated in this brief paragraph is but the

[89] "Ut in Monasteriis opera apostolatus, ad normam art. 1, § 2, praevio beneplacito Ordinarii loci necnon Superioris Regularis, si adsit, exerceantur, approbatio S. Sedis requiritur."—*Statuta, 1961,* Art. 6, § 1.

[90] Cf. *supra,* pp. 127-128.

[91] "In operum apostolatus exercitio Sorores normas ab Ordinario loci impertitas sequantur."—*Statuta, 1961,* Art. 6, § 2.

logical consequence of the position of the local ordinary as the immediate pastor of his flock, who possesses the right of governing his diocese in spiritual and temporal matters, including, consequently, any works of the apostolate which might be entrusted to the care of the extern sisters.[92]

ARTICLE 2
SEVENTH ARTICLE OF THE STATUTES: CLOTHING OF THE EXTERN SISTERS

A. *Paragraph One: Form of the Habit*

> The habit of the sisters should be the same as that of the nuns, suitably accommodated, however, by the Chapter to the purpose of external service according to the circumstances of time and place.[93]

Article 26 of the Statutes of 1931 already prescribed that the extern sisters wear the same habit as the cloistered nuns, permitting adaptation to the particular circumstances of the extern sisters, after consultation with the local ordinary.[94] However, according to the Statutes of 1961, no consultation of the ordinary is required to make suitable accommodations in the habit for extern sisters. Instead, the Chapter of the monastery is empowered to decide this matter. It must be noted that this paragraph permits adaptations and alterations, provided the habit of the extern sisters remains essentially the same as that of the cloistered nuns. These variations must not be so great as to result in a habit for the extern sisters which is entirely different from that worn by the nuns. It would seem that the Chapter may, in virtue of the permission granted in the present paragraph, make those alterations in the habit of the Order which are necessary for the extern sisters efficiently to carry out their duties. To make alterations in the habit of the extern sisters which

[92] Cf. canons 294, § 1; 314; 315; 323, § 1; 334-336.

[93] "Habitus Sororum idem sit ac Monialium, ad finem tamen servitii externi pro rerum et locorum adiunctis convenienter a Capitulo aptatus."—*Statuta, 1961*, Art. 7, § 1.

[94] Cf. *supra*. p. 95.

are not a help to efficient performance of duty, but rather serve to distinguish the extern sisters as a separate class apart from the nuns, is to exceed the power here granted to the Chapter, and to fail against the wish of the Holy See that both groups of religious be clothed in the same habit.

B. *Paragraph Two: Uniformity in Federations*

> With regard to the religious habit in monasteries of one and the same federation, the sisters, as far as possible, should be dressed in the same way.[95]

To comply with the wishes of the Holy See in regard to uniform clothing for the extern sisters in the various monasteries of a federation, some consideration must be given by the federation to the matter contained in this paragraph. Since the Chapter of a single monastery is empowered to authorize such accommodations for the extern sisters of that particular house,[96] it seems that the Chapter of a federation would be competent to determine this matter for all the houses of the federation, always keeping in mind the prescription of § 1, namely, that the habit of the extern sisters must be essentially the same as that of the nuns. Beyond this determination of the Chapter, no further permission or confirmation is required, unless the particular statutes of the federation require further formalities or confirmations of decisions made by the Chapter.

[95] "In Monasteriis unius eiusdemque Foederationis, Sorores, quoad habitum religiosum, eodem, quantum potest, modo vestiantur."—*Statuta, 1961,* Art. 7, § 2.

[96] *Ibid.,* § 1; cf. *supra,* p. 161.

CHAPTER X

THE STATUTES OF 1961—CHAPTER II: CONCERNING THE RECEPTION AND PROFESSION OF THE EXTERN SISTERS

The six articles which make up this portion of the Statutes contain legislation pertaining to the reception, postulancy, novitiate and profession of the extern sisters.[1]

Section I
Admittance to the Order and Postulancy

ARTICLE 1
EIGHTH ARTICLE OF THE STATUTES: QUALITIES OF EXTERN SISTER CANDIDATES

> In the admission and training of extern sisters, the same conditions are to be observed as those prescribed by the Constitutions for the nuns of the monastery, with due considerations given, however, to their special function. The superioress with her Council should take care to accept only those aspirants who have mature judgment and more than ordinary piety, so that they may give good example, especially outside the monastery in their dealings with secular persons.[2]

In consequence of the present Article, it is the general rule that, in the acceptance and training of extern sisters in a

[1] *Statuta, 1961,* Caput II, "De Sororum Servitio Externo Addictarum Cooptatione."

[2] "In admittendis et instituendis Sororibus servitio externo destinatis, eaedem prorsus condiciones serventur quae pro Monialibus respectivi Monasterii vi Constitutionum praescribuntur, ratione tamen semper habita ipsarum peculiaris muneris. Curet autem Antistita cum suo Consilio, ut adspirantes unice acceptet quae maturi sint iudicii, quaeque pietate non communi fulgeant, ea mente ut exemplo praeluceant, maxime extra Monasterium, in usu cum saecularibus."—*Statuta, 1961,* Art. 8.

given Order, the Constitutions are to be followed, just as they are in the case of the cloistered nuns. However, since account must be taken of the special role of the extern sisters, there will be certain notable exceptions to this general rule. It has been shown that, except in those cases where the Constitutions expressly treat of the service rendered by the extern sisters, the Statutes of 1961 take precedence over these norms.[3] For example, this second Chapter of the Statutes contains special regulations concerning the postulancy, novitiate and profession of extern sisters.[4] In practice, therefore, the postulancy, novitiate and profession of extern sisters will be regulated, insofar as the specific matters included in these special norms are concerned, not by the Constitutions of their Order, but by the law of the Statutes.[5] Moreover, in view of the special juridical status of the extern sisters, it must be recognized that certain matters in the Constitutions of an Order, even though they may not be expressly repealed by some Article of the Statutes of 1961, are nevertheless inapplicable to extern sisters. In this category would fall, for example, those Articles of the Constitutions of an institute which refer to the preparation for and the making of solemn profession, the effects of solemn profession, and the observance of the papal enclosure. The Statutes for Extern Sisters

[3] *Statuta, 1961,* Art. 2; cf. *supra,* pp. 122-123, 132-133.

[4] Cf. *Statuta, 1961,* Art. 9, 10, 12.

[5] Following are examples of some cases where this principle is to be applied: Article 27 of the Constitutions of the Order of St. Clare specifies a postulancy of six months' duration; however, in the case of extern sisters in this Order, the norm of Article 9, § 1, of the Statutes of 1961 must be observed, since this article demands a postulancy of one year, with certain provisions for shortening or lengthening the time. Article 56 of the same Constitutions, as well as Articles 205 and 211 of the Constitutions of the Poor Clare Colettines, specify a novitiate of one year; Article 10, § 1, of the Statutes of 1961, however, demands a two-year novitiate, and must be observed in the case of extern sisters in these Orders. With regard to the profession to be made at the end of the novitiate, the norms of Article 86 of the Constitutions of the Order of St. Clare and Article 232 of the Colettine Constitutions must give place to the prescriptions of Article 12, § 1, of the Statutes of 1961.

place these religious in a position which is simply not envisioned by such Articles of the Constitutions, which are therefore completely inapplicable in regard to the extern sisters.

ARTICLE 2
NINTH ARTICLE OF THE STATUTES: THE POSTULANCY

A. *Paragraph One: Duration of the Postulancy*

> The postulancy lasts one year; but the superioress, with the advice of her Council, may reduce this time to six months or prolong it for another six months beyond the year, according as the postulant seems to need a longer or shorter preparation for the novitiate.[6]

This paragraph incorporates the norm of Article 21 of the Statutes of 1931; however, the power to shorten the postulancy to only six months is new in the Statutes of 1961.[7] The shortening or lengthening of the postulancy is to be done at the discretion of the superioress of the monastery, after consultation with her Council. Although the Statutes speak expressly only of a reduction or prolongation of six months, it seems that, in conformity with the axiom that one who has power to do more can also do that which is less, the superioress could also prescribe that the postulancy be shortened or lengthened by a period which is less than six months. Moreover, these alterations in the duration of the postulancy may not be set up as a general policy for all, but may be made only in individual cases. After all, this paragraph explicitly states that any change made in the duration of the postulancy is to be "according as the postulant seems to need a longer or shorter preparation for the

[6] "Postulatus annum perduret: quod tamen tempus Antistita, audito suo Consilio, ad sex menses contrahere poterit vel ad alios sex menses, ultra annum, prorogare, prout postulantis ad novitiatum opportuna praeparatio exigere videatur."—*Statuta, 1961*, Art. 9, § 1.

[7] Cf. *supra*, p. 94.

novitiate."[8] It is the express intention of the legislator that the ordinary norm for all be a postulancy of one year; decisions to alter this period of time are to be made as the need requires them in individual cases.

B. *Paragraph Two: Place of the Postulancy*

> The postulancy should be made in the residence of the sisters in order that the postulants may be trained and tested in their proper duties.
>
> Nevertheless, in accordance with the judgment of the superioress and her Council, and with the approval of the local ordinary and of the regular superior if there be one, the postulancy can be made within the monastery, that is, within the cloister of the nuns, without prejudice, however, to the Statutes of the Federation in the case of a federated monastery, or to Article 4, § 2.[9]

According to the norm of this paragraph, the postulancy is to be made in the place of residence of the extern sisters, so that those who aspire to that position in the monastery may be trained in their proper duties. In those monasteries where, in virtue of Article 4, § 1, of the Statutes, the quarters of the extern sisters are, by papal indult, located within the papal enclosure, the extern postulants will likewise live within the cloister in the section set aside for the extern sisters.[10] Moreover, even in those monasteries where the quarters of the extern sisters are situated outside the papal enclosure, the extern postulancy can be made within the cloister of the nuns, in accordance with the judgment of the superioress and her Council, together with the approval of the local

[8] "... prout postulantis ad novitiatum opportuna praeparatio exigere videatur."—*Statuta, 1961,* Art. 9, § 1.

[9] "Postulatus in habitatione Sororum peragatur, ut in officiis propriis postulantes exerceantur et probentur.

Attamen de iudicio Antistitae eiusque Consilii et de beneplacito Ordinarii loci necnon Superioris Regularis, si adsit, postulatus intra Monasterium peragi poterit, scilicet intra clausuram Monialium, salvis Statutis Foederationis, si de Monasterio foederato agatur, et salvo Art. 4, § 2."—*Ibid.,* § 2.

[10] Cf. *supra,* pp. 149-154.

ordinary and the regular superior, if there be one. Since the Statutes do not clearly specify that the consent of the Council must be obtained, it suffices for the superioress simply to consult this body in the matter.[11] A papal indult is not required in such a case, since it is not the dwelling of the extern sisters as such which is located within the cloister, but only the residence of the postulants. However, if the Statutes of the federation contain prescriptions concerning this matter, these Statutes will take precedence over the norms of the present paragraph; monasteries belonging to that federation must abide by its Statutes.

Finally, the provision exists that these conditions for the making of the postulancy within the papal enclosure be without prejudice to Article 4, § 2, of the Statutes. This means that, even though the postulants may live within the cloister of the nuns, they are not bound by the law of enclosure. Hence they can, according to the judgment of the superioress, leave the enclosure for external service, for the work of the monastery, or for some other just and reasonable cause.[12]

SECTION II
THE NOVITIATE

ARTICLE 1
TENTH ARTICLE OF THE STATUTES: QUALITIES OF THE NOVITIATE

A. *Paragraph One: Duration and Conditions for Validity of the Novitiate*

> The novitiate is to last for two years. The first of these years is strictly canonical; and, although the novices of this class are not bound by the law of papal cloister, the year is to be spent together with the cloistered novices within the enclosure of the monastery or of some other monastery that belongs to the group of federated monasteries. This year of

[11] Cf. *supra*, pp. 142-143.
[12] Cf. *supra*, pp. 155-157.

> novitiate, in order to be valid, must be a complete and continuous year according to the norm of the law.[13]

The first or strictly canonical year of novitiate is necessary for the validity of the profession which is made at the end of the second year of novitiate. However, in accord with the norms of Canon Law, the second year of noviceship is not required for the validity of the novitiate and the subsequent profession.[14] Even though the omission of this second year of novitiate would not affect the validity of an extern sister's profession, only the Holy See can grant a dispensation from it. These extern sisters belong to an institute of pontifical law and, according to a decision of the Code Commission, local ordinaries can dispense from the second year of noviceship only when there is question of religious institutes of diocesan approval.[15]

According to this paragraph, the first year of novitiate of the extern sister novices is to be made, together with the cloistered novices, within the enclosure of the monastery. In the Statutes of 1931 it was stated that this first year of the novitiate, to be valid, had to be a complete and continuous year, spent within the cloister of the monastery.[16] Is the requirement that the novitiate be made within the monastic cloister still demanded for the validity of the novitiate under the Statutes of 1961? In the opinion of the writer, the making of the novitiate by extern sisters within the papal enclosure is demanded no longer for the validity, but only for

[13] "Novitiatus in duos annos protrahatur, quorum prior sit stricte canonicus et, licet novitiae huiusmodi lege clausurae papalis non teneantur, intra clausuram proprii Monasterii una cum novitiis vel, si agatur de Foederatione, alius etiam Monasterii Foederationis, peragendus erit. Hic, ut valeat, debet esse integer et continuus ad normam iuris."—*Statuta, 1961*, Art. 10, § 1.

[14] "Si longius tempus in constitutionibus pro novitiatu praescribatur, illud ad validitatem professionis non requiritur, nisi in eisdem constitutionibus aliud expresse dicatur."—Canon 555, § 2.

[15] Comm. Pont., 12 febr., 1935—*AAS*, XXVII (1935), 92.

[16] "Novitiatus duos annos durabit, quorum primus erit stricte canonicus. Hic, ut valeat, debet esse integer et continuus, intra claustra monasterii peragendus."—*Statuta, 1931*, Art. 27; cf. *supra*, p. 95.

the lawfulness of the novitiate. The present paragraph states clearly: "This year, in order to be valid, must be a complete and continuous year according to the norm of the law."[17] Thus, the Statutes of 1961 deliberately omit from the enumeration of specific requirements for a valid novitiate the demand that it be made within the enclosure, a demand which was explicitly included in that same enumeration as found in the Statutes of 1931. The Statutes of 1961 merely mention that the novitiate of the extern sisters is to be made together with the other novices in the enclosure; there is no express or equivalent invalidating clause in the law. Therefore, in conformity with the norm of canon 11, it must be concluded that the matter in question is no longer required for the validity of the novitiate.[18] It is true that, according to the norms of the Code of Canon Law, the novitiate, to be valid, must be made in the house of novitiate.[19] However, it is quite possible for the novices to dwell in the house of the novitiate without at the same time living in the novitiate proper, which, according to canon 564, § 1, is to be segregated from the part of the house wherein the professed religious dwell. Therefore, neither can this provision of the Code of Canon Law be cited as a proof for the invalidity of the novitiate of an extern sister which is made outside the papal enclosure.

The Statutes provide that the novitiate is to be made in the cloister of the novice's own monastery. Moreover, in the case of monasteries which are federated, the Statutes permit that the novitiate be made within the enclosure of some other monastry of the federation. This concession opens the way for the establishment of a common novitiate for the extern sisters of all the monasteries in the federation, should this prove desirable in a given case.

[17] "Hic, ut valeat, debet esse integer et continuus ad normam iuris." —*Statuta, 1961,* Art. 10, § 1.

[18] "Irritantes aut inhabilitantes eae tantum leges habendae sunt, quibus aut actum esse nullum aut inhabilem esse personam expresse vel aequivalenter statuitur."—Canon 11.

[19] Cf. canon 555, § 1, 3°.

Finally, although the extern sister novices are directed to dwell, during the first year of their novitiate, within the papal cloister, this paragraph specifically exempts them from the observance of the enclosure of the nuns. Therefore, in accordance with Article 4, § 2, they may, according to the judgment of the superioress, leave the cloister for external service, for the work of the monastery, or for some other just and reasonable cause.[20]

B. *Paragraph Two: Second Year of Novitiate*

> For the proper training of the novices in their external duties, the second year of the novitiate will ordinarily be made in the proper residence of the sisters under the vigilance of a specially designated sister, who is to give an account to the mistress of novices. Two months before profession, the novices shall refrain completely from external service and remain within the novitiate of the monastery so that there, under the direction of the mistress of novices, they may more peacefully prepare themselves for profession.[21]

The extern novices who are making the second year of their novitiate are to spend this time in the proper residence of the extern sisters, a practice which was already required under the Statutes of 1931.[22] Thus, it is evident that these novices will live outside the papal enclosure or within its confines, depending on whether the residence of the extern sisters is situated inside or outside the cloister of the nuns.[23] As the present paragraph indicates, the purpose of this arrangement whereby the novices who are making the second

[20] Cf. *supra*, pp. 155-157.

[21] "Ut novitiae in muneribus externis exerceantur, alter novitiatus annus ordinarie peragitur in propria Sororum habitatione, sub vigilantia Sororis ad hoc deputatae, quae Magistrae novitiarum rationem reddit. Duobus vero ante professionem mensibus, novitiae a servitio externo omnino abstineant et intra Monasterii novitiatum permaneant, ut ibi, sub directione Magistrae novitiarum, tranquillius ad professionem se praeparare valeant."—*Statuta, 1961*, Art. 10, § 2.

[22] *Statuta, 1931*, Art. 34; cf. *supra*, p. 96.

[23] Cf. *supra*, pp. 155-157.

year of their novitiate dwell together with the professed extern sisters is to provide adequate training for them in the duties they will be expected to perform as professed religious. Nevertheless, it must not be forgotten that the purpose of the second year of novitiate, according to the Sacred Congregation of Religious, must always remain the cultivation of the spiritual life; the external service performed by these novices must ever keep in mind this primary purpose of the novitiate.[24] One of the extern sisters is to exercise a special watchfulness and direction in regard to the second-year novices, and to keep the mistress of novices informed concerning their progress. According to the mind of the Sacred Congregation of Religious, this sister must be competent to instruct the novices in their duties, a religious who can teach and lead them by word and example.[25]

Two months before they are to make profession of their first vows, the novices who have been living in the quarters of the extern sisters are to return to the novitiate, once again living together with the other novices inside the papal enclosure. This procedure was already enjoined in the Instruction of 1921 of the Sacred Congregation of Religious,[26] and was incorporated into Article 36 of the Statutes of 1931. The situation of these novices is thus similar to that of the novices who are completing the first year of the novitiate, i.e., they dwell within the cloister of the monastery, but are not subject to the law of papal enclosure. During these two months, the novices are directed by the Statutes to refrain completely from external service so that, remaining in the novitiate, they may prepare for their profession under the direction of the mistress of novices. They may, of course, be employed within the enclosure for work, just as is the practice in regard to the cloistered novices. Moreover, although these novices may not be *employed in the service* of

[24] Instr. S. C. de Rel., 3 nov. 1921—*AAS*, XIII (1921), 539-540; cf. *supra*, p. 96, nota 126.

[25] *Loc. cit.*

[26] Instructio de secundo novitiatus anno—*AAS*, XIII (1921), 539-540.

the monastery, it seems that, in accord with Article 4, § 2, of the Statutes, they may be assigned to the performance of occasional work outside the enclosure, and the superioress may even permit them to go out of the cloister for other just and reasonable causes, provided the discipline and purpose of the novitiate are not violated.[27] This is possible since the Statutes order those novices who are preparing for profession to abstain only from *employment in the external service* of the monastery, i.e., more or less habitual employment outside the cloister. The Statutes themeslves make a distinction between such service and the other work of the monastery, as well as other just causes.[28]

C. *Paragraph Three: Second Year of Novitiate within Cloister*

> In accordance with the judgment of the superioress and her Council, and with the approval of the local ordinary and of the regular superior, if there be one, the novices can make also the second year of their novitiate within the monastery, without, however, being bound by the papal cloister.[29]

With the approval of the local ordinary and of the regular superior, if there be one, the superioress, after consultation with her Council, may determine that the second year of novitiate, as well as the first, be made within the enclosure. A papal indult is not required in this case, since there is question, not of placing the quarters of all the extern sisters inside the papal cloister, but simply of the novices of the second year. As has already been shown,[30] these novices

[27] Cf. *supra*, pp. 154-157.

[28] "Sororibus quae habitualiter intra clausuram degunt, cum lege clausurae papalis non teneantur, pro servitio vel alio opere externo Monasterii vel ob aliam iustam et rationabilem causam, de iudicio Antistitae licet e clausura egredi."—*Statuta, 1961*, Art. 4, §2.

[29] "De iudicio Antistitae eiusque Consilii et accedente beneplacito Ordinarii loci necnon Superioris Regularis, si adsit, etiam alter annus intra Monasterium peragi potest, quin novitiae lege clausurae papalis teneantur."—*Ibid.*, Art. 10, § 3.

[30] Cf. *supra*, pp. 156-157.

of the second year who are living within the enclosure without being bound by it may be allowed to go out of the cloister under the terms of Article 4, § 2, of these Statutes.

D. *Paragraph Four: Training of the Novices*

> In the training of the novices for the religious life, while instructions and conferences are to be given in the same way as is prescribed in the Constitutions for the novitiate of the nuns, special care should be taken with reference to the instructions regarding the external affairs and works for which the novices are destined.[31]

With regard to these conferences and instructions in the religious life, this paragraph guarantees the religious formation of the extern sisters in accordance with the Rule and Constitutions of the institute to which, according to Article 2, these sisters are obliged. The Statutes do not prescribe any definite means for imparting the instructions in the external affairs for which the extern sisters are destined. Therefore, each monastery is at liberty to adopt its own means, consistent with its own Constitutions and customs, for exercising the special care demanded in the present paragraph for the training of the extern sisters.

ARTICLE 2
ELEVENTH ARTICLE OF THE STATUTES: NOVITIATE MUST BE MADE FOR PROPER CLASS

> The novitiate made for extern sisters is not valid for choir nuns or for lay sisters; nor is the novitiate made for choir nuns or for lay sisters valid for extern sisters. (Canon 558)[32]

[31] "In informandis novitiis ad vitam religiosam, dum instructiones et collationes impertiuntur eodem prorsus modo ac de novitiatu Monialium in Constitutionibus praescriptum est, specialis cura habeatur in edocendis illis circa negotia et opera externa quibus destinantur." —*Statuta, 1961,* Art. 10, § 4.

[32] "Novitiatus pro Sororibus servitio externo addictis peractus pro Monialibus choristis vel conversis non valet, neque valet pro Sororibus externis novitiatus qui pro choristis vel conversis peractus est (can. 558).—*Ibid.,* Art. 11.

This article, as the text itself indicates, is simply an application of the law of the Code to monasteries of nuns which are served by extern sisters; it was already incorporated into the Statutes for Extern Sisters in 1931.[33] According to the norm of canon 558, in institutes where there are two classes of members, the novitiate made for one class is not valid for the other class. As the present Article indicates, there is question in these monasteries of nuns not of two, but of three, separate classes of religious, scil., choir nuns, lay sisters and extern sisters. This Article makes it abundantly clear that the extern sisters are members of a distinct third class within their Order, since the making of the novitiate for extern sisters lacks validity for profession on the part either of a choir nun or of a lay sister.[34]

Section III
Profession and Last Will

ARTICLE 1
TWELFTH ARTICLE OF THE STATUTES: PROFESSION

A. *Paragraph One: Duration of Vows*

> At the completion of the novitiate, the novice is to make profession of simple temporary vows for six years; these are to be renewed annually, at least during the first three-year period. At the end of six years, she is to make profession of simple perpetual vows or to return to the world.[35]

According to the norm of the Statutes, the first profession which is made at the termination of the novitiate is for one year. Moreover, the first two renewals of profession

[33] *Statuta, 1931,* Art. 28.

[34] Concerning this existence of three separate classes of religious within the Order, cf. *supra,* p. 129.

[35] "Expleto novitiatu, novitia professionem emittat votorum simplicium temporariorum per sex annos, quovis anno renovandam saltem primo triennio; elapso vero sexennio professionem votorum pariter simplicium, sed perpetuorum, emittat aut ad saeculum redeat."—*Statuta, 1961,* Art. 12, § 1.

must be made for periods of one year each. At the conclusion of the first three years of temporary profession, this paragraph allows an option with regard to the final three years of temporary vows, according to the pleasure of each monastery and the circumstances of individual cases. This option is based on the fact that an annual renewal is demanded "at least during the first three-year period." After that period it is, of course, permitted to continue the practice of an annual renewal of profession through the following three years. Or, if it be preferred, the profession for the final three years of temporary vows may be made at one and the same time. Under the terms of this Article, it would also be allowed to make a renewal of profession for the first year of this final period, followed by a single renewal for the final two years of temporary vows. This arrangement is similar to that set up in the Statutes of 1931. However, those former Statutes prescribed a mandatory renewal of temporary vows every year for each of the six years of temporary profession; there was no option in regard to the final three years of temporary profession. Moreover, the Statutes of 1931 provided for an extension of the period of temporary vows, up to six months beyond the six-year period.[36] This concession has been removed from the current Statutes, which demand that at the end of the six years of temporary vows the extern sister either make perpetual profession of simple vows, or return to the world.

1. Formalities for Admission to and Exclusion from Perpetual Profession

As has been pointed out, until the promulgation of the Statutes of 1961, the extern sisters were not directly bound to observe the Constitutions of the Order to which they belonged.[37] Thus, the formalities connected with admitting extern sisters to profession, or excluding them from the taking of vows, were governed not by the Constitutions of the institute, but by the Statutes for Extern Sisters. According-

[36] *Statuta, 1931,* Art. 44; cf. *supra,* pp. 97-98.

[37] Cf. *supra,* pp. 83-84, 106-107.

ingly, these Constitutions, seeking to regulate only the profession of the cloistered nuns, in most cases do not provide for the case of the extern sisters who take simple perpetual vows. Thus, for the validity of religious profession, the Constitutions of the Order of St. Clare, as well as the Constitutions of the Poor Clare Colettines, demand the approval of the Chapter of the monastery, stating that this vote is deliberative for simple profession, and only consultative in the case of solemn profession.[38] Since the perpetual profession made by the extern sisters is not solemn like that of the nuns, it would seem, at first consideration, on the basis of these Articles of the Constitutions, that the Chapter would have a deliberative vote in admitting extern sisters to final vows. However, in the opinion of the writer, the Constitutions are simply incorporating in these Articles the requirements of Canon Law in canon 575, § 2, that the vote of the Council or Chapter for the first temporary profession is deliberative, while that for the subsequent perpetual profession, be it solemn or simple, is only consultative.[39] Since, at the time these Constitutions were approved, the only perpetual profession envisioned was solemn profession, they simply omitted all reference to simple perpetual profession, which was made only by the extern sisters and was governed by the Statutes of 1931. However, now that the profession of the extern sisters is to be governed by the Constitutions, it seems that, especially in view of canon 575, § 2, cited above, the admission of extern sisters to perpetual profession should be regulated by the prescriptions of the Constitutions for solemn profession, and not by those for simple profession which, as is apparent from canon 575, seek to cover only the case of simple temporary vows. The Chapter, then, has only a consultative vote in admitting an extern sister to simple perpetual vows, unless, in some Order, the Constitutions should explicitly provide otherwise.

[38] *Const., OSC,* Art. 89, 2°; *Const., PCC,* Art. 235, 2°.

[39] "Suffragium Consilii seu Capituli pro prima professione temporaria est deliberativum; pro subsequente professione perpetua, sollemni vel simplici, est consultivum tantum."—Canon 575, § 2.

A similar situation arises in the consideration of the formalities prescribed in the Constitutions for excluding a sister from final profession. Both the Constitutions of the Order of St. Clare and those of the Poor Clare Colettines, for example, mention the power of the abbess of the monastery to exclude a religious from solemn profession. The former norms allow this to be done with the consultative vote of the Council, the latter with the deliberative vote of the Council.[40] However, for reasons similar to those presented above in connection with admission to final profession,[41] no mention at all is made of the formalities necessary for excluding a religious from taking simple perpetual vows. However, it seems that these norms of the Constitutions are simply adapting the prescriptions of the common law to their particular Order, making mention only of solemn profession, the sole type of perpetual profession envisioned by the Constitutions. This contention is supported by the fact that Article 101 of the Constitutions of the Order of St. Clare makes specific reference to canon 637, which refers to exclusion from perpetual profession, not distinguishing between simple and solemn vows.[42] Thus, unless the Constitutions of an institute provide otherwise, it would seem that the same formalities should be observed for the exclusion of an extern sister from simple perpetual profession as for the exclusion of a nun from solemn profession.

2. Formalities for Admission to and Exclusion from Renewal of Temporary Profession

Further problems in this regard are presented by the renewals of temporary profession prescribed by the Statutes. According to Article 19 of the Statutes of 1931, it was necessary for the superioress to obtain the consent of her Council before admitting the extern sisters to the annual

[40] *Const., OSC,* Art. 101; *Const., PCC,* Art. 247.

[41] Cf. *supra,* pp. 175-176.

[42] "... pariter religio ob iustas ac rationabiles causas eundem potest a renovandis votis temporariis vel ab emittenda professione perpetua excludere.—Canon 637.

renewal of temporary vows. Is the advice or consent of the Council or Chapter required for the admission of the extern sisters to the renewals of temporary profession which are prescribed in the present paragraph of the Statutes of 1961? The Statutes themselves contain no mention whatsoever of such a vote of the Council or Chapter. Moreover, the Constitutions of Orders of nuns, not at all envisioning the renewal of profession by extern sisters, treat only of the deliberative vote of the Council or Chapter for the first temporary profession, and the consultative vote before solemn vows.[43] Ordinarily, the only renewal of temporary profession to which the Constitutions advert is the one that receives mention in canon 574, § 2, i.e., when there is a desire to prolong the period of probation before their admission to perpetual vows by having them renew their temporary profession.[44] However, the Constitutions simply do not envision the set policy of a regular renewal of profession such as that which is prescribed in the Statutes of 1961. Therefore, it does not seem that the formalities prescribed by the Constitutions to prolong the period of probation in an individual case should be adopted in the matter under consideration. After all, the Constitutions are dealing with a cloistered nun who, at the conclusion of her three-year period of temporary vows is required, apart from the ordinary procedure of making solemn profession, to renew her temporary vows for a period which may range up to three years. The case at hand is rather that of an extern sister who, at the conclusion of a one-year period of temporary vows, is required according to the ordinary norms of the law to renew those vows.

The conclusion of all this is that, while the deliberative vote of the Council or Chapter is required for the admission of an extern sister to her first temporary profession, and the consultative vote of the Council or Chapter must be

[43] Cf. *supra*, p. 176.

[44] Hoc tempus legitimus Superior potest, renovata a religioso temporaria professione, prorogare, non tamen ultra aliud triennium."—Canon 574, § 2; cf. *Const., OSC,* Art. 87; cf. *Const., PCC,* Art. 233.

taken before a sister is admitted to perpetual profession,[45] no permission or consultation of the Council or the Chapter is prescribed for the admission of an extern sister to the prescribed renewal of temporary vows, unless the Constitutions of some institute should explicitly make provision to that effect. When these renewals are due, the superioress herself can simply allow them to take place without any further advice or consent. This opinion finds ample support among the authors, who point out that, although the Council or Chapter may have a controlling voice when there is question of first temporary profession, "the competent superior does not even need their advice for subsequent temporary professions necessary because of annual profession required by the constitutions."[46] In the case of the extern sisters, it is the Statutes of 1961 which require this annual profession, and not the Constitutions of the institute. However, it is the writer's contention that the Statutes for Extern Sisters are equivalent to the Constitutions in this regard. The text of Beste cited in footnote 46 bears this out, since he states flatly that, once first temporary profession has been made, the superioress is not bound by any law to seek the vote of her Council or Chapter for subsequent temporary professions, unless the Constitutions provide otherwise.[47] He makes no distinction whether the subsequent professions of temporary vows are prescribed by the Constitutions themselves or by some other body of law, such as the Statutes of 1961.

A final question concerns the formalities requisite for the exclusion of an extern sister from the annual renewal of temporary vows. As has been stated, the Constitutions

[45] Cf. canon 575, § 2; *Const., OSC,* Art. 89, 2°; *Const., PCC,* Art. 235, 2°; cf. *supra,* p. 176.

[46] Abbo-Hannan, *The Sacred Canons,* I, 594; "Unice pro *prima* professione temporaria suffragatio erit necessaria; igitur pro subsequentibus professionibus temporariis et pro prorogatione votorum superior nulla lege ad expetendum suffragium sui consilii vel capituli adigitur, nisi aliud in constitutionibus caveatur."—Beste, *Introductio in Codicem,* p. 387.

[47] *Loc. cit.*

of most Orders of nuns do not envision the policy of an annual renewal of temporary vows;[48] consequently there are no prescriptions in these Constitutions concerning the formalities to be observed in the exclusion of a sister from this renewal. Is it sufficient for the superioress simply to withhold permission for the sister in question to renew her vows, or is some further action demanded in such a case?

One solution to this problem is based upon the principle of law that, when an express prescription of law is wanting in a certain matter, the norm is to be taken from laws enacted in similar cases.[49] According to this view, should the Constitutions of a given institute contain prescribed formalities for the exclusion of a professed sister from final vows, these same formalities ought to be observed if it is desired to exclude an extern sister from the renewal of her temporary vows. For example, the Constitutions of the Poor Clare Colettines require the consent of the discreets before the abbess can exclude a nun from the profession of solemn vows.[50] With the application of this norm to the case of renewal of temporary profession by an extern sister, it would seem that a Colettine abbess would have to obtain the consent of her discreets to exclude an extern sister from the renewal of her temporary vows. Similarly, other Orders would have to observe such formalities as their Constitutions might require in order to effect this exclusion.[51] Indeed, this view is in accord with the practice which was prescribed by the Statutes of 1931, which demanded the consent of the Council for the superioress to refuse admittance to the renewal of temporary profession.[52]

However, arguments can also be advanced to show that, regardless of what procedure the Constitutions may specify

[48] Cf. *supra*, p. 178.

[49] Cf. canon 20.

[50] *Const.*, *PCC*, Art. 247.

[51] The Constitutions of the Order of St. Clare, for instance, demand not the consent of the discreets, but merely that the abbess consult them before acting.—*Const.*, *OSC*, Art. 101.

[52] *Statuta, 1931*, Art. 114.

for excluding a professed sister from final vows, the superioress herself, without the observance of any of these formalities, can exclude an extern sister from the renewal of her temporary vows. Even after the superioress, in accordance with canon 575, § 2, and the Constitutions of her institute, has obtained the favorable deliberative vote of the Council or Chapter to admit a novice to first temporary profession, she is still not coerced to admit that novice to profession.[53] In the present case, where neither the Statutes nor the Constitutions require the consent or the advice of the Council, it is *a fortiori* true that the superioress can, at her own discretion, exclude a sister from the renewal of her temporary profession.

Moreover, the Constitutions, such as the ones cited, which supply a norm of procedure in these cases of exclusion from the renewal of temporary vows bear reference solely to solemn vows, since they look only to the case of the profession of nuns. Inasmuch as laws which limit the free exercise of rights are subject to a strict interpretation,[54] it does not seem permissible to limit the right of the superioress to exclude a sister from the renewal of her temporary profession on the basis of a law which deals with solemn profession.

Finally, in cases where the Constitutions of an institute do not specify any intervention of the Council or Chapter at all, many authors admit that the superioress need not seek their advice for the exclusion of a sister even from perpetual profession.[55] Thus, there is no reason to main-

[53] "Can. 105, n. 1. 'Si consensus exigatur, Superior contra earundem votum invalide agit.' Vi huius statuti superior agere nequit contra votum consiliariorum (seniorum, assistentium, definitorum, coetus consultorum); minime vero cogitur exinde illud facere, quod maioritas consiliariorum faciendum deciderit; potest enim etiam ab agendo prorsus desistere."—Beste, *op. cit.*, p. 161; cf. Abbo-Hannan, *op. cit.* I, 153.

[54] Cf. canon 19.

[55] " 'Ab emittenda professione perpetua excludere.' Illud ius exclusionis competit superiori, quem determinant constitutiones, vel, silentibus constitutionibus, superiori, qui religiosum ad professionem

tain that she need seek such advice or consent regarding the question of exclusion from the renewal of temporary vows, when no such formalities are prescribed by the Constitutions. Indeed, the Constitutions do not even envision the taking of temporary vows on an annual basis.

B. *Paragraph Two: The Rite of Profession*

> In the making of profession, the rite of each monastery should be observed, with the necessary changes, however, being made. The first religious profession following the novitiate is made by the sisters within the cloister of the monastery; the renewals of vows, as well as the perpetual profession, are to be made outside of the cloister at the choir grille of the nuns. However, in accordance with the judgment of the superioress and her Council, and with the approval of the local ordinary and of the regular superior if there be one, these too may be made within the cloister.[56]

1. The Ceremony of Profession

According to the General Statutes of Nuns accompanying

admittere potest ad normam can. 543 coll. can. 575, § 2. Suffragium consilii vel capituli, licet satius et convenientius petatur, necessarium non esse videtur ad talem recusationem."—Beste, *op. cit.*, p. 430; Abbo-Hannan, *op. cit.*, I, 656. Schäfer contradicts this view: "Silentibus autem Constitutionibus competit exclusio sicut admissio Superiori maiori e can. 543, 575, § 1. . . . Cum pro admissione requiratur suffragium Consilii, consequenter pro negatione admissionis Consilium suffragare debet (cf. can. 543); in casu agitur de suffragio consultivo, proinde Superior non tenetur stare suffragiis Consilii sui (cf. can. 575, § 2)."—Schäfer, *De Religiosis ad normam Codicis Iuris Canonici* (ed. quarta aucta et emendata, Romae: Typis Polyglottis Vaticanis, Editrice "Apostolato Cattolico," 1947), n. 1522, pp. 905-906.

[56] "In emittenda professione servetur ritus sui cuiusque Monasterii, mutatis quae mutari debeant. Prima professio religiosa, quae novitiatum sequitur, emittitur a Sororibus intra clausuram Monasterii; renovationes autem votorum, sicut et professio perpetua, fiant extra clausuram, ad crates chori Monialium. Attamen, de iudicio Antistitae eiusque Consilii et de beneplacito Ordinarii loci atque Superioris Regularis, si adsit, hae etiam intra clausuram peragi possunt."—*Statuta, 1961*, Art. 12, § 2,

the Apostolic Constitution *Sponsa Christi,* the ancient solemn formulae for the consecration of virgins, which are in the Roman Pontifical, are reserved to nuns.[57] Therefore, if any of the profession ceremonies used by the nuns of the monastery contain portions which are drawn from the rite for the Blessing and Consecration of Virgins,[58] these particular sections are to be omitted from the profession ceremony of extern sisters. Ordinarily, such ceremonies would be found in the rite for solemn profession of the nuns of the monastery, but not in the rite for the first profession of nuns, nor in that for the perpetual profession of sisters in congregations of simple vows. Thus, the extern sisters in a given monastery would follow the rite in use for solemn profession in making their simple perpetual profession, changing or omitting those parts which are reserved to the nuns.[59] Moreover, since the Statutes themselves call

[57] Cf. "Statuta Generalia Monialium," Art. III, n. 3—*AAS,* XLIII (1951), 16.

[58] "De Benedictione et Consecratione Virginum," *Pontificale Romanum* (Mechliniae: Dessain, 1895), Pars I, pp. 180-207.

[59] For example, a comparison of the profession ceremonies in use in monasteries of the Order of St. Clare and the Poor Clare Colettines with the rite for the Blessing and Consecration of Virgins reveals the following facts. The rite for the profession of temporary vows in the Second Order of St. Francis ("Ritus Professionis Votorum Temporariorum in II Ordine," *Rituale Romano-Seraphicum Ordinis Fratrum Minorum* [ed. 3., Romae: Schola Typographica "Pax et Bonum," 1955], Titulus VI, Caput II, pp. 383-394) contains no sections which are strictly proper to the solemn consecration of virgins; therefore, in making their first profession, the Poor Clare extern sisters simply use this rite in its entirety. However, certain parts of the ceremony for solemn profession in the Second Order ("Ritus Professionis Votorum Solemnium in II Ordine," *Ibid.,* Caput III, pp. 398-419) do contain elements which are strictly proper to the solemn consecration of virgins, necessitating the following alterations when the rite is employed at the simple perpetual profession ceremony of extern sisters: a) the Litany of All Saints is omitted; b) the Solemn Preface for Virgins is omitted, and the preceding prayer of the Ritual, *Exaudi Domine,* is simply concluded in the tone of the Oration: *Per omnia saecula saeculorum.* R. *Amen;* c) the prayer at the presentation of the ring, *Desponso te,* is omitted and, in its place, at the presentation of the ring, is recited the formula given on p. 464 of the Roman-

for necessary changes to be made in the rite of profession for extern sisters, it appears that the local ordinary or religious superior who has jurisdiction over the monastery could, without further permission of the Holy See, authorize such alterations in the ceremony of an individual monastery. It would likewise seem desirable, in the case of federated monasteries, that the members agree definitely on the changes to be made in the ceremony for the profession of extern sisters, so as to establish a uniform norm of observance in all the monasteries of the federation.

With regard to the ceremony to be employed for the annual renewal of vows, the monastery may have a rite which is to be used when it is necessary for a nun to renew her temporary vows.[60] It seems that this rite should also be used for the annual renewal of temporary vows by the extern sisters, if it is available. In the absence of such a ceremony, a monastery might continue to follow the method used in the past for the renewal of profession by extern sisters, or possibly adapt the ceremony of temporary profession for the occasion.

2. The Place of Profession

The Statutes prescribe that the first temporary profession be pronounced within the papal enclosure. This is quite natural since, according to Article 10, § 2, the final two months of the novitiate are to be spent within the papal enclosure. However, it should be noted that extern novices, even though they are actually dwelling within the papal cloister, are never bound to the observance of the law of enclosure.[61] Therefore, should a given monastery have a longstanding custom to the contrary, it seems that, for just and reasonable causes, the extern novices may be permitted

Seraphic Ritual, *Accipe Soror carissima;* d) the presentation to the Abbess *(Suscipe, Reverenda Mater)* is to be omitted.

[60] The *Rituale Romano-Seraphicum,* Title VI, Chapter II, Appendix II, pp. 396-397, lists a ceremony for the renewal of temporary vows in the Second Order.

[61] Cf. *Statuta, 1961,* Art. 10, §§ 1 and 3.

to make their first temporary profession outside the enclosure.[62]

Great freedom is granted with regard to the renewals of temporary profession and the making of perpetual profession. Ordinarily these ceremonies are to take place outside the papal enclosure. But, in accordance with the judgment of the superioress, after consultation with her Council, and with the approval of the local ordinary and the regular superior, if there be one, these rites may also take place within the cloister of the monastery.

C. *Paragraph Three: Formula of Profession*

> The formula of profession should be the same as that of the nuns, with the necessary additions and changes; each profession of the sisters must be made in the quality of an extern sister according to the Rule and Constitutions of the monastery and the special Statutes for Extern Sisters approved by the Apostolic See.[63]

The formula of profession used by the extern sisters is to be essentially the same as that used by the nuns of the monastery, with certain additions and alterations. According to the present paragraph, the formula must express the fact that the profession is being made in the quality of an extern sister, according to the Rule and Constitutions of the monastery, as well as the Statutes for Extern Sisters which are approved by the Holy See. It seems that, just as the local or religious ordinary to whom a monastery is subject may authorize the necessary changes in the rite of profession,[64] so too he may approve the changes which

[62] Concerning the status of such longstanding customs, cf. *infra*, pp. 216-218.

[63] "Formula professionis eadem sit ac pro Monialibus, cum necessariis additionibus et mutationibus; quaelibet enim Sororum professio emitti debet in qualitate Sororis externo servitio Monasterii addictae, secundum Regulam et Constitutiones Monasterii, nec non propria Statuta pro Sororibus externis a Sede Apostolica approbata."—*Statuta, 1961*, Art. 12. § 3.

[64] Cf. *supra*, p. 184.

must be made in the wording of the form of profession. Here, too, it would be good for all the monasteries belonging to a federation to agree on the formulae of temporary and perpetual profession to be used by extern sisters in all member monasteries.[65]

[65] The formulae of profession used by the Order of St. Clare are found in the *Rituale Romano-Seraphicum,* pp. 389, 396-397, 409; Article 18 of the Constitutions of the Poor Clare Colettines gives the formula for the Colettines. Following are examples of formulae of profession, adapted from these sources. They contain the necessary additions and changes for extern sisters, in accordance with the demands of this paragraph of the Statutes:

1) *Formulae for the profession and renewal of temporary vows*

a) For the Order of St. Clare:

I, Sister N. N., intending to make this profession according to the norms of the Sacred Canons concerning simple and temporary vows to be made in our Order, do vow and promise to Almighty God, to the blessed Mary ever Virgin, to our blessed Father Francis, to our blessed Mother Clare, to all the Saints and to you, Mother (for one year; for two years; for three years) to live as an extern sister under the Rule of the Poor Sisters of our holy Mother Clare, confirmed by the Lord Pope Innocent, in obedience, in poverty and in chastity, according to the Sacred Canons, our Constitutions, and the Statutes for Extern Sisters approved by the Apostolic See.

b) For the Colettine Poor Clares:

I, Sister N. N., vow and promise God and the Blessed Virgin Mary, the blessed Francis, the blessed Clare, all the Saints and you, Mother, to observe for a period of (one; two; three) year(s), as an extern sister, the form of life of the poor Sisters of St. Clare, given by the same blessed Francis to the same St. Clare and confirmed by the Lord Pope Innocent IV, living in obedience, in poverty and in chastity, according to our Constitutions and the Statutes for Extern Sisters approved by the Apostolic See.

2) *Formulae for the profession of perpetual vows*

a) For the Order of St. Clare:

I, Sister N. N., do vow and promise to Almighty God, to the Blessed Mary ever Virgin, to our blessed Father Francis, to our blessed Mother Clare, to all the Saints and to you, Mother, to live during the whole time of my life as an extern sister under the Rule of the Poor Sisters of our holy Mother Clare, confirmed by the Lord Pope Innocent, in obedience, in poverty and in chastity, according to the Sacred Canons, our Constitutions, and the Statutes for Extern Sisters approved by the Apostolic See.

ARTICLE 2
THIRTEENTH ARTICLE OF THE STATUTES: THE PROPERTY OF THE SISTERS

A. *Paragraph One: Provisions during the Lifetime of a Sister and the Last Will*

> Without prejudice to the prescriptions of the Constitutions concerning the cession of administration and the disposition of the use and usufruct of property, according to the norm of the common law (canon 569, § 1, and canon 580, § 1), every professed sister of simple vows, whether perpetual or temporary, unless something else is provided in the Constitutions, retains the ownership of her property and her capacity to acquire other property. Lest, however, the extern sisters be solicitous about their property, even before their profession of temporary vows they shall freely make a civilly valid will concerning their present property as well as whatever may come to them in the future. They may not change this will without the permission of the Holy See or, if the matter is urgent and there is no time for recourse to the Holy See, without permission of the superioress of the monastery in which the sister is actually living.[66]

b) For the Colettine Poor Clares:

I, Sister N. N., vow and promise God and the Blessed Virgin Mary, the blessed Francis, the blessed Clare, all the Saints and you, Mother, to observe during the whole time of my life, as an extern sister, the form of life of the poor Sisters of St. Clare, given by the same blessed Francis to the same St. Clare and confirmed by the Lord Pope Innocent IV, living in obedience, in poverty and in chastity, according to our Constitutions and the Statutes for Extern Sisters approved by the Apostolic See.

[66] "Salvis Constitutionum praescriptis circa cessionem administrationis et dispositionem de usu et usufructu bonorum, ad norman iuris communis (can. 569, § 1, ac can. 580, § 1), quaelibet professa a votis simplicibus sive perpetuis sive temporariis, nisi aliud in iisdem Constitutionibus cautum sit, conservat proprietatem bonorum et capacitatem alia bona acquirendi. Sorores tamen externo servitio Monasterii addictae, ne sollicitae sint circa bona propria et iam ante professionem votorum temporariorum testamentum civiliter validum de bonis praesentibus vel forte obventuris libere condant; quod mutare ipsis non licebit sine venia S. Sedis, vel si res urgeat nec tempus suppetat ad

The norms of this paragraph, and indeed of this entire Article of the Statutes, are drawn from the common law and current practice of the Holy See, with some minor adaptations to fit the situation of the extern sisters. The text of the paragraph itself refers to the common law of canon 569, § 1, which regulates the cession of administration and the disposition of the use and usufruct of property. According to the Statutes, the prescriptions of the Constitutions of an institute are to take precedence in all of these matters, whereas canon 569, § 1, expressly accords such precedence to the Constitutions only in the matter of the disposition of use and usufruct. As a matter of fact, since these norms are to be observed whenever a novice makes temporary vows at her first profession, they are usually incorporated into the Constitutions of Orders of nuns, perhaps with some slight alterations.[67]

The declaration that each professed sister retains the ownership of her goods and the capacity to acquire additional goods is based on canon 580, § 1. This provision, too, is ordinarily included in the Constitutions of nuns, but without reference to simple perpetual profession, since the only perpetual profession envisioned in these Constitutions is a solemn profession.[68]

The remainder of this paragraph, treating of the making and changing of the civilly valid will, is drawn from canon 569, § 3, and canon 583, 2°.[69] Since the law does not require such a will and testament from members of Orders who are destined to make solemn profession, but only from

eam recurrendi, sine licentia Antistitae Monasterii in quo Soror actu degit."—*Statuta, 1961,* Art. 13, § 1.

[67] Cf. *Const., PCC,* Art. 224; cf. *Const., OSC,* Art. 80. These latter Constitutions add the provision that the cession of administration of a sister's goods may not be made to the monastery.

[68] *Const., OSC,* Art. 95; *Const., PCC,* Art. 239. Both these sets of Constitutions treat only of temporary vows, omitting any reference to perpetual vows.

[69] Concerning this matter of the will of canon 569, § 3, cf. O'Brien, "The Vow of Poverty and Its Civil Law Implications," *The Jurist,* XXI, No. 4 (October, 1961), 441-444.

novices in religious Congregations,[70] the Constitutions of Orders of nuns ordinarily make no mention at all of this will. Consequently, it was necessary to insert these regulations concerning the will into the Statutes of 1961, since the extern sisters do not make the complete renunciation of goods which is demanded by canon 581, § 1, for those who take solemn vows.

It is of interest to note that, although canon 569, § 3, contains no such prescription, the Statutes demand that the will made by the extern sisters before temporary vows be civilly valid. This is in accord with the mind and practice of the Sacred Congregation of Religious as evidenced in private replies, namely, that the will mentioned in canon 569, § 3, should be a valid one according to civil law, without prejudice to canon 1513, which safeguards the validity in canon law of wills in favor of pious causes, even though they may be civilly invalid. If a novice, before profession, can not make a will which is valid according to civil law, or if the will must be deferred for some other grave cause, it is best to simply omit the drafting of the will. Such a novice has no obligation to make a will until she can do so validly before the civil law, or until the excusing cause ceases. In fact, a will which is invalid at civil law is equally invalid at canon law, except as regards bequests to a pious cause. However, once civil capacity has been attained or the excusing cause has ceased, a civilly valid will must be made as soon as possible. In this case no permission of the Holy See is required, and the freedom of the testator is in no way restricted.[71]

An exception to the principle that a will which is invalid at civil law is likewise invalid at canon law is the case of a will made in favor of a pious cause. Even though a novice may lack testamentary capacity before the civil law, she may still make a will in favor of such a pious cause; this will

[70] Cf. Canon 569, § 3; cf. O'Brien, *ibid.*, p. 443.

[71] S. C. de Rel., 26 mart., 1957—Prot. N. 13101/56, in *Commentarium pro Religiosis*, XXXVII (1958), 56; cf. *Gutiérrez*, "De Testamento Novitiorum," *Ibid.*, pp. 56-58; cf. O'Brien, *ibid*, pp. 442-443.

is canonically valid and binding in conscience, even though the civil law may consider it invalid.[72] The present paragraph of the Statutes which demands that the will made by the extern novices be civilly valid should, in the opinion of the writer, be applied to wills in favor of pious causes in the light of the norm of canon 1513, § 2: "In last wills favoring the Church, there shall be observed, if it can be done, the formalities required by the civil law; but if they were not observed, the heirs shall be admonished to carry out the intention of the testator." Thus, an extern novice who desires to make a will in favor of a pious cause should, if at all possible, observe the formalities of the civil law. If, however, for some reason the observance of these civil formalities was not possible, the will should later be ratified before the civil law when this becomes possible.[73]

Once a valid will has been made, it may not be changed without the permission of the Holy See. The Statutes state that in urgent cases, when there is no time to apply to the Holy See, the permission can be granted by the superioress of the monastery. This is in accord with the demand of canon 583, 2°, which requires that permission be obtained from the major superior in urgent cases, since the superioress of an independent monastery, even though it may belong to a monastic congregation or a federation, is considered a major superior.[74]

B. *Paragraph Two: Renunciation of Property Forbidden*

> Without prejudice to an indult granted by the Holy See, the sisters can not renounce their property or alienate it without compensation.[75]

The norm of this paragraph is taken from the law of canon 583, 1°, with the provision that, if any institute should

[72] Cf. canon 1513, § 2; O'Brien, *ibid.*, p. 443.

[73] *Loc. cit.*

[74] Cf. canons 488, 8°; 490.

[75] "Salvo indulto a S. Sede concesso, ipsae Sorores nequent bonis suis renuntiare seu titulo gratuito eadem abdicare."—*Statuta, 1961,* Art. 13, § 2.

have an indult from the Holy See in this matter, that indult is to retain its force.[76] Inasmuch as this canon treats of the case of religious Congregations in which simple perpetual vows are taken, its norm is not ordinarily incorporated into the Constitutions of nuns, since the latter provide for the renunciation of goods to be made before solemn profession according to the norm of canon 581, § 1.[77] The Statutes, therefore, wishing to make provision for extern sisters who take simple perpetual vows without a renunciation of possessions, include here the same norm as that which is applied in religious congregations, wherein the members make profession of simple vows.

C. *Paragraph Three: Changes in Cession and Disposition*

> The cession or disposition which is treated in canon 569 can be changed by a professed sister, not indeed at her own choice, unless the Constitutions allow this, but with the permission of her superioress as well as of the local ordinary and of the regular superior if there be one, provided the change, if it involves a notable part of her property, is not made in favor of the monastery. In the case of her departure from the monastery the cession and disposition lose their force.[78]

The norms of this paragraph are taken from the law of canon 580, § 3, and are frequently incorporated into the Constitutions of nuns.[79] It is noteworthy that the Code does not require the permission of the superioress of the monas-

[76] "Professis a votis simplicibus in Congregationibus religiosis non licet per actum inter vivos dominium bonorum suorum titulo gratioso abdicare."—Canon 583, 1°.

[77] *Const., OSC,* Art. 106; *Const., PCC,* Art. 242.

[78] "Cessionem vel dispositionem de qua in can. 569 professa mutare potest, non quidem proprio arbitrio, nisi Constitutiones id sinant, sed de Antistitae, necnon de Ordinarii loci et Superioris Regularis, si adsit, licentia, dummodo mutatio, quae notabilem bonorum partem respiciat, non fiat in favorem Monasterii; per discessum autem e Monasterio eiusmodi cessio ac dispositio vim habere desinit."—*Statuta, 1961,* Art. 13, § 3.

[79] *Const., OSC,* Art. 96; *Const., PCC,* Art. 240.

tery in order to make this change, nor is such a requirement by any means universal in the Constitutions of the various institutes.[80] However, in the case of extern sisters, the present paragraph quite clearly demands not only the permission of the local ordinary and the regular superior, if the monastery is subject to one, but also that of the superioress of the monastery. Thus, if an extern sister wishes to make a change in her cession or disposition, she must obtain the permission of the superioress of her monastery, whether or not this formality is prescribed by the Constitutions of her Order.

D. *Paragraph Four: Acquisition of Property for the Monastery*

> Whatever a sister acquires by her own industry, or in consideration of the monastery, she acquires for the monastery.[81]

This norm is taken from canon 580, § 2, and is frequently incorporated into the Constitutions of nuns.[82]

[80] Neither of the Articles cited in footnote 79 makes mention of such a requirement.

[81] "Quidquid autem industria sua vel intuitu Monasterii acquirit, Monasterio acquirit."—*Statuta, 1961*, Art. 13, § 4.

[82] *Const., OSC*, Art. 95; *Const., PCC*, Art. 239.

CHAPTER XI

THE STATUTES OF 1961—CHAPTER III: CONCERNING THE RELIGIOUS DISCIPLINE OF THE EXTERN SISTERS

This Chapter, in six Articles, treats of the religious discipline which is to be observed in regard to the extern sisters.[1]

SECTION I
GOVERNMENT AND COMMON LIFE OF THE EXTERN SISTERS

ARTICLE 1
FOURTEENTH ARTICLE OF THE STATUTES: AUTHORITY OF THE SUPERIORESS

A. *Paragraph One: Subjection to the Superioress*

> The sisters, like the nuns, are subject to the superioress of the monastery in all things, in regard both to religious discipline and to the service they are to render. It is the duty of the superioress to prescribe the order of their spiritual exercises and to provide with motherly care whatever is necessary for the common life and for their individual needs.[2]

The prescriptions of this paragraph are simply the logical consequence of the fact that the extern sisters are members of the Order and the monastery they serve. Quite naturally they are subject to the superioress of the monastery, who is obliged, in virtue of her office and according to the Con-

[1] *Statuta, 1961,* Caput III, "De Sororum Servitio Externo Addictarum Disciplina."

[2] "Sorores, haud secus ac Moniales, Antistitae Monasterii subiciuntur in omnibus, sive quoad religiosam disciplinam sive quoad servitium ab ipsis praestandum. Antistitae autem est habitualiter ordinem exercitiorum Sororibus praescribere necnon quidquid necessarium eis ad vitam sive communem sive individualem ducendam materna cura providere."—*Ibid.,* Art. 14, § 1.

stitutions of each monastery, to exercise maternal care over all her subjects.[3]

B. *Paragraph Two: Supervision of the Extern Sisters*

> The superioress can delegate one of the extern sisters or a nun, choosing a religious who is prudent, of mature age and perpetually professed to see to it that everything pertaining to discipline or work is conducted properly according to the directions of the superioress. This sister shall prudently report all called for information to the superioress, or to some other nun designated for this, and from her receive instructions.[4]

The norm of this paragraph is basically the same as Article 10 of the Statutes of 1931.[5] However, the new Statutes permit the task of overseeing the work and religious discipline of the extern sisters to be performed not only by one of the extern sisters, but also, if it be so desired, by one of the cloistered nuns. But the Statutes of 1961 do not grant the nun who is appointed to this office permission to leave the papal enclosure. Ordinarily, therefore, it would seem better to appoint an extern sister to fulfil this office. However, according to the Instruction *Inter cetera,* the need of looking after the house where the extern sisters live is a just and canonical cause for seeking certain dispensations and habitual faculties from the Holy See.[6] Therefore, should it seem desirable to appoint a nun to fill this office, an indult should be obtained from the Holy See to allow her to leave the enclosure for her supervision of the extern sisters.

[3] *Ibid.*, Art. 2; cf. *supra*, pp. 129, 132-133.

[4] "Deputare poterit Antistita unam ex Sororibus servitio externo addictis vel Monialem prudentia et aetate provectam votorumque perpetuorum professam, cuius munus sit vigilandi ut omnia, quae ad disciplinam et servitium spectent, ordinate iuxta ipsius Antistitae mandata procedant. Haec vero Soror ad Antistitam vel ad aliam Monialem ad hoc designatam prudenter ea referat quae referenda sunt et ab illa instructiones recipiat."—*Statuta, 1961,* Art. 14, § 2.

[5] Cf. *supra*, p. 92.

[6] Instructio *Inter cetera*, n. 24, 5°; *Statuta, 1961,* Art. 5; cf. *supra*, pp. 116, 159.

ARTICLE 2

FIFTEENTH ARTICLE OF THE STATUTES: RELIGIOUS EXERCISES

A. *Paragraph One: Exercises of the Rule and Constitutions*

> The superioress should see to it that the extern sisters perform the religious exercises which are indicated in the Rule and the Constitutions, with the exception of those which are proper to the choir nuns.[7]

Although many of the exercises performed by religious are the same in all institutes, the precise determination of the exercises required of the members of a given institute is made in the Rule and the Constitutions, according to the spirit and character of the community concerned.[8] The Statutes of 1931 contained detailed regulations concerning the religious exercises of the extern sisters.[9] The present Statutes simply point to the norms of the Rule and the Constitutions to which the extern sisters are bound in virtue of their profession in the Order. The superioress has the obligation to see to it that the extern sisters perform those religious exercises which the Rule and the Constitutions of the institute

[7] "Curet Antistita ut Sorores servitio externo Monasterii addictae exercitia pietatis peragant quae in Regula et Constitutionibus continentur, exceptis illis quae propria sunt Monialium choro addictarum." —*Statuta, 1961*, Art. 15, § 1.

[8] A survey of the Constitutions of the Order of St. Clare and of the Poor Clare Colettines indicates that the following may be considered religious exercises prescribed by the Constitutions of the institute: attendance at Holy Mass and reception of Holy Communion; recitation of the Divine Office or the Office of the "*Paters*"; meditation; spiritual reading; confession; visits to the Blessed Sacrament; taking of the discipline; chapter of faults; recitation of the Rosary; Way of the Cross; particular and general examinations of conscience; special devotions, e.g. in honor of St. Clare; devotional renewal of vows and various annual consecrations; days of recollection; retreats; processions; Holy Week services; conferences on the religious life; instructions in Christian doctrine. These and similar occupations fall under the general classification of religious exercises *(exercitia pietatis)*.

[9] *Statuta, 1931*, Cap. V et VI, Art. 72-87.

prescribe, with the exception of those which are proper to the nuns.

Although the exercises proper to choir nuns may vary from one Order to another, the one exercise which is generally proper to them is the recitation of the Divine Office, not only in choir, but also privately, if they are solemnly professed.[10] Hence, in virtue of this paragraph, the recitation of the Divine Office is not obligatory for extern sisters, unless the Rule or the Constitutions of an institute should prescribe the Office as the proper prayer not only of the choir nuns, but of all the members of the institute, including the extern sisters. The Statutes do not specify a particular form of Office to be used by the extern sisters; they leave this matter entirely to the judgment of the individual Orders. The Rule or Constitutions of an institute may contain some prescriptions concerning this matter. In many cases, however, these particular norms, promulgated at a time when the extern sisters were not even envisioned as members of the Order, will contain no mention at all of the Office to be said by these religious. In such cases, should the Constitutions prescribe a form of Office to be said by the lay sisters (*conversae*) of the institute, it seems that this same Office might fittingly be adopted for use also by the extern sisters.[11] Should the Constitutions make no such provision, it would be the function of the superioress, together with her

[10] Cf. canon 610; *Const., OSC*, Art. 152-153; *Const., PCC*, Art. 40-41.

[11] Chapter III of the Rule of St. Clare describes the Office of the lay sisters, which consists of the recitation of the *Pater noster* seventy-six times. Mention of this Office is made in the Constitutions of the Order of St. Clare, Article 153, and in the Constitutions of the Poor Clare Colettines, Article 41. The Rule of St. Clare, in Chapter III, clearly envisions some Office as obligatory for all the religious. Since the extern sisters are not bound to recite the Divine Office, which is proper to the choir nuns, it is reasonable to conclude that the Office to which the extern sisters are bound is that of the *Pater noster*. This conclusion is in complete accord with longstanding practice and tradition, since the Poor Clare extern sisters have for many years considered the Office of the "*Paters*" as their proper Office.

Council, to decide what Office is to be recited by the extern sisters, choosing perhaps the Little Office of the Blessed Virgin, a shortened vernacular form of the Divine Office, or even, in a proper case, the Divine Office recited by the nuns who are bound to choir.[12]

No matter which Office is appointed for the extern sisters, it does not seem that they are under a grave obligation to recite it, since it is not the practice of the Holy See to place such an obligation upon sisters of simple vows. Rather, the degree of obligation is determined by the particular law of each institute, thus making the recitation of the Office binding at most under pain of venial sin, and in most cases not under pain of sin at all.[13] Thus, the degree of gravity of this obligation of extern sisters to recite the Office is inferred not from the gravity of the obligation in this matter as it rests upon nuns of the Order,[14] but rather from the obligations of members of religious congregations who, like the extern sisters, take only simple vows.[15]

B. *Paragraph Two: Communion and Confession*

> Also with regard to Holy Communion and to confession, the prescriptions contained in the Constitutions for the nuns are to be observed.[16]

[12] The authority of the superioress to make such a decision is based upon Article 14, § 1, of these Statutes, wherein she is given the duty to determine the order of the spiritual exercises performed by the extern sisters.

[13] "Apud Congregationes religiosas obligatio chori ex solis Constitutionibus metienda est.... Nullatenus ergo inducenda est in omnes religiones quae ex Constitutionibus choro obligantur, obligatio gravis, quae ex praesenti canone colligeretur (contra Augustine, in h. 1.)."—Vermeersch-Creusen, *Epitome Iuris Canonici* (3 vols., 7 ed., Mechliniae-Romae: Dessain, 1949), I, n. 768, p. 581.

[14] *Loc. cit.*

[15] This same basis is employed by the Statutes themselves in determining the obligations of the extern sisters. Thus, the common cloister set up by Art. 3, par. 1, is that prescribed for the houses of Congregations of women by Canon 604. The will to be made according to Art. 13, par. 1, is the same as that prescribed for novices in religious Congregations by Canon 569, par. 3.

[16] "Pro S. Communione et pro Confessione pariter quae in Constitu-

The Statutes of 1931 devoted an entire Chapter of eleven Articles to these matters.[17] Since the extern sisters are now bound to the observance of the Constitutions, the Statutes of 1961 merely direct that the extern sisters observe the norms contained in the Constitutions, in the same manner as these are observed by the cloistered nuns.

C. *Paragraph Three: Occasional Confessions*

> For an occasional confession the sisters enjoy the right which is granted to women religious not bound by the papal cloister, namely, if a sister, for her peace of conscience, goes to a confessor approved for women by the local ordinary, the confession is valid and licit, when made in a church or an oratory, even a semi-public one, or in any other place legitimately designated for the confessions of women or of women religious, or legitimately designated as such for a particular confession (can. 522).[18]

For the most part, as the reference cited in the Statutes themselves indicates, this paragraph simply incorporates the norms of canon 522, which treats of the occasional confessor. Although the application of this law to the case of the extern sisters is essentially the same as for other religious, certain points in this paragraph are worthy of comment.

The Statutes speak of the right to approach an occasional confessor as "the right which is granted to women religious not bound by the papal cloister.[19] Does this mean to

tionibus pro Monialibus praescribuntur serventur."—*Statuta, 1961*, Art. 15, § 2.

[17] *Statuta, 1931*, Cap. V, Art. 72-82.

[18] "Pro Confessione occasionali peragenda frui possunt facultatibus quibus religiosis clausurae papali non obstrictis uti licet, nempe: si Soror ad suae conscientiae tranquillitatem, confessarium adeat ab Ordinario loci pro mulieribus approbatum, confessio peracta in qualibet ecclesia vel oratorio etiam semipublico vel alio loco pro confessionibus mulierum vel religiosarum legitime destinato aut etiam per modum actus designato, valida et licita est (can. 522)."—*Statuta, 1961*, Art. 15, § 3.

[19] "... facultatibus quibus religiosis clausurae papali non obstrictis uti licet, ..."—*Loc. cit.*

imply that there are no occasions when a nun bound by the obligation of the papal enclosure would be able to make use of the concessions of canon 522? In the opinion of the writer, the Statutes do not at all mean to exclude the possibility of an occasional confession by a nun bound to the papal cloister. Rather, they simply indicate that, as a matter of fact, in the ordinary course of events, such occasional confessions are usually made by women religious who are not bound by the papal enclosure, since the opportunity for cloistered nuns to make such a confession is indeed rather limited. True, the law of canon 522 treats of a woman religious who "*goes to* a confessor approved by the local ordinary for the confessions of women."[20] Now, while it is true that a cloistered nun cannot leave the enclosure in order to seek out an occasional confessor, it is also true that the Code Commission has declared that, under the provisions of canon 522, the religious herself may call the occasional confessor to the monastery to hear her confession in a legitimate place.[21] It is not at all difficult to imagine a situation in which a cloistered nun would legitimately request that an occasional confessor come to the monastery to hear her confession. For this reason it seems better to maintain that, when the Statutes mention the right which is granted to women religious not bound by the papal cloister, they are simply making reference to the more usual situation in which the norms of canon 522 are applied.

Both canon 522 and the present paragraph list churches and semi-public oratories as places where an occasional confession can be both licitly and validly made. In addition, the Statutes add that such a confession is also valid and licit if made in another place legitimately destined for the

[20] "Si . . . aliqua religiosa . . . confessarium adeat ab Ordinario loci pro mulieribus approbatum . . ."—Canon 522.

[21] "An verbum 'adeat' canonis 522 sit ita intelligendum ut confessarius advocari nequeat per ipsam religiosam ad loca confessionibus mulierum vel religiosarum legitime destinata. R. Negative."—Comm. Pont., 28 dec. 1927—*AAS*, XX (1928), 61; cf. Beste, *op. cit.*, p. 345; Abbo-Hannan, *op. cit.*, I, 537.

confessions of women or women religious, or in a place which is legitimately designated as such for a particular confession.[22] The additions to this Article of the Statutes are the result of two interpretations given by the Pontifical Commission. The first of these replies confirms the fact that occasional confessions are licit and valid only if they are made in a church, a semi-public oratory, *or in a place legitimately destined for hearing the confessions of women.*[23] The second and later interpretation states that the place legitimately destined for the confessions of women religious, mentioned in the former reply, is to be understood not only of a place habitually designated for the hearing of these confessions, but also of a place designated for individual confessions (*per modum actus*) or chosen according to the norm of canon 910, § 1.[24] The expanded number of places for licit and valid occasional confession over and above those mentioned in canon 522 is, then, a reflection of the official interpretations of the Code Commission. These interpretations, which are included in the Statutes, are applied to the extern sisters in the same way as to other women religious.[25]

[22] "... confessio peracta ... alio loco confessionibus mulierum vel religiosarum legitime destinato aut etiam per modum actus designato, valida et licita est."—*Statuta, 1961*, Art. 15, § 3.

[23] "Utrum verba canonis 522: *confessio in qualibet ecclesia vel oratorio etiam semipublico peracta valida et licita est,* ita intelligenda sint, ut confessio extra ea loca peracta non tantum illicita, sed etiam invalida sit. Resp. Canon 522 ita est intelligendus, ut confessiones, quas ad suae conscientiae tranquillitatem religiosae peragunt apud confessarium ab Ordinario loci pro mulieribus approbatum, licitae et validae sint, dummodo fiant in ecclesia vel oratorio etiam semipublico, aut in loco ad audiendas confessiones mulierum *legitime* destinato."—Comm. Pont., 24 nov. 1920—*AAS*, XII (1920), 575.

[24] "Utrum verba: *loco legitime destinato,* de quibus in interpretatione diei 24 nov. 1920 ad can. 522, intelligenda sint tantum de loco habitualiter designato, an etiam de loco per modum actus designato vel ad normam can. 910, § 1, electo. Resp. Negative ad primam partem; affirmative ad secundam."—Comm. Pont., 12 febr. 1935—*AAS*, XXVII (1935), 92.

[25] Beste, *op. cit.*, pp. 346-347; Abbo-Hannan, *op. cit.*, I, 537-538; Vermeersch-Creusen, *op. cit.*, I, n. 644, p. 482.

D. *Paragraph Four: Performing Spiritual Exercises inside the Cloister*

> With the consent of the superioress and her Council, and the approval of the local ordinary and of the regular superior if there be one, the spiritual exercises mentioned in § 1 may be performed by the extern sisters inside the cloister of the nuns.[26]

The situation envisioned in this paragraph is obviously one in which the dwelling place of the extern sisters is located outside the papal enclosure; in monasteries where the sisters live within the papal enclosure, no further permission or formalities are demanded to admit them to religious exercises together with the nuns.[27] With the observance of certain formalities, the extern sisters who live outside the cloister of the nuns may be admitted to the enclosure for the religious exercises mentioned in § 1 of this same Article 15, i.e., those exercises which are listed in the Rule and the Constitutions.[28] One of the formalities demanded is the consent of the superioress and her Council.[29] In the view of the writer, the wording of this requirement demands the consent not only of the superioress herself, but also the consent of her Council, which therefore has a deliberative vote in the matter. The wording used here differs from such phrases as "according to the judgment of the superioress and her Council," and "the superioress with her Council," which indicate only consultative intervention on the part of the Council.[30] Here the Latin construction specifies not merely the judgment of the superioress in conjunction with her Council, but requires the consent of the superioress and her

[26] "Pia exercitia spiritualia, de quibus supra in par. 1, consentiente Antistita eiusque Consilio et approbante Ordinario loci ac Superiore Regulari, si adsit, Sorores servitio externo addictae intra clausuram Monialium peragere poterunt."—*Statuta, 1961*, Art. 15, § 4.

[27] *Ibid.*, Art. 4, § 1; cf. *supra*, pp. 151-152.

[28] "... exercitia pietatis peragant quae in Regula et Constitutionibus continentur, ..."—*Ibid.*, Art. 15, § 1.

[29] "... consentiente Antistita eiusque Consilio ..."—*Ibid.*, § 4.

[30] Cf. *supra*, pp. 142-143.

Council as well. This interpretation is supported by the fact that Article 3, § 2, of the Statutes clearly demands that the superioress obtain the consent of her Council to permit the extern sisters to enter the enclosure occasionally for reasons of devotion, e.g., religious exercises.[31] Now if, under the prescriptions of Article 3, § 2, the consent of the Council is obviously required for the superioress to admit the extern sisters within the enclosure even *occasionally* for religious exercises, it would hardly be consistent to maintain that, after only consulting her Council and without their consent, the same superioress, under the norms of Article 15, § 4, could admit them to the enclosure *regularly and constantly* for religious exercises, and this despite the fact that the law specifically calls for the consent of the superioress and her Council.

This paragraph of Article 15 provides expressly for those religious exercises alone which are listed in the Rule and the Constitutions. Does this mean that permission can not, in virtue of the Statutes, be granted to the extern sisters to enter the enclosure for religious exercises which are not specifically mentioned in the Rule and the Constitutions? In view of the generous and liberal spirit which pervades these Statutes, such a strict interpretation does not seem to be at all necessary. Moreover, it is a general principle that laws which grant favors such as this are subject to a broad interpretation.[32] Thus, according to this view, among the exercises for which the extern sisters may enter the enclosure under the provisions of the present paragraph are included not only the exercises prescribed by the Rule and the Constitutions, but also those which are performed according to the customs and usage of individual monasteries.

[31] "... ius est Antistitae, de consensu sui Consilii atque probante Ordinario loci et Superiore Regulari, si adsit, permittendi ut Sorores servitio externo addictae interdum intra clausuram Monasterii, pietatis vel instructionis causa, sicuti et ad convescendum et animos recreandos, cum Monialibus conveniant, ..."—*Statuta, 1961,* Art. 3, § 2; cf. *supra,* pp. 137-138.

[32] "Favores convenit ampliari."—Regula 15, R. J. in VI°; cf. can. 19.

ARTICLE 3
SIXTEENTH ARTICLE OF THE STATUTES: COMMON LIFE

> As far as possible, the religious duties mentioned in the preceding Article shall be performed in common by the sisters.
> The sisters should also eat and recreate in common.[33]

The norms of this Article are almost identical with the prescriptions which were embodied in Articles 91 and 92 of the Statutes of 1931.[34] Naturally, the practice of the exercises of the common life mentioned in this Article will depend upon whether the residence of the extern sisters is located outside the papal enclosure, or within the confines of the cloister of the nuns. In the latter case, the extern sisters will quite naturally perform their religious exercises, eat and recreate together with the cloistered nuns. In cases where the extern dwelling is located outside the papal cloister, it has been shown that, according to the norms of Article 3, § 2, the extern sisters may occasionally be allowed to enter the enclosure for purposes of devotion or instruction, as well as for meals and recreation.[35] Moreover, under the provisions of Article 15, § 4, they may be permitted to enter the enclosure regularly to perform their spiritual exercises together with the nuns.[36] Apart from the times when the extern sisters enter the enclosure under the provisions of these Articles, they will perform their spiritual exercises, eat and recreate in their own quarters. The present Article requires that at these times, insofar as this is possible, the religious exercises mentioned in Article 15, § 1, be performed in common; moreover, when the extern sisters eat and

[33] "Pietatis officia de quibus in superiori articulo, in communi, quantum fieri potest, a Sororibus persolvantur.
In communi quoque Sorores se reficiant atque recreentur."—*Statuta, 1961,* Art. 16.

[34] Cf. *supra,* p. 102.

[35] Cf. *supra,* pp. 136-142.

[36] Cf. *supra,* pp. 201-202.

recreate in their own quarters apart from the nuns, they are to do so in common. In this manner the observance of the common life is safeguarded for the extern sisters who dwell outside the papal cloister, and constitute a distinct section of the community which does not share fully in the common life of the cloistered religious.

It will be noted that this Article requires that the religious exercises be performed in common *insofar as this is possible,* a condition which is not included in the prescription that the sisters eat and recreate in common. One possible reason for this difference could be the fact that the work and duties of the sisters will require that they sometimes miss the common religious exercises; indeed, their duties may make it impossible to have some of the exercises in common at all. This will not so readily be the situation in regard to meals and recreation, although here too there will certainly be occasions when it will not be possible for all the extern sisters to be present.

ARTICLE 4
SEVENTEENTH ARTICLE OF THE STATUTES: ABSTINENCE AND FASTING

> With regard to the laws of abstinence and fasting proper to each Order by reason of the Rule and Constitutions, the superioress should treat the extern sisters maternally, dispensing in these matters insofar as there is real need. It is desirable that in each Order, or at least in each federation, there be set up some uniform norm for the observance of such particular laws by the extern sisters.[37]

Since the extern sisters are members of the Order and monastery they serve, and, as such, are bound to observe the

[37] "Antistita materne se gerat cum Sororibus servitio externo addictis quoad leges abstinentiae et ieiunii cuique Ordini proprias vi Regulae aut Constitutionum, dispensando in illis, quatenus vere opus sit. Optandum est ut in singulis Ordinibus aut saltem Foederationibus norma quaedam aequalis quoad observantiam huiusmodi legum propriarum, ad Sorores quod pertinent, statuatur."—*Statuta, 1961,* Art. 17.

Rule and the Constitutions of the institute, they are also obliged to observe the abstinence and fasting of the Order as it is prescribed for them in the Rule and Constitutions.[38] In other words, they are bound to abstain and to fast in the same manner as the cloistered nuns, unless a dispensation is granted in their favor.

According to the tenor of this Article, the superioress should not be hesitant to grant dispensations from the abstinence and the fasts which are prescribed by the Rule and the Constitutions whenever a real need exists. Thus, a dispensation is certainly in order on days when the manual labor performed by the extern sisters is especially heavy and tiring, as well as on days when it is necessary for them to do a good deal of travelling about outside the monastery. Should it be necessary for the extern sisters to take a meal outside the monastery, the superioress might well dispense them from the observance of the abstinence and fasting of the Order, in order to obviate undue inconveniences and difficulty.

According to the mind of the Statutes, each Order, or at least each federation, should establish a uniform norm for the observance by the extern sisters of the abstinence and fasts prescribed by the Rule and the Constitutions, always allowing some leeway for differences in individual monasteries. Should the Order or the federation set up no norm of this kind, the superioress with the advice of her Council might well establish a general norm to be observed by the extern sisters of the monastery. In formulating such a norm, the best policy will be to require that they observe, as closely as possible, the same general practice in this regard as the nuns, especially where the extern sisters eat together with the nuns. This policy, of course, must always leave room for execptions in individual cases and for charitable dispensations in the situations mentioned in the preceding paragraph. It follows, then, that the degree to which the extern sisters are bound to observe the abstinence and fast-

[38] *Ibid.*, Art. 2.

ing of the Rule and the Constitutions will depend, in practice, on the decision of the superioress in regard to the dispensations to be granted.

Section II
Discipline of the Cloister

Article 1
Eighteenth Article of the Statutes: Leaving and Remaining Outside the Monastery

A. *Paragraph One: Conditions for Leaving the Monastery*

> The sisters should remain at home, diligently engaging in prayer and work; and they should not go outside except to care for the business of the monastery or for some other reasonable cause, and with the express permission of the superioress; nor should they leave the house alone without a just cause and the permission of the superioress. When they go out, they should be mindful of their state in their conduct and speech with seculars; and, by manifesting modesty, piety, meekness, urbanity, and the greatest reverence, they should be a source of edification to others in all their actions.[39]

1. Reasons for Leaving the Monastery

The present paragraph specifies the conditions under which the extern sisters may be permitted to leave the precincts of the monastery. First of all, they may be permitted to go out of the house whenever it is necessary for them to transact business for the monastery. Examples of this are very numerous, including such matters as shopping, questing for alms and, in general, anything which may be necessary or useful for the smooth functioning of the monastery. The

[39] "Domi maneant Sorores, orationi et labori diligenter incumbentes, neque foras exeant nisi ad negotia Monasterii agenda aliave rationabili de causa, de Antistitae expressa licentia; non tamen absque iusta causa et Antistitae venia, singulae e domo egrediantur. Exeuntes autem, in modo agendi et loquendi cum saecularibus meminerint condicionis suae, et modestia, pietate, mansuetudine, urbanitate maximaque reverentia enitentes, in omnibus suis actibus ceteris sint aedificationi."—*Statuta, 1961,* Art. 18, § 1.

experience of each convent will indicate precisely which items fall into this category. Moreover, any other reasonable cause will justify permission for the extern sisters to leave the monastery; there is no need for a serious reason to permit such absence. Thus, the extern sisters might be allowed to go out to attend some notable religious celebration or civic event, to represent the community at the funeral of a benefactor, or a relative of one of the nuns, or even to visit some historic and educational site. Of course, no matter what may be the reason for going out, when the extern sisters leave the monastery they must obtain the express permission of the superioress. With regard to those matters outside the monastery which recur frequently and regularly, it would be wise for the superioress to set up a general policy whereby the extern sisters would automatically have her express permission to leave the cloister to perform such service. This permission on the part of the superioress would still be express, although it would also be a habitual permission.

2. Going Out Alone

The extern sisters are not to leave the monastery alone, unless there exists a just cause for so doing, and then only with the permission of the superioress. This prohibition refers only to departure from the precincts of the monastery; there is nothing to forbid an extern sister who lives within the papal enclosure to leave the confines of the cloister without a companion.[40] Nor would it be against the norm of this paragraph for an extern sister who lives outside the papal enclosure to leave the episcopal enclosure which exists in the residence of the extern sisters,[41] and, without a companion, to go into the parlors or the monastery yard.

It is important to note that the Statutes require only a *just* cause for the superioress to permit an extern sister to go out of the monastery by herself. This is a more liberal norm than that of canon 607, adopted by Article 99 of the

[40] *Ibid.*, Art. 4, § 2; cf. *supra*, pp. 154-155.

[41] *Statuta, 1961*, Art. 3, § 2; cf. *supra*, pp. 134-135.

Statutes of 1931, which lays upon the superiors and ordinaries the obligation of seeing to it that women religious do not go out alone except in a case of necessity.[42] To allow an extern sister to go out by herself, the present Article only requires that there be a just cause, i.e., a good reason for going out without a companion. There need be no necessity; the convenience and utility of the monastery constitute sufficient reason for the superioress to permit an extern sister to leave the monastery without a companion. There is no requirement that, should another extern sister not be available as a companion, a lay woman be called upon to act in this capacity. The mere fact that no extern sister is available as a companion is enough reason for a sister to go out alone.

In practice, according to the circumstances of each monastery, there will be many and varied situations where this permission to leave the monastery without a companion may find application. For example, if one sister is able to do the shopping alone while the other extern sisters are occupied with work about the monastery, the one sister can be given permission to go out without a companion. Again, suppose that there are only two extern sisters in a given monastery, one of whom is slightly ill or rather elderly, so that it is difficult for her to accompany the other sister. Such a situation, according to the demands of charity, should be viewed as offering a just cause for the other sister to go out alone. Certainly, in monasteries where there is only one extern sister, there need be no scruple about her leaving the convent without a companion. Nor, in any of these cases, is a permission beyond that of the superioress required. Here, too, when habitual egress without a companion is demanded, it seems that the superioress may grant such a permission whenever some regularly recurring situation presents itself.

[42] "Antistitae et Ordinarii locorum serio advigilent ne religiosae, citra casum necessitatis, singulae extra domum pergant."—Canon 607.

B. *Paragraph Two: Conditions for Living outside the Monastery*

> The superioress may not permit the sisters to live outside their own house except for a just cause and for as short a time as possible; for an absence which exceeds a month, there is required the permission of the local ordinary and of the regular superior, if there be one; for an absence, moreover, which lasts beyond six months, the permission of the Apostolic See is necessary.[43]

This paragraph refers to a situation in which it would be necessary for extern sisters to live outside their convent. Unless the provisions of this paragraph are observed, they can not even live in another monastery of the same Order. This, of course, is without prejudice to the particular Statutes of a federation which are approved by the Holy See. The General Statutes of Nuns which accompanied the Apostolic Constitution *Sponsa Christi* provide for the drafting of such statutes. Special norms may regulate the faculty and the moral obligation of mutually asking for and granting to other monasteries such nuns as may be thought necessary for the government of the monasteries, for the training of novices in a common novitiate, or for the supplying of other moral or material needs of the monasteries or of the nuns.[44] Moreover, the Instruction of the Sacred Congregation of Religious on the same Apostolic Constitution recognizes among the purposes and advantages of federations the possibility of a common novitiate, the interchange of nuns for government and training, and the possibility of a mutual temporary exchange of subjects. This Instruction also envisions a permanent assignment because of health or another

[43] "Antistitae fas non est permittere ut Sorores extra propriam domum degant, nisi iusta de causa atque ad tempus quo fieri potest brevius; pro absentia vero quae mensem excedat, requiritur Ordinarii loci et Superioris Regularis, si adsit, licentia; pro absentia autem quae ultra sex menses protrahatur, necessaria est Sedis Apostolicae venia." —*Statuta, 1961*, Art. 18, § 2.

[44] "Statuta Generalia Monialium," Art. VII, § 8, 3°—*AAS*, XLIII (1951), 19.

moral or material need.[45] The norms of federations drawn up to include these elements, insofar as they pertain to extern sisters, would take precedence over the requirements laid down in the present paragraph.

This paragraph contains a modification of canon 606, § 2, which demands a just and grave cause for permitting a religious to remain outside a house of her own institute. It is likewise a change from the Statutes of 1931, which specified a serious reason for the superioress to permit an extern sister to remain outside her convent.[46] The present Statutes make no mention of a grave cause, but require only a just reason for an extern sister to dwell outside her own monastery, whether or not this be in another monastery of the same Order. Examples of such just causes are not difficult to find. For example, an extern sister might be sent to her home for a visit, or to help out for some time in another monastery. She might be sent to a hospital for treatment under the provisions of this paragraph. Again, an extern sister, under the provisions of this Article, could be sent to attend a liturgical convention, or to take a course in practical nursing.

The permissions necessary to allow an extern sister to live outside her own monastery depend upon the length of time for which she is to be away from home. According to the Statutes, this time is to be as short as possible; in other words, permission may be granted for as long as the just cause exists. No mention is made in this paragraph of absences which do not exceed one month's duration; hence, unless the Constitutions determine otherwise, the permission of the superioress suffices for such an absence. For an absence which exceeds one month in duration, the permission of the local ordinary and of the regular superior, if the monastery is subject to one, is required; this permission may be granted for a period up to and including six months.[47] How-

[45] Instr., S. C. de Rel., 23 nov. 1950, Art. XXII, 2°, 3°, 4°—*AAS*, XLIII (1951), 42.

[46] *Statuta, 1931*, Art. 100; cf. *supra*, p. 103.

[47] This same provision was contained in Article 100 of the Statutes

ever, if the extern sister is to be away from her monastery for a period which exceeds six months, it is necessary to obtain the permission of the Holy See.[48] The local ordinary and the regular superior, if there be one, should also be approached in regard to permission for absences which exceed six months, since their permission is required for an absence in excess of one month; moreover, it will be upon their recommendations that the Holy See will grant its permission for the extern sister to remain away from home for more than six months. With regard to absences which exceed six months, the Statutes do not explicitly incorporate the norm of canon 606, § 2, which permits an absence of more than six months for the purpose of study without the permission of the Holy See.[49] Despite the fact that the Statutes, in this present paragraph, are obviously adapting the norm of canon 606, § 2, to the case of the extern sisters, it is by no means certain that the omission of this exception for studies is intended to exclude extern sisters from the benefits of this concession of the common law. Therefore, in accord with the principles of canon law,[50] extern sisters may be permitted to remain away from their monastery for the purpose of study for more than six months, and this without the permission of the Holy See.

ARTICLE 2
NINETEENTH ARTICLE OF THE STATUTES: SICK AND AGED EXTERN SISTERS

A. *Paragraph One: Sick Extern Sisters*

A sick sister who, in the judgment of the doctor

of 1931, except that it was not necessary to obtain the permission of the regular superior, if the monastery was subject to one. Canon 606, § 2, makes no requirement such as this for absences of six months or less.

[48] Article 100 of the Statutes of 1931 contained an identical prescription.

[49] "... pro absentia vero quae sex menses excedat, nisi causa studiorum intercedat, semper Apostolicae Sedis venia requiritur."—Canon 606, § 2.

[50] Cf. canon 23.

> or the superioress, can not be conveniently cared for in her external residence, may be brought into the cloister; and her cloistered sister religious should take care of her with the greatest charity, offering their assistance with kindness and solicitude.[51]

The norm of this paragraph is extremely liberal in granting admittance to the enclosure in the case of those extern sisters who fall ill. All that is required to bring the sister to the infirmary within the papal enclosure is the judgment of either the physician or the superioress that she can not conveniently be cared for in the residence of the extern sisters. It is not demanded that it be very difficult or impossible to care for the sick sister in the residence of the extern sisters; should taking care of her there involve inconvenience, that constitutes sufficient reason to take the ailing sister within the enclosure. There is no need for special formalities or permissions beyond this judgment of the physician or the superioress.[52]

B. *Paragraph Two: The Aged Extern Sisters*

> Likewise, aged sisters who have become incapable of external service, or who can not receive proper assistance in the residence of the extern sisters, may be admitted into the monastery with the permission of the superioress, granted with the consent of the Council, and with the approval of the local ordinary and of the regular superior, if there be one.[53]

Despite the fact that it requires more formalities for the

[51] "Soror infirma quae, iudicio medici aut Antistitae, in externa habitatione commode curari nequeat, intra clausuram feratur, eique maxima cum caritate adsint consorores claustrales, auxilium benevole seduloque praestantes."—*Statuta, 1961,* Art. 19, § 1.

[52] Article 107 of the Statutes of 1931 called for the permission of the local ordinary to take a sick extern sister inside the enclosure.

[53] "Ita pariter Sorores senio confectae, quae ad externum servitium evaserint inhabiles, quaeque in externa domo convenienti auxilio priventur, cum licentia Antistitae, de consensu Consilii concedenda, et probante Ordinario loci necnon Superiore Regulari, si adsit, in Monasterium admitti poterunt."—*Statuta, 1961,* Art. 19, § 2.

admittance of these elderly sisters than are demanded by the preceding paragraph of this Article in the case of sick sisters,[54] this paragraph is nevertheless quite liberal in its scope. The elderly sisters included under this norm are not those who are sick in the sense that they suffer from some disease or bodily infirmity; such cases would be included under the norms of the preceding paragraph. Rather, they are sisters who have been enfeebled by old age, and are unable any longer to function in the external service of the monastery. No serious cause is demanded to make use of the permission granted in this paragraph; rather, when it is inconvenient to care for an aged sister in the quarters of the extern sisters, she may, with due observance of the formalities described in the Statutes, be taken inside the cloister. No papal indult is required, but only the permission of the local ordinary and the regular superior, if the monastery is subject to one. In addition to these permissions, the superioress needs the consent of her Council to admit an elderly extern sister to residence inside the enclosure.

C. *Paragraph Three: Precautions to Protect Religious Discipline*

> The superioress, however, must be vigilant lest, on account of this, the discipline of the nuns suffer harm, especially the spirit of recollection, which should always flourish within the cloister.[55]

This paragraph reflects a warning similar to the one given in Article 4, § 1, concerning the precautions to be taken lest the permanent dwelling of the extern sisters within the enclosure occasion harm to the recollection of the monastery.[56]

[54] Article 108 of the Statutes of 1931 specified only the permission of the local ordinary in the case of these aged sisters who were to be admitted to the cloister.

[55] "Advigilet autem Antistita ne hac occasione Monialium disciplina, praesertim vero spiritus recollectionis, quae perpetuo intra clausuram vigere debet, detrimentum patiatur."—*Statuta, 1961,* Art. 19, § 3.

[56] Cf. also Art. 3, §§ 2 and 3, for similar prescriptions to be observed when there is contact between the extern sisters and the cloistered nuns.

CHAPTER XII

THE APPROBATION OF THE STATUTES OF 1961

> The Sacred Congregation of Religious, having made its report to His Holiness John XXIII, by Divine Providence Pope, in the Audience granted to His Eminence the Cardinal Prefect on the 21st of March, 1961, now, in fulfilment of the commission given it in the Apostolic Constitution *Sponsa Christi,* of November 21, 1950 (AAS, Vol. 43, p. 5), and in virtue of the faculties granted to it, hereby decrees and ordains that the present Norms and Statutes for sisters dedicated to the external service in monasteries be observed.
>
> All things to the contrary notwithstanding.
>
> Given at Rome, March 25, 1961.
>
> Valerius Cardinal Valeri, Prefect
>
> L. ✠ S.
>
> Fr. Paul Philippe, O.P., Secretary[1]

In this formula of approbation, it is stated that the Sacred Congregation is acting in fulfilment of the commission given it in the Apostolic Constitution *Sponsa Christi.* The reference apparently is to the closing words of that document which provide that the Sacred Congregation of Religious attend to the administration of the entire Constitution and of the General Statutes of Nuns which accompany it. The Sacred Congregation was further empowered to accomplish

[1] "S. Congregatio negotiis Religiosorum sodalium praeposita, facta relatione Ss.mo D. N. Ioanni Div. Prov. Pp. XXIII in Audientia E.mo Cardinali Praefecto die 21 Martii 1961 concessa, pro munere ipsi a Constitutione Apostolica 'Sponsa Christi' diei 21 Novembris 1950 (A. A. S. vol. XXXXIII, p. 5) commisso et vigore facultatum eidem concessarum, praesentes Normas et Statuta pro sororibus servitio externo in Monasteriis addictis, observanda esse statuit ac mandat.
Contrariis quibuslibet non obstantibus.
Datum Romae, 25 Martii, 1961.

Valerius Card. Valeri, *Praefectus*

L. ✠ S.

Fr. Paulus Philippe, O.P., *a Secretis*

by papal authority, through instructions, declarations, responses and other such documents, everything which concerns putting the Constitution effectively into practice and securing a faithful and prompt observance of the Statutes.[2]

In commanding that the Statutes of 1961 be observed by extern sisters, the Sacred Congregation states that this is to be done, "all things to the contrary notwithstanding."[3] It is important to examine the force of this last clause, in order to determine the status of previous laws, customs, privileges and indults pertaining to extern sisters.

SECTION I
CONTRARY LAWS

It is the opinion of reliable authors that the clause, "all things to the contrary notwithstanding," serves to abrogate contrary laws, whether they be universal or particular laws.[4] Therefore, with regard to matter wherein the Statutes of 1961 contain prescriptions which are contrary to those of the Code of Canon Law, the Statutes are to take precedence, because of this clause which abrogates contrary universal law insofar as extern sisters are concerned. In virtue of this same clause, the provisions of the Statutes serve to abrogate contrary norms which may be contained in the Rules and Constitutions of various institutes. In effect, this is the same principle as that embodied in Article 2 of the Statutes, which states that, although the extern sisters have

[2] *AAS*, XLIII (1951), 37-44.

[3] "Contrariis quibuslibet non obstantibus."

[4] "Caeterum in fine ipsius Decreti apposita adest specialis quoque clausula derogatoria, nimirum 'contrariis quibuscumque minime obstantibus,' per quam contraria omnia censentur abrogata ac si essent in specie expressa."—*ASS*, XXXIX (1906), 493: "Nihil enim obstat legem novam versari totam in abroganda lege superiore. Huiusmodi formulae sunt: 'Contrariis non obstantibus quibuscumque,' . . . Omnes illae formulae, prima quoque, revocant ius etiam particulare legi contrarium; id enim non abrogatur, 'nisi aliud in ipsa (lege) expresse caveatur.' "—Van Hove, *De Legibus Ecclesiasticis* (Mechliniae-Romae: H. Dessain, 1930), Vol. I, Tom. II, n. 345, p. 352; Michiels, *Normae Generales*, I, 660; Beste, *op. cit.*, p. 87.

the same Rule and Constitutions as the nuns, they are also subject to the Statutes which derogate from some of the prescriptions of the Rule and the Constitutions.[5] Finally, as has been shown, these Statutes of 1961 completely abrogate the Statutes of 1931, since the later Statutes entirely revise the subject matter of the older norms.[6]

SECTION II
CONTRARY CUSTOMS

According to canon 30, customs contrary to the law, or outside the scope of the law, are revoked by a contrary law. However, unless it makes express mention of them, a law does not revoke centenary or immemorial customs, nor does a universal law abolish particular customs.[7] The question now arises whether the clause, "all things to the contrary notwithstanding," serves to revoke privileged or particular customs. Concerning this point there is indeed much discussion but also a notable lack of agreement on the part of reliable authors.[8] Because of the uncertainty, it may be

[5] Cf. *supra*, pp. 132-133.

[6] Cf. *supra*, pp. 120-122.

[7] "Firmo praescripto can. 5, consuetudo contra legem vel praeter legem per contrariam consuetudinem aut legem revocatur; sed, nisi expressam de iisdem mentionem fecerit, lex non revocat consuetudines centenarias aut immemorabiles, nec lex generalis consuetudines particulares."—Canon 30.

[8] "Nam clausula finalis decreti '*A primis*,' quae sonat: 'quibuscumque contrariis minime obstantibus' abrogat omnes consuetudines et leges, etsi speciales, contrarias, ac si essent in specie expressae (cfr. Laymann, 1. I, t. 11, c. 1, n. 12 in VI; Acta S. Sedis, l.c. p. 493)."—S. Rom. Rotae *Decisiones*, IV (1912), Dec. II, n. 4, p. 14; "Saepe in actibus pontificiis occurrit *alia mentio*: 'Contrariis non obstantibus quibuscumque.' Contendunt hanc formulam habere sensum omnino generalem et abrogare 'omnes consuetudines et leges, etsi speciales, contrarias, ac si essent in specie expressae' (1); (1 Ita S. C. Concilii, *Romana et aliarum. Excardinationis et S. Ordinationis*, 15 Septembris 1906, *ASS*, t. 39, 1906, p. 493, in voto consultoris. Huius verba refert S. R. Rota *Londonen. Incardinationis*, 4 ianuarii 1912, *S. Romane Rotae decisiones seu sententiae*, t. 4, Romae, 1917, p. 14, n. 4.—Cf. G. Michiels, *Normae Generales i.c.*, I, p. 469.—Sententiae allatae provocant ad P. Laymann, *Ius canonicum*, Dilingae, 1666, L. I., tit. 2,

said that the revocatory force of the clause in question is doubtful; and a doubtful revocation of existing customary law amounts to no revocation at all.[9] Therefore, the Statutes of 1961, which are approved "all things to the contrary notwithstanding," do not revoke contrary customs which are centenary or immemorial,[10] nor those which are par-

de constitutionibus, in fine, ad c. 1, *de constitutionibus* in VI°, qui hanc theoriam tenet agendo, non de clausula 'Contrariis non obstantibus quibuscumque,' sed de clausula 'Non obstante quocumque statuto aut consuetudine in contrarium.' Iam vero haec ultima clausula, ex clara dispositione can. 30, nullo modo derogat consuetudinibus privilegiatis.) addunt formulas abrogatorias hodie habere maiorem efficaciam quam antiquis temporibus ideoque recte dici posse, hodie vix ullam consuetudinem contrariam sustineri, si lex posterior manifesto et certe contrarium statuerit (2). ([2] Ph. Maroto, *Institutiones i.c.*, I, no. 254;— H. I. Cicognani, *Ius can.*, II, p. 175.) Indubium est clausulas derogatorias hodie maiorem habere efficaciam ad abrogandas dispositiones contrarias, in specie formulam 'non obstantibus quibuscumque' esse late interpretandam. Quod autem particularis consuetudo contraria abrogari possit per legem generalem manifesto contrariam, absque formula revocationis, aut consuetudo privilegiata aboleri possit sine eius expressa mentione, per formulam 'Contrariis non obstantibus quibuscumque.' conciliari non posse videtur cum dispositione clara canonis 30. Hac autem formula abrogari consuetudines non privilegiatas, videtur admittendum."—Van Hove, *De consuetudine,* (Mechliniae-Romae, Dessain, 1933), Vol. I, Tom. III, Tit. II, n. 258, p. 226; "De clausula 'contrariis non obstantibus quibuscunque' dubitatur, num sufficiat ad supprimendam contrariam consuetudinem particularem."—Beste, *op. cit.*, p. 97; "The clause, *non obstante consuetudine contraria,* does not affect particular customs, and it is doubtful whether this is the effect of the clause, *contrariis non obstantibus quibuscumque.*" Abbo Hannan, *op. cit.*, I, 59.

[9] Cf. canons 15 and 23.

[10] Further proof of this conclusion, insofar as immemorial customs are concerned, is based upon private correspondence during the year 1958 with the authorities of the Sacred Congregation of Religious. The correspondence deals with Rubric n. 3 on p. 366 of the *Rituale Romano-Seraphicum,* pertaining to the Rite of Investiture in the Second Order. This rubric provides that, in monasteries where there is an immemorial custom allowing it, the candidates to be invested as cloistered novices may leave the enclosure before Mass and go to the outside chapel for the ceremony. However, no. 19 of the Instruction *Inter cetera* states that postulants may not leave the enclosure on the occasion of their clothing, profession, Communion or for any such

ticular, even though not privileged. Hence, monasteries, federations and even entire Orders may continue to abide by legitimate particular customs which were in force at the time the Statutes took effect. It does not matter whether these customs are centenary or immemorial, since the uncertainty of the revocatory effect of the Statutes extends to all particular customs, privileged or not. Conversely, because of the element of doubt involved in this matter, it seems that, should a given monastery, federation or Order decide to cease observing a particular custom, privileged or not, and to follow the norm of the Statutes, such a course of action might safely be adopted.

SECTION III
CONTRARY PRIVILEGES AND INDULTS

According to the norms of the Code of Canon Law, indults and privileges are not revoked by contrary law, unless an adverse provision be made in that law.[11] Because of its uncertain revocatory force, it is apparent that the clause, "all

reason. At the end of this Instruction is appended the same clause which appears at the conclusion of the 1961 Statutes, "all things to the contrary notwithstanding." The Sacred Congregation of Religious was asked privately whether the immemorial particular custom mentioned in Rubric n. 3 might still be observed in view of n. 19 of the Instruction *Inter cetera.* The first reply, on March 24, 1958, stated that the prescription of *Inter cetera* was to be applied to this custom, which could, therefore, no longer be observed. This reply recommended obtaining a dispensation in order to continue the practice, citing as one reason for the dispensation the fact that the practice was a longstanding custom. However, after further correspondence with the authorities of the Sacred Congregation, a second reply was forthcoming on May 8, 1958; this second response was a reversal of the former reply of March 24. According to the reply of May 8, the Instruction *Inter cetera* sets down a general rule, which does not affect particular ancient customs or indults, adding that, if the Congregation had desired to include even such cases, it could and would have said so quite explicitly. The clause, "all things to the contrary notwithstanding," is a general phrase covering ordinary instances, not privileged customs such as the one in question.

[11] Cans. 71 and 60.

things to the contrary notwithstanding," by no means constitutes a certain revocation of such indults and privileges, and therefore has no effect on them.[12] Therefore, monasteries, federations or Orders which, before the promulgation of the Statutes of 1961, possessed indults or privileges contrary to the Statutes, may continue to make use of those favors.

[12] "*Clausula 'contrariis quibusque non obstantibus'* probabilius non revocat privilegia per actum peculiarem concessa, neque privilegia praescriptione vel consuetudine immemorabili aut centenaria acquisita." —Michiels, *Normae Generales*, II, 607.

CONCLUSIONS

CHAPTER I

According to Roman Law, the external service of monasteries of women was carried out by men called commissaries *(apocrisiarii).* Although there was a strict separation of these men from contact with the nuns, they lived in a dwelling near the monastery. In this way the *apocrisiarii* were able to perform certain spiritual ministrations for the benefit of the nuns.

CHAPTER II

In some of the early Benedictine convents of nuns, where the cloister was not so strictly observed, the nuns themselves were able to perform the external service of the monastery. With regard to those Benedictine monasteries where the cloister forbade any egress on the part of the nuns, the external service was usually carried out by clerics and monks who were attached to the monasteries, in varying degrees of dependence upon them. Some assistance was also furnished by male and female lay servants. Cistercians, Camaldulese and Carthusians adopted similar arrangements.

CHAPTER III

1. The original serving sisters envisioned by the Rule of St. Clare were nuns, just as were the cloistered sisters; however, an exception to the strict rule of enclosure was made for them, so that they might carry out the business of the monastery. Even after the Church withdrew this exception and demanded that all nuns observe perpetual cloister, it was some time before this practice was eliminated.

2. Many monasteries of the Poor Clares were attended by several Friars Minor, known as friars almsgatherers *(fratres eleemosynarii),* who looked after the spiritual and temporal welfare of the nuns. Eventually this became such

a burden on the Friars that they sought to be relieved of any responsibility for the Poor Clares. This desire on the part of the Friars precipitated a controversy with the nuns, in which the Holy See was several times forced to intervene.

3. Some of the monasteries of the Poor Clares were served by lay brothers (*conversi*), who promised obedience directly to the abbess. Especially after 1336, when the serving sisters were definitely forbidden to go out of the enclosure, the role of male and female servants became of great importance in Poor Clare monasteries.

CHAPTER IV

1. Once it was definitely forbidden for any professed nun to leave the enclosure, the sole method of providing for the external needs of the monasteries was the employment of lay servants, or of male religious. Despite the fact that it was not always easy to find such persons, the attitude of the Church towards the strictness of the cloister for nuns remained firm, being restated by the Council of Trent.

2. In order to alleviate the hardships caused to the nuns by this strict rule of enclosure, the Constitution *Circa pastoralis,* of 1566, made certain exceptions to the inviolable rule of enclosure. This Constitution permitted a temporary exclaustration for certain lay sisters who, although they were true nuns, were temporarily engaged in the service of the monastery.

3. In the Constitution *Deo sacris,* of 1572, Gregory XIII, taking note of the still existing needs in many monasteries, set aside certain revenues for their support. He withdrew the concessions of the Constitution *Circa pastoralis* with regard to those monasteries where daily sustenance was adequately provided without the collection of alms by the nuns themselves.

4. Since the papal constitutions forbade the reception of any lay sisters *(conversae)* exclusively for external service, these became completely cloistered and performed menial tasks within the enclosure. Exit of nuns from their mona-

steries in order to quest became a rarity, as this work was taken over by lay servants and the extern sisters who began to develop at that time.

CHAPTER V

As the practice of permitting professed nuns to leave the cloister disappeared, the employment of male and female servants for outside work and questing became more common among the various Orders. These lay servants lived near the monastery, and were accorded a quasi-religious dignity. The number of these lay servants began to decline as the institution of extern sisters gained prominence.

CHAPTER VI

1. The institution of extern sisters in the present-day concept consists of women religious of simple vows who, attached to a monastery of nuns as members of the religious family, care for the external necessities of the convent. It originated with the *Soeurs Tourières* of the Visitation Nuns in the 17th century.

2. The institution of extern sisters spread rapidly to other Orders of nuns. The growing progress of the status of simple profession in institutes of women religious brought changes and improvement in the condition of the extern sisters. Thus there was great impetus given to the development of the extern sisters in the latter part of the 19th century.

3. In 1888, the extern sisters of all monasteries of Poor Clares subject to the jurisdiction of the bishops were permitted to take the three simple vows of poverty, chastity and obedience, to be observed according to the Rule of the Third Order of St. Francis, which was approved in 1521. This Rule was adapted to the extern sisters by means of certain declarations and explanations appended to each chapter. Numerous other institutes followed this example, each obtaining its own particular Statutes for extern sisters. In 1931, desiring to bring some unity into the legislation for ex-

tern sisters, the Sacred Congregation of Religious promulgated special statutes to be observed by the extern sisters in all institutes.

CHAPTER VII

1. Under the Statutes of 1931, the extern sisters professed the same Rule as the nuns, and were members of the same Order, even though they made no solemn profession. In some cases, especially among the Poor Clares, there was great uncertainty concerning the obligation of the extern sisters to adopt the Statutes of 1931. The result was a great deal of legal confusion, not only on the part of the nuns, but of the ecclesiastical authorities as well.

2. The Statutes of 1931 conferred many benefits on the extern sisters, in effect setting up a new canonical institution, the members of which participated in the condition of both monastic nuns and sisters of simple vows.

3. The Statutes of 1931 took the place of the Constitutions of the Order as far as the extern sisters were concerned. In attempting to reconcile the prescriptions of the Statutes with those of the Constitutions to which the nuns were bound, many difficulties arose because of conflicting norms. The obvious need to perfect the Statutes for Extern Sisters led to the drafting of the present legislation for extern sisters, the Statutes of 1961.

CHAPTER VIII

1. The Statutes of 1961 brought up to date the legislation concerning extern sisters by adapting it to recent papal documents concerning nuns, by non-mention of the prescriptions of the common law already contained in the Constitutions of nuns, and by accommodating the norms for extern sisters to the Rules and Constitutions of the Orders to which the sisters belong.

2. The Statutes of 1961 effected the complete abrogation of the Statutes of 1931. Moreover, they set up definite rules

to determine the relationship of the Statutes to the particular law of the various institutes.

CHAPTER IX

1. The Statutes set down certain definite formalities which must be observed in order to introduce extern sisters into a monastery. However, the matter is often complicated by the provisions of some Constitutions which prescribe other additional or different formalities to introduce extern sisters. Since such Constitutions treat expressly of the service of the extern sisters, they take precedence over the requirements of the Statutes.

2. Under the 1961 Statutes, the extern sisters are members of the Order and monastery which they serve. They are bound to the observance of the same Rule and Constitutions as the cloistered nuns, except in those matters wherein the Statutes repeal certain prescriptions of these particular norms.

3. The Statutes set down regulations for the entrance of extern sisters into the enclosure for purposes of devotion and instruction, as well as for meals, recreation and work. These regulations are quite liberal and it is conceivable that, with regard to the last of these purposes, the permission granted in virtue of Article 3, § 3, may be extended to cover even daily entrance.

4. When the extern sisters live habitually in the papal enclosure, the separation from the nuns enjoined by the Statutes is achieved in practice if the extern sisters reside in a special section of the papal cloister.

5. Although the local superioress has a right of vigilance over the quarters of the extern sisters, this does not confer on her the right to leave the enclosure to supervise the extern sisters. A papal indult is required if she desires to do this.

6. In adapting the habit of the Order to the needs of the extern sisters, the alterations shall not be of such extent that the habit of the extern sisters is essentially different from that of the cloistered nuns.

CHAPTER X

1. The Statutes contain special regulations concerning the postulancy, novitiate and profession of extern sisters. As far as these matters are concerned, the extern sisters are regulated not by their own Constitutions, but by the norms of the Statutes, which take precedence over the Constitutions.

2. The Statutes provide great freedom in the determination of the place where the postulancy and the second year of novitiate shall be made. The requirement that the first year of novitiate be made within the cloister no longer affects the validity of the novitiate.

3. The matter of the annual renewal of temporary vows is complicated by the fact that the Constitutions of most institutes of nuns simply do not envision any such arrangement, and contain no provisions for it. Very probably there are no special formalities demanded for the superioress to admit a sister to these renewals, or to exclude her from them.

4. Since the Constitutions of institutes of nuns envision the fact that all the religious make solemn profession, and do not cover the case of the extern sisters, the Statutes prescribe the making of a civilly valid will on the part of the extern sisters, who, since they profess only simple perpetual vows, retain the ownership of their goods.

CHAPTER XI

1. The superioress, whose duty it is to direct the extern sisters and care for their spiritual and temporal welfare, should see that the extern sisters perform the religious exercises delineated in the Rule and Constitutions, with the exception of those which are proper to the choir nuns. Thus the extern sisters are not bound to recite the Divine Office, but will have their own Office in accordance with the prevailing practice in their Order.

2. In those monasteries where the extern sisters live apart from the cloistered nuns, they are, insofar as this is possible,

to maintain among themselves the observance of the common life.

3. Although the extern sisters are bound to observe the laws of fast and abstinence of their Order, just as the nuns, reasons for dispensation from these obligations can readily be found.

4. The Statutes are very liberal in requiring only a just and reasonable cause for the extern sisters to leave the monastery precincts. With regard to the matter of going out alone they are considerably more lenient than the Code of Canon Law.

5. The Statutes are quite liberal in the requirements they set for bringing the sick and aged extern sisters within the enclosure.

CHAPTER XII

1. Previous laws which are contrary to the Statutes, whether universal or particular, are abrogated by the Statutes.

2. Neither privileged nor particular customs are revoked by contrary provisions of the Statutes. Contrary privileges and indults likewise remain intact.

APPENDIX

THE INSTRUCTION AND STATUTES OF 1961

The characteristic condition of nuns living within cloister is such that, in order to safeguard their life of recollection, they need some persons to take care of the business and affairs of the monastery outside the cloister. Accordingly, there have always been pious women, who usually lived outside the cloister and who were not bound by any obligations which, properly appraised, could be called obligations of the religious life. These women were called oblates, mandataries, portresses, or some other such name.

In the course of time, however, these pious women expressed a desire for a more intimate participation in the life of the cloistered nuns; and in various places they were permitted to bind themselves to the external service of the monastery, by making a special resolution, promise, oath, or vow. Moreover, there have been rules, constitutions, and special statutes which were approved by the Holy See and which consecrated as it were, this resolve to live the religious life.

In modern times, the decree of the Sacred Congregation of Religious, *Conditio plurium monasteriorum,* of July 16, 1931, confirmed and duly regulated their status as sisters of simple religious vows. These sisters were declared to be "members of the community they serve and participants in the same spiritual goods as the nuns." (*Statutes for the Extern Sisters of Monasteries of Nuns of Every Order,* no. 4.) Lest, however, the juridical incorporation of the sisters into the community should endanger the contemplative life of the nuns, a general norm was laid down according to which the sisters were to live in a part of the monastery outside of the papal cloister.

The experience of the last thirty years, however, has clearly shown that a number of things in the Statutes of

1931 need to be improved through an adaptation of them to more recent pontifical documents concerning cloistered nuns, through non-mention of certain prescriptions of the common law which are already included in the Constitutions of nuns, and through a closer adjustment to the Rules and Constitutions of the Second Order to which the sisters belong. Accordingly, the Sacred Congregation of Religious has decided to make a new and shorter, but nonetheless complete, edition of the aforementioned Statutes, without prejudice, however, to the following points.

1. Those monasteries of nuns which do not have extern sisters, and do not need them, since the external service of the monastery is taken care of by trustworthy secular persons who have been chosen with the consent of the local ordinary and who live outside of the cloister, are not obliged to introduce this class of sisters.

2. Where the Rule or Constitutions of a given Order expressly prescribe and regulate the external service of sisters for a monastery of nuns, the canonical dispositions regulating this service retain their full force, provided they are not contrary either to the sacred canons or to the Apostolic Constitution *Sponsa Christi.*

3. If, for the better observance of the spirit of their own foundation and vocation, the nuns of an Order wish to insert into their own Constitutions special provisions for the external service of the monastery, they are free to draw up such dispositions. These, however, are to be submitted for the approval of the Sacred Congregation of Religious.

After a similar approval by the same Congregation, provisions of the same sort may also be inserted into the Statutes of those federations erected by the Holy See which observe within the same Order a somewhat diversified practice of regular observance. However, the prescriptions which may be added to the Constitutions or to the Statutes of a federation, according to the nature of the Order, must conform to the following general Statutes.

CHAPTER I

CONCERNING THE DUTIES AND DWELLING PLACE OF THE EXTERN SISTERS

ARTICLE 1

§ 1. With the consent of the Chapter and with the approval of the local Ordinary, as well as that of the regular superior if they are subject to one, monasteries of nuns may introduce extern sisters, whose principal duty is to serve the monastery by attending to external business which can not be done by the cloistered nuns.

§ 2. Moderate works of the apostolate connected with the monastery but performed outside the papal cloister may be considered as included in the external services to which the sisters are destined.

ARTICLE 2

The extern sisters are members of the community of their monastery, and, in the order of precedence, come after the choir nuns and the lay sisters *(conversae);* they profess the same Rule and Constitutions as their sister religious, the nuns, but in virtue of their proper office they are subject to the present Statutes, which repeal some prescriptions of the Rule and Constitutions.

ARTICLE 3

§ 1. Without prejudice to Article 4, the extern sisters have a residence which is annexed to the monastery and which is subject to the common cloister (see canon 604 and the Instruction *Inter cetera,* n. 73), though not situated within the limits of the papal cloister of the nuns (see the Instruction *Inter cetera,* n. 11, b; 44, b). Accordingly, they may not enter the part of the monastery reserved for the nuns, except in accordance with the provisions made in these Statutes.

§ 2. Without prejudice to the stricter law of individual monasteries, the superioress, with the consent of her Council and with the approval of the local ordinary and of the regular superior if there be one, has the right to permit the extern sisters to meet at times with the nuns inside the cloister of the monastery for purposes of devotion or instruction, as well as for eating and recreating together, care being taken that nothing detrimental follows from this. At these times, the sisters, even if questioned imprudently, should refrain from relating things they have seen or heard outside the monastery; they should especially keep silent about matters which do not set a good example or which can disturb peace and application of mind. The superioress with her councilors should carefully watch over these matters; and, if the entrance of the sisters into the monastery becomes an occasion for abuses, suitable remedies should be applied.

§ 3. In accordance with the judgment of the superioress and her Council, together with the previous and at least general approval of the local ordinary and of the regular superior if there be one, the sisters living outside the cloister may at times be employed for the internal duties and works of the monastery, care being taken that they do not habitually associate with the nuns.

§ 4. What is said in this Article about the entrance of the sisters into the cloister applies also to postulants and to novices of the second year of novitiate.

ARTICLE 4

§1. With due regard to the spirit and character of each Order as well as the number of nuns living in the monastery, monasteries, after a previous vote of the Chapter and, in the case of monasteries belonging to a federation, after hearing the Council of the federation, may, with the approval of the Holy See, determine that the extern sisters shall live habitually within the limits of the cloister of the monastery, even though they are not bound by the law of papal cloister. In this case precautions must be taken so that this association of the sisters with the nuns who are bound by the law of enclosure does not harm the spirit of recollection; besides other precautions, a kind of separation should be instituted within the cloister similar to that prescribed for the novitiate (canon 564, § 1), and the sisters should be forbidden to relate to the nuns the things that happen outside of the cloister.

§ 2. Since they are not bound by the law of papal cloister, sisters who habitually live within the cloister may, at the discretion of the superioress, leave the cloister for the service or other external work of the monastery, or for some other just and reasonable cause.

Without prejudice to the discipline and the purpose of the postulancy and the novitiate (canon 565), the same provision holds also for novices even of the first year of the novitiate and for the postulants, if the postulancy, according to the norm of Article 9, § 2, is conducted within the cloister.

ARTICLE 5

The residence and other places outside the limits of the cloister which are destined for the extern sisters are subject, according to the norms of law, to the vigilance and visitation not only of the local ordinary and of the regular superior, if there be one, but also, with all due prescriptions on the matter being observed, to the vigilance and visitation of the Superioress of the monastery and of the moderator of the federation, in the case of federated monasteries (see the Instruction *Inter cetera,* n. 24, 5°).

ARTICLE 6

§ 1. To engage in works of the apostolate in monasteries in a stable manner, according to the norm of Article 1, § 2, besides the previous approval of the local ordinary and of the regular superior, if there be one, the approbation of the Holy See is required.

§ 2. In carrying out the works of the apostolate, the sisters should follow norms set down by the local ordinary.

ARTICLE 7

§ 1. The habit of the sisters should be the same as that of the nuns, suitably accommodated, however, by the Chapter to the purpose of external service according to the circumstances of time and place.

§ 2. With regard to the religious habit in monasteries of one and the same federation, the sisters, as far as possible, should be dressed in the same way.

CHAPTER II
CONCERNING THE RECEPTION AND PROFESSION OF THE EXTERN SISTERS

ARTICLE 8

In the admission and training of extern sisters, exactly the same conditions are to be observed as those prescribed by the Constitutions for the nuns of the monastery, with due consideration given, however, to their special function. The superioress with her Council should take care to accept only those aspirants who have mature judgment and more than ordinary piety, so that they may give good example, especially outside the monastery in their dealings with secular persons.

ARTICLE 9

§ 1. The postulancy lasts one year; but the superioress, with the advice of her Council, may reduce this time to six months or prolong it for another six months beyond the year, according as the postulant seems to need a longer or shorter preparation for the novitiate.

§ 2. The postulancy should be made in the residence of the sisters in order that the postulants may be trained and tested in their proper duties.

Nevertheless, in accordance with the judgment of the superioress and her Council, and the approval of the local ordinary and of the regular superior if there be one, the postulancy can be made within the monastery, that is, within the cloister of the nuns, without prejudice, however, to the Statutes of the federation in the case of a federated monastery, or to Article 4, § 2.

ARTICLE 10

§ 1. The novitiate is to last for two years. The first of these years is strictly canonical; and, although the novices of this class are not bound by the law of papal cloister, the year is to be spent together with the cloistered novices within the enclosure of the monastery, or of some other monastery that belongs to the group of federated monasteries. This year of novitiate, in order to be valid, must be a complete and continuous year according to the norm of the law.

§ 2. For the proper training of the novices in their external duties, the second year of the novitiate will ordinarily be made in the proper residence of the sisters under the vigilance of a specially designated sister, who is to give an account to the mistress of novices. Two months before profession, the novices shall refrain completely from external service and remain within the novitiate of the monastery so that there, under the direction of the mistress of novices, they may more peacefully prepare themselves for profession.

§ 3. In accordance with the judgment of the superioress and her Council, and with the approval of the local ordinary and of the regular superior, if there be one, the novices can make also the second year of their novitiate within the monastery, without, however, being bound by the papal cloister.

§ 4. In the training of the novices for the religious life, while instructions and conferences are to be given in the same way as is prescribed in the Constitutions for the novitiate of the nuns, special care should be taken with reference to the instructions regarding the external affairs and works for which the novices are destined.

ARTICLE 11

The novitiate made for extern sisters is not valid for choir nuns or for lay sisters; nor is the novitiate made for choir nuns or for lay sisters valid for extern sisters (Canon 558).

ARTICLE 12

§ 1. At the completion of the novitiate, the novice is to make profession of simple temporary vows for six years;

these are to be renewed annually, at least during the first three-year period. At the end of six years, she is to make profession of simple perpetual vows or to return to the world.

§ 2. In the making of profession, the rite of each monastery should be observed, with the necessary changes, however, being made. The first religious profession following the novitiate is made by the sisters within the cloister of the monastery; the renewals of vows, as well as the perpetual profession, are to be made outside of the cloister at the choir grille of the nuns. However, in accordance with the judgment of the superioress and her Council, and with the approval of the local ordinary and of the regular superior if there be one, these too may be made within the cloister.

§ 3. The formula of profession should be the same as that of the nuns, with the necessary additions and changes; each profession of the sisters must be made in the quality of an extern sister according to the Rule and Constitutions of the monastery and the special Statutes for Extern Sisters approved by the Apostolic See.

ARTICLE 13

§ 1. Without prejudice to the prescriptions of the Constitutions concerning the cession of administration and the disposition of the use and usufruct of property, according to the norm of the common law (canon 569, § 1, and canon 580, § 1), every professed sister of simple vows, whether perpetual or temporary, unless something else is provided in the Constitutions, retains the ownership of her property and her capacity to acquire other property. Lest, however, the extern sisters be solicitous about their property, even before their profession of temporary vows they shall freely make a civilly valid will concerning their present property as well as whatever may come to them in the future. They may not change this will without the permission of the Holy See or, if the matter is urgent and there is no time for recourse to the Holy See, without permission of the superioress of the monastery in which the sister is actually living.

§ 2. Without prejudice to an indult granted by the Holy

See, the sisters can not renounce their property or alienate it without compensation.

§ 3. The cession or disposition which is treated in canon 569 can be changed by a professed sister, not indeed at her own choice, unless the Constitutions allow this, but with the permission of the local ordinary and of the regular superior if there be one, provided the change, if it involves a notable part of her property, is not made in favor of the monastery. In the case of her departure from the monastery the cession and disposition lose their force.

§ 4. Whatever a sister acquires by her own industry, or in consideration of the monastery, she acquires for the monastery.

CHAPTER III
CONCERNING THE RELIGIOUS DISCIPLINE OF THE EXTERN SISTERS

ARTICLE 14

§ 1. The sisters, like the nuns, are subject to the superioress of the monastery in all things, in regard both to religious discipline and to the service they are to render. It is the duty of the superioress to prescribe the order of their spiritual exercises and to provide with motherly care whatever is necessary for the common life and for their individual needs.

§ 2. The superioress can delegate one of the extern sisters or a nun, choosing a religious who is prudent, of mature age and perpetually professed to see to it that everything pertaining to discipline or work is conducted properly according to the directions of the superioress. This sister shall prudently report all called for information to the superioress, or to some other nun designated for this, and from her receive instructions.

ARTICLE 15

§ 1. The superioress should see to it that the extern sisters perform the religious exercises which are indicated in the Rule and the Constitutions, with the exception of those which are proper to the choir nuns.

§ 2. Also with regard to Holy Communion and to confession, the prescriptions contained in the Constitutions for the nuns are to be observed.

§ 3. For an occasional confession the sisters enjoy the right which is granted to women religious not bound by the papal cloister, namely, if a sister, for her peace of conscience, goes to a confessor approved for women by the local ordinary, the confession is valid and licit, when made in a church or an oratory, even a semi-public one, or in any other place legitimately designated for the confessions of women or of women religious, or legitimately designated as such for a particular confession (can. 522).

§ 4. With the consent of the superioress and her council, and the approval of the local ordinary and of the regular superior if there be one, the spiritual exercises mentioned in § 1 may be performed by the extern sisters inside the cloister of the nuns.

ARTICLE 16

As far as possible, the religious duties mentioned in the preceding Article shall be performed in common by the sisters.

The sisters should also eat and recreate in common.

ARTICLE 17

With regard to the laws of abstinence and fasting proper to each Order by reason of the Rule and Constitutions, the superioress should treat the extern sisters maternally, dispensing in these matters insofar as there is real need. It is desirable that in each Order, or at least in each federation, there be set up some uniform norm for the observance of such particular laws by the extern sisters.

ARTICLE 18

§ 1. The sisters should remain at home, diligently engaging in prayer and work; and they should not go outside except to care for the business of the monastery or for some other reasonable cause, and with the express permission of the superioress; nor should they leave the house alone without a just cause and the permission of the superioress. When they go out, they should be mindful of their state in their conduct and speech with seculars; and, by manifesting modesty, piety, meekness, urbanity and the greatest reverence, they should be a source of edification to others in all their actions.

§ 2. The superioress may not permit the sisters to live outside their own house except for a just cause and for as short a time as possible; for an absence which exceeds a month, there is required the permission of the local ordinary and of the regular superior, if there be one; for an absence, moreover, which lasts beyond six months, the permission of the Apostolic See is necessary.

ARTICLE 19

§ 1. A sick sister who, in the judgment of the doctor or the superioress, can not be conveniently cared for in her external residence, may be brought into the cloister; and her cloistered sister religious should take care of her with the greatest charity, offering their assistance with kindness and solicitude.

§ 2. Likewise, aged sisters who have become incapable of external service, or who can not receive proper assistance in the residence of the extern sisters, may be admitted into the monastery with the permission of the superioress, granted with the consent of the Council, and with the approval of the local ordinary and of the regular superior, if there be one.

§ 3. The superioress, however, must be vigilant lest, on account of this, the discipline of the nuns suffer harm, especially the spirit of recollection, which should always flourish within the cloister.

The Sacred Congregation of Religious, having made its report to His Holiness John XXIII, by Divine Providence Pope, in the Audience granted to His Eminence the Cardinal

Prefect on the 21st of March, 1961, now, in fulfilment of the commission given in the Apostolic Constitution *Sponsa Christi,* of November 21, 1950 (AAS, Vol. 43, p. 5), and in virtue of the faculties granted to it, hereby decrees and ordains that the present Norms and Statutes for sisters dedicated to the external service in monasteries be observed.

All things to the contrary notwithstanding.

Given at Rome, March 25, 1961.

Valerius Cardinal Valeri, *Prefect*

L. ✠ S.

Fr. Paul Philippe, O.P., *Secretary*

BIBLIOGRAPHY

Sources

Acta Apostolicae Sedis, Commentarium Officiale, Romae, 1909-1929; Civitate Vaticana, 1929-

Acta Ordinis Minorum, Vol. I-XVI, ad Claras Aquas prope Florentiam, 1882-1897; *Acta Ordinis Fratrum Minorum,* a Vol. XVII, ad Claras Aquas prope Florentiam, 1898-

Acta Sanctae Sedis, 41 vols., Romae, 1865-1908.

Alessandri, Laetus, et Pennacchi, Franciscus, *Bullarium Pontificium quod exstat in Archivo Sacri Conventus S. Francisci Assisiensis* (nunc apud publicam Bibliothecam Assisii), ad Claras Aquas prope Florentiam: Typ. Collegii S. Bonaventurae, 1920.

Bouscaren, T. Lincoln, *The Canon Law Digest,* 4 vols. and Supplements through 1958-1961, Milwaukee: Bruce and Company, 1934-1962.

Bullarium Franciscanum, 8 vols., Vol. I-IV ed. a Joanne Sbaralea, Romae, 1759-1780, Vol. V-VIII ed. a Eubel, Romae, 1897-1908.

Bullarium Romanum seu *Bullarum, Diplomatum et Privilegiorum Sanctorum Romanorum Pontificum* Taurinensis Ed., 24 vols., Augustae Taurinorum, 1857-1872.

Canones et Decreta Concilii Tridentini, ed. Neapolitana quam edidit Ioseph Pelella, Neapoli, 1859.

Codex Iuris Canonici, Pii X Pontificis Maximi iussu digestus, Benedicti Papae XV auctoritate promulgatus, Romae: Typis polyglottis Vaticanis, 1917; reimpressio, 1948.

Codicis Iuris Canonici Fontes, cura Emi Petri Card. Gasparri editi, 9 vols., VII-IX *ed. cura et studio Emi Iustiniani Card. Serédi,* Romae (postea Civitate Vaticana): Typis Polyglottis, 1923-1939.

Collectanea in usum Secretariae Sacrae Congregationis Episcoporum et Regularium, cura A. Bizzarri Archiepiscopi Philippensis Secretarii edita, Romae: S. C. De Prop. Fide, 1885.

Corpus Iuris Canonici, editio Lipsiensis secunda curas ad librorum manu scriptorum et editionis Romanae fidem recognovit et adnotatione critica instruxit Aemilius Friedburg, 2 vols., Vol. I, *Decretum Magistri Gratiani,* Lipsiae, 1879, Vol. II, *Decretalium Collectiones,* Lipsiae, 1881.

Corpus Iuris Civilis, 3 vols., Vol. I, *Institutiones,* quas recognovit P. Krueger; *Digesta,* quae recognovit T. Mommsen et retractavit P. Krueger, 15. ed.; Vol. II, *Codex Iustinianus,* quem recognovit et retractavit P. Krueger, 10. ed., Vol. III, *Novellae Constitu-*

tiones, a R. Schoell; opus Schoellii morte interceptum absolvit G. Kroll, 5. ed., Berolini: apud Weidmannos, 1928-1929.

Coutumier et Directoire pour les Soeurs Religieuses de la Visitation Sainte-Marie, Annecy, 1850.

Hardouin, J., *Acta Conciliorum et Epistolae Decretales ac Constitutiones Summorum Pontificum*, 12 vols., Parisiis, 1714-1715.

Mansi, Joannes Dominicus, *Sacrorum Conciliorum Nova et Amplissima Collectio*, 53 vols., Florentiae, Venetiis, Parisiis, Arnhem, Lipsiae, 1759-1927.

Normae secundum quas S. Congr. Episcoporum et Regularium procedere solet in Approbandis Novis Institutis Votorum Simplicium, Romae, 1901.

Pontificale Romanum, Mechliniae: Dessain, 1895.

Règles de St. Augustin et Constitutions de la Visitation, Annecy, 1889.

Regula et Constitutiones Generales Ordinis Fratrum Minorum, Romae: Curia Generalis Ordinis, 1953.

Regula S. Clarae et Constitutiones pro Monialibus Clarissis Reformationis a Sancta Coleta, Romae: Curia Generalitia Ordinis Fratrum Minorum, 1932.

Regulae et Constitutiones Generales Monialium Ordinis Sanctae Clarae, Romae: Curia Generalitia Ordinis Fratrum Minorum, 1941.

Rituale Romano-Seraphicum Ordinis Fratrum Minorum, 3. ed., Romae, 1955.

S. Romanae Rotae Decisiones seu Sententiae ab anno 1909, Romae: Typis Polyglottis Vaticanis, 1912-

Statuta Capitulorum Generalium Ordinis Cisterciensis ab anno 1116 ad annum 1786, quae edidit D. Josephus-Maria Canivez, 8 vols., Louvain: Bureaux de la Revue, 1933.

Reference Works

Abbo, John A.-Hannan, Jerome D., *The Sacred Canons*, 2. rev. ed., 2 vols., St. Louis: Herder, 1960.

Beste, Udalricus, *Introductio in Codicem*, ed. altera, Collegeville, Minnesota: St. John's Abbey Press, 1944.

Bollandistae, *Acta Sanctorum*, ed. novissima curante Joanne Carnandet, 68 vols., Parisiis, 1863-

Bonacina, Martinus, *Tractatus de clausura, et poenis eam violantibus impositis*, Venetiis, 1626.

Bouix, D., *Tractatus de Jure Regularium*, 2 vols., Parisiis, 1857.

Bourdillon, A. F. C., *The Order of Minoresses in England*, British Society of Franciscan Studies, Vol. XII, Manchester: University Press, 1926.

Ferraris, Lucius, *Bibliotheca canonica iuridica moralis theologica*, ed. novissima mendis expurgata, 9 vols., Romae: S. C. de Prop. Fide, 1885-1899.

Frémiot de Chantal, St. Jane Frances, *Answers of the Blessed Mother Jane Frances Frémiot*, translated by B. Rayment, Georgetown, 1834.

Holzapfel, Heribert, *Manuale Historiae Ordinis Fratrum Minorum*, Latine redditum a G. Haselbeck, Friburgi Brisgoviae, 1909.

Ledwolorz, Adolphus, *Epitome Iuris Religiosorum*, 2 vols., pro manuscripto, Romae, Pontificium Athenaeum Antonianum.

Lucidi, Angelus, *De Visitatione Sacrorum Liminum*, Instructio S. C. Concilii, 3. ed., purgata et aucta per P. Iosephum Schneider, 3 vols., Romae, 1883.

Mabillon, Johannes, *Annales Ordinis S. Benedicti*, ed. prima Italica a quamplurimis mendis, quae in Parisiensen irrepserant, ad auctoris mentem expurgata, 6 vols., Lucae, 1739.

Michiels, Gommarus, *Normae Generales Iuris Canonici*, ed. altera, 2 vols., Parisiis-Tornaci-Romae: Desclée, 1949.

———, *Principia Generalia de Personis in Ecclesia*, ed. altera, Parisiis-Tornaci-Romae: Desclée, 1955.

Migne, P. J., *Patrologiae Cursus Completus, Series Latina*, 221 vols., Parisiis, 1864-1884.

Mittarelli, D. Johannes Benedictus, et Costadini, D. Anselmus, *Annales Camaldulenses Ordinis S. Benedicti*, 9 vols., Venetiis, 1755.

Monstrolii, D. Carolus le Couteulx, *Annales Ordinis Cartusiensis ab anno 1084 ad annum 1429*, 7 vols., Typis Cartusiae S. Mariae de Pratis, 1888.

Pellizzari, Franciscus, *Tractatio de Monialibus*, Venetiis, 1651; ed. novissima, aucta et correcta iuxta animadversiones Sacrae Indicis Congregationis a Joanne Francisco Montani, Romae, 1761.

Petra, Vincentius, *Commentaria ad Constitutiones Apostolicas seu Bullas Singulas Summorum Pontificum in Bullario Romano contentas secundum collectionem Cherubini*, 5 vols., Romae, 1708.

Schäfer, Timotheus, *De Religiosis ad Norman Codicis Iuris Canonici*, 4. ed. actua et emendata, Romae: Typis Polyglottis Vaticanis, 1947.

Van Hove, Alphonsus, *Commentarium Lovaniense in Codicem Iuris Canonici*, 1 vol. in 5 toms., Tom. II, *De Legibus Ecclesiasticis*, Romae: Dessain, 1930; Tom. III, *De Consuetudine et de Temporis Supputatione*, Romae: Dessain, 1933.

Vermeersch, A.-Creusen, I., *Epitome Iuris Canonici*, 3 vols., 7. ed., Mechliniae-Romae, H. Dessain, 1949.

Waddingus, Lucas; Joannes de Luca Veneto; Iosephus Maris de Ancona; Caietanus Michelesius Asculanus; Stanislaus Melchiorrus de Cerreto; Chiappini, Anicetus; Pandzic, Basilius; *Annales Minorum*, 31 vols., Vol. I-XXX, Ad Claras Aquas prope Florentiam, 1931-1951; Vol. XXXI, Romae, 1956.

Articles

Bergh, E., "Actes du Saint-Siège—S. Congregation des Religieux," *Nouvelle Revue Théologique,* LXXXIII (1961), 1095-1096.

D'Ambrosio, Franciscus X., "Sorores externae monasteriorum monialium," *Apollinaris,* IV (1931), 397-409.

Gutiérrez, Anastasius, "De Testamento Novitiorum," *Commentarium pro Religiosis et Missionariis,* XXXVII (1958), 56-68.

Hofmeister, Philipp, "Von den Nonnenklöstern," *Archiv für katholisches Kirchenrecht,* CXIV (1934), 353-437.

La Puma, Vincentius, "De Sororibus Externis," *Commentarium pro Religiosis,* XII (1931), 426-430.

Lazzeri, Zephyrinus, "Documenta de Controversia inter Clarissas et Fratres Minores," *Archivum Franciscanum Historicum,* III (1910), 664-679, IV (1911), 74-94.

Lépicier, Alexius Henricus, "Le 'Suore esterne' nei monasteri di clausura," *Il Monitore Ecclesiastico,* Ser. V, Vol. III (1931), 330-333.

O'Brien, Romaeus W., "The Vow of Poverty and Its Civil Law Implications," *The Jurist,* XXI (1961), 435-450.

Vermeersch, Arturus, "De externis monasteriorum Sororibus," *Periodica,* XXI (1932), 43-51.

Dictionaries

Lexicon of the Latin Language, ed. by F. P. Leverett, Philadelphia: J. B. Lippincott Co., 1895.

Periodicals

Apollinaris, Romae, 1928-

Archiv für katholisches Kirchenrecht, Innsbruck, 1857-1861, Mainz, 1862-

Archivum Franciscanum Historicum, ad Claras Aquas prope Florentiam, 1908-

Commentarium pro Religiosis, Romae, 1920-1934; *Commentarium pro Religiosis et Missionariis,* a Vol. XVI, Romae, 1935-

Il Monitore Ecclesiastico, Romae, 1876-1948; *Monitor Ecclesiasticus,* Romae, 1949-

Jurist, The, Washington, D.C., 1941-

Nouvelle Revue Théologique, Paris, 1869-

Periodica de Re Canonica et Morali, Brugis, 1920-1927; *Periodica de Re Morali, Canonica, Liturgica,* Brugis, 1927-1936, et Romae, 1937-

Review for Religious, Topeka, Kans., 1942-

ABBREVIATIONS

AAS—*Acta Apostolicae Sedis*
Answers—Answers of the Blessed Mother Jane Frances Frémiot
Art.—Article
ASS—*Acta Sanctae Sedis*
Bonac.—Bonacina
Bull. Fran.—*Bullarium Franciscanum*
Bull. Rom.—*Bullarium Romanum*
C.—*Codex Iustiniani, caput*
can.—*canon*
cap.—*caput*
C.I.C.—*Codex Iuris Canonici*
col.—column
Comm. Pont.—*Commissio Pontificia ad Codicis Canones Authentice Interpretandos*
Conc. Trident.—*Concilium Tridentinum*
Const.—*Constitutio, Règles de St. Augustin de Constitutions de la Visitation*
Const., OSC—*Regulae et Constitutiones Generales Monialium Ordinis Sanctae Clarae*
Const., PCC—*Regula S. Clarae et Constitutiones pro Monialibus Clarissis Reformationis a Sancta Coleta*
Coutumier—*Coutumier et Directoire pour les Soeurs Religieuses de la Visitation Sainte-Marie*
ed.—*editio, edita*
Fasc.—*Fasciculus*
Fontes—*Codicis Iuris Canonici Fontes*
Instr.—*Instructio*
in VI°—*Liber Sextus Bonifatii VIII*
Lib.—*Liber*
N.—*Novellae Constitutiones, numerus*
Prot. n.—Protocol number
R. J.—*Regulae Juris*
S.C. Concilii—*Sacra Congregatio Concilii*
S. C. de Prop. Fide—*Sacra Congregation de Propaganda Fide*
S. C. de Rel.—*Sacra Congregatio de Religiosis*
S. C. Ep. et Reg.—*Sacra Congregatio Episcoporum et Regularium*
sess.—*sessio*
Statuta, 1931—*Statuta a sororibus externis Monasteriorum Monialium cuiusque Ordinis servanda*
Statuta, 1961—*Instructio et Statuta de Sororibus externo Monasteriorum servitio addictis*
tit.—*titulus*
Tom.—*Tomus*

ALPHABETICAL INDEX

BIOGRAPHICAL NOTE

Dismas W. Bonner was born in Fort Wayne, Indiana, on September 15, 1929. He received his elementary education at St. Patrick Parochial School of that city, and was graduated from Central Catholic High School in Fort Wayne. After attending Purdue University at West Lafayette, Indiana, from 1947 to 1950, he began preparatory studies for the priesthood at St. Joseph Seminary, Westmont, Illinois. He entered the Franciscan Novitiate at Teutopolis, Illinois, in 1951. At the conclusion of his philosophical studies in Our Lady of Angels Seminary, Cleveland, Ohio, he received the degree of Bachelor of Arts from Quincy College, Quincy, Illinois. His theological studies were completed at St. Joseph Seminary, Teutopolis, Illinois, where he was ordained to the priesthood on June 24, 1958.

After assignments to St. Bernard Parish, St. Bernard, Nebraska, and Alverna Retreat House, Indianapolis, Indiana, he was enrolled in the School of Canon Law at the Pontifical University of St. Anthony in Rome, where he received the degree of the Baccalaureate in Canon Law in June, 1961. In September of that year, he transferred to the School of Canon Law of the Catholic University of America, where he received the degree of Licentiate in Canon Law in June, 1962.

CANON LAW STUDIES*

430. Bonner, Rev. Dismas W., O.F.M., B.A., J.C.L., Extern Sisters in Monasteries of Nuns.

431. Bowen, Rev. Henry G., A.B., Ph.B. S.T.L., J.C.L., The Juridic Authority of the Church over the Non-baptized. (*microfilm*)

432. Calhoun, Rev. John C., B.A., S.T.B., J.C.L., The Restraint of the Exercise of One's Rights.

433. Goeke, Rev. John W., B.A., J.C.L., The Laws of the State of Kentucky Affecting Church Property (*microfilm*)

434. Swierzowski, Rev. Stanislaus J., S.T.L., M.S., J.C.L., Church Parties in Civil Separation and Divorce Cases.

435. Voegtle, Brother Leonard A., F.M.S., B.A., M.A., J.C.L., Canonical Reasons for the Rejection of Candidates to Final Vows. (*microfilm*)

* For a complete list of the available numbers of this series apply to the Catholic University of America Press, 620 Michigan Avenue, N.E., Washington 17, D.C., for a general catalogue.

www.ingramcontent.com/pod-product-compliance
Lightning Source LLC
LaVergne TN
LVHW050252080826
844660LV00012B/626